Garfield
Left Speechless
COMICS WITHOUT WORDS

BY JIM DAVIS

Ballantine Books • New York

A Ballantine Books Trade Paperback Original

Copyright © 2012 by PAWS, Inc. All Rights Reserved.
"GARFIELD" and the GARFIELD characters are trademarks of PAWS, Inc.

Published in the United States by Ballantine Books, an imprint of The Random House Publishing Group,
a division of Random House, Inc., New York.

BALLANTINE and colophon are registered trademarks of Random House, Inc.

ISBN 978-0-345-53058-5

Printed in the United States of America

www.ballantinebooks.com

9 8 7 6 5 4 3 2 1

FOREWORD

In the early '50s, I attended Fowlerton Elementary School, which housed six grades in three rooms. There was no kindergarten and no *Sesame Street*. We learned to read in the first grade, and not before. As a result, the first comic strip I ever read ("followed" rather) was *Henry*, because it didn't have any dialogue. I got to follow a story. It made me laugh, and I couldn't even read! It was magic. . . .

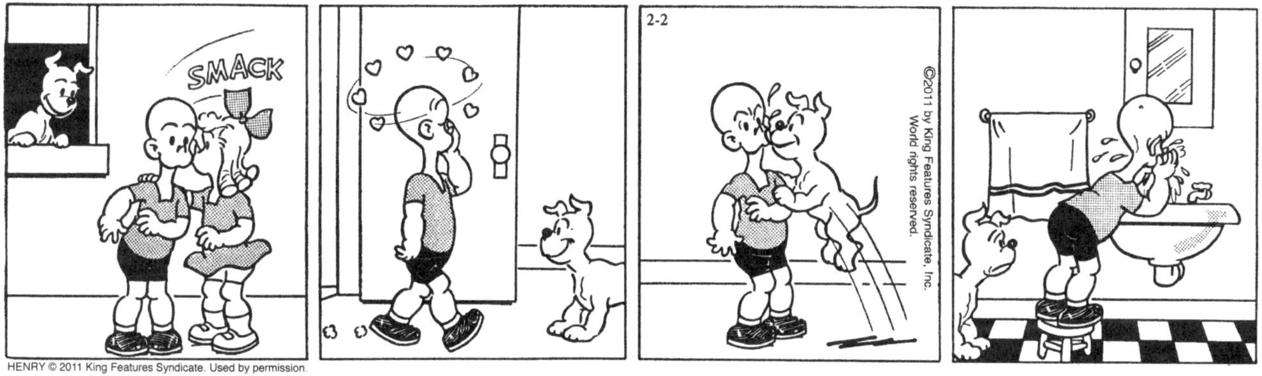
SMACK
2-2
©2011 by King Features Syndicate, Inc.
World rights reserved.

To this day, I am still a big fan of a well-turned gag performed in pantomime. Sir Laurence Olivier had nothing on Charlie Chaplin!

I have discovered that gags without dialogue are harder to craft; like baking a cake from scratch rather than out of a box. So please enjoy this home-cooked batch of comfort strips; my homage to all things wordless and wonderful.

JIM DAVIS

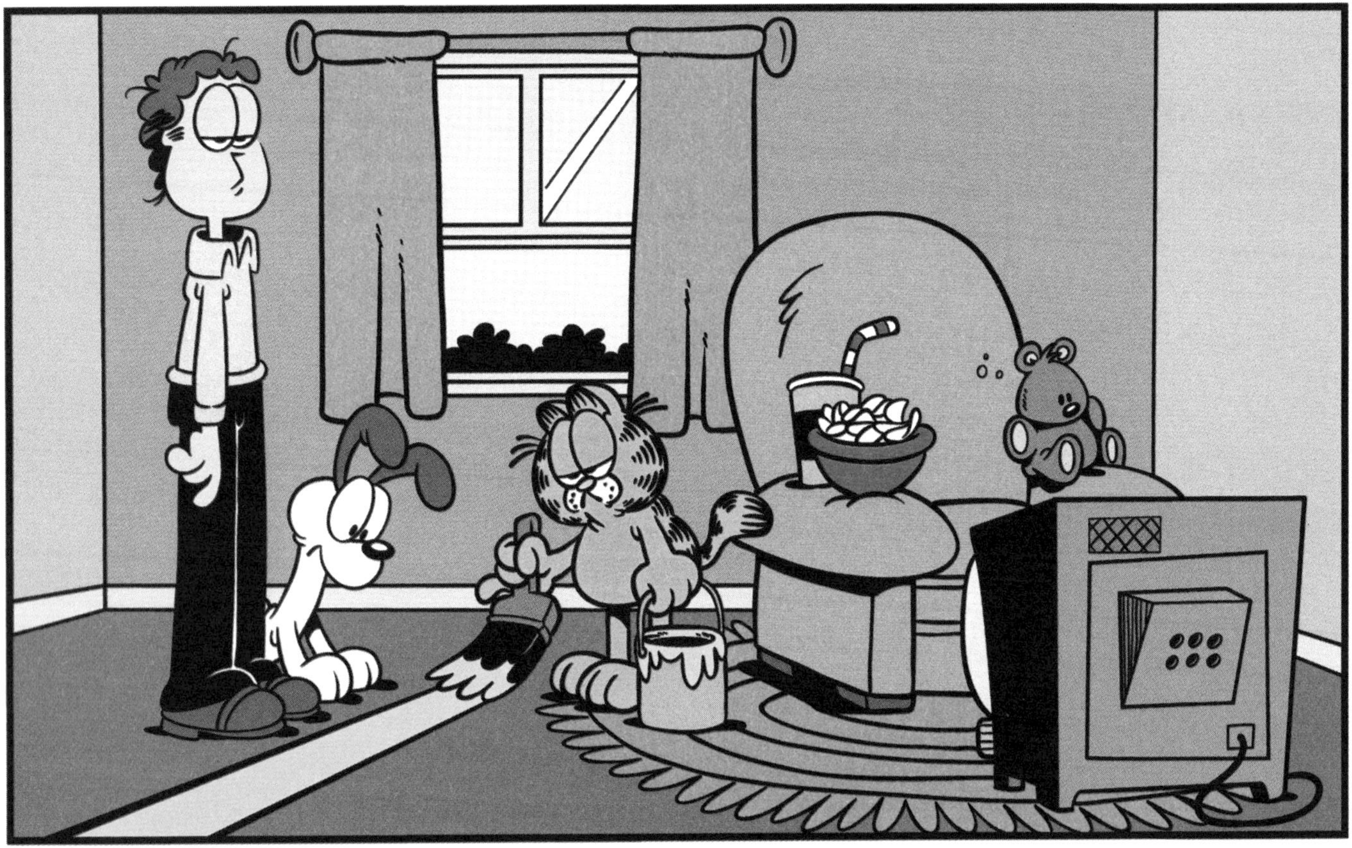

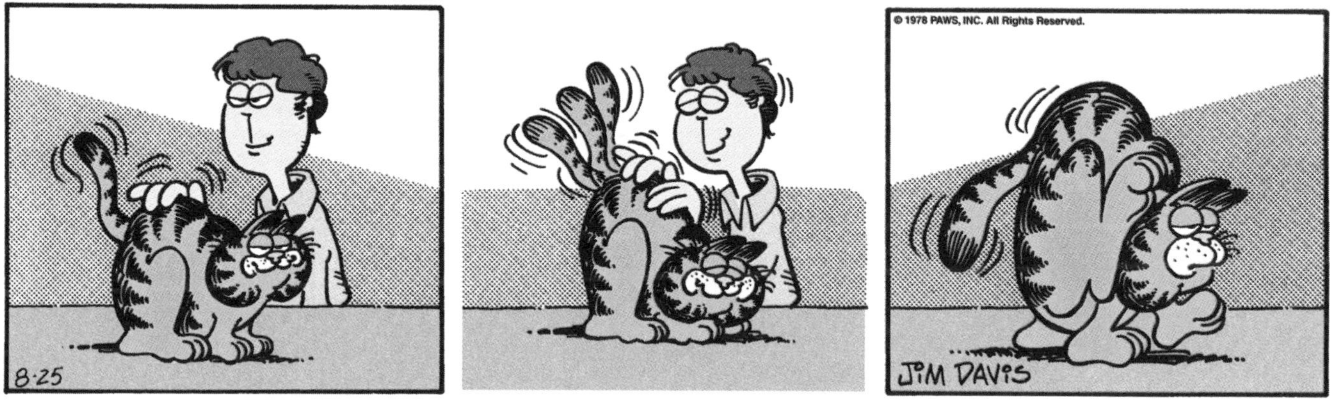
8-25
© 1978 PAWS, INC. All Rights Reserved.
JIM DAVIS

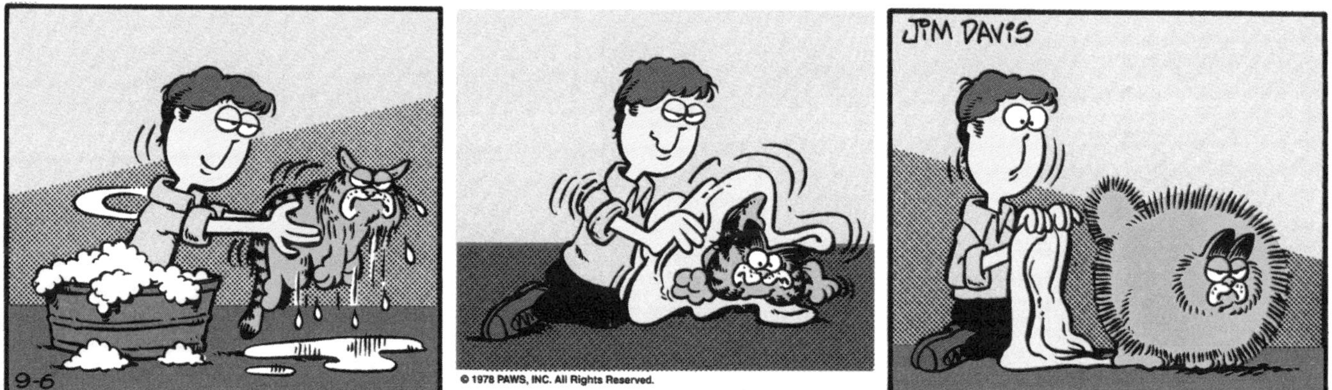
9-6
© 1978 PAWS, INC. All Rights Reserved.
JIM DAVIS

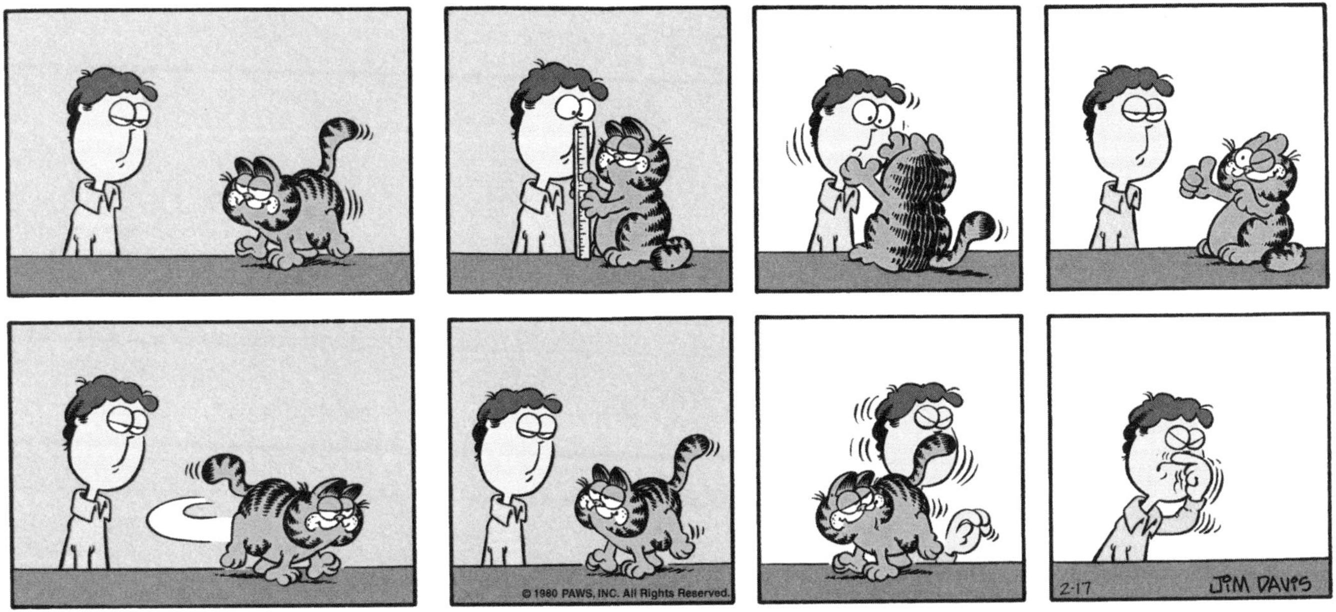
© 1980 PAWS, INC. All Rights Reserved.
2-17
JIM DAVIS

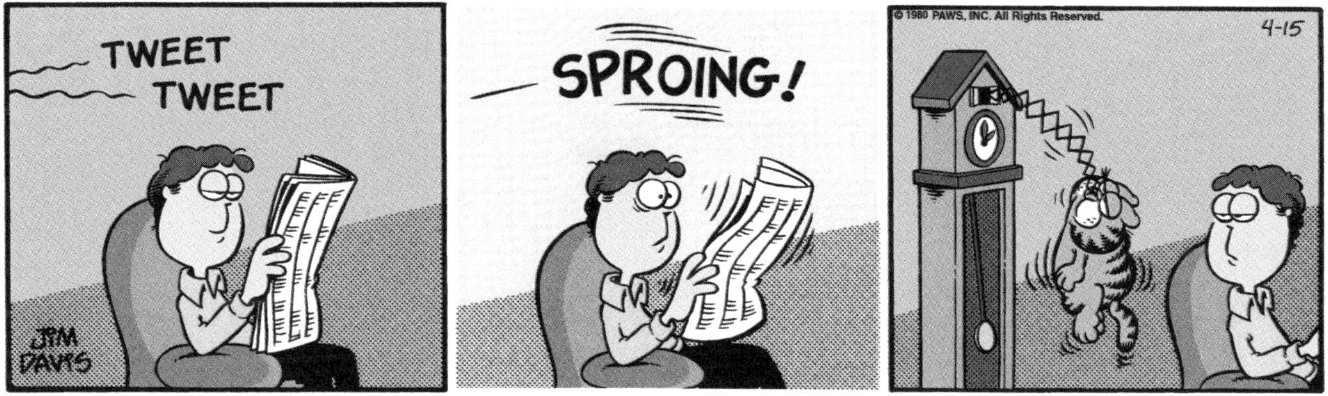
TWEET
TWEET
JIM DAVIS
SPROING!
© 1980 PAWS, INC. All Rights Reserved.
4-15

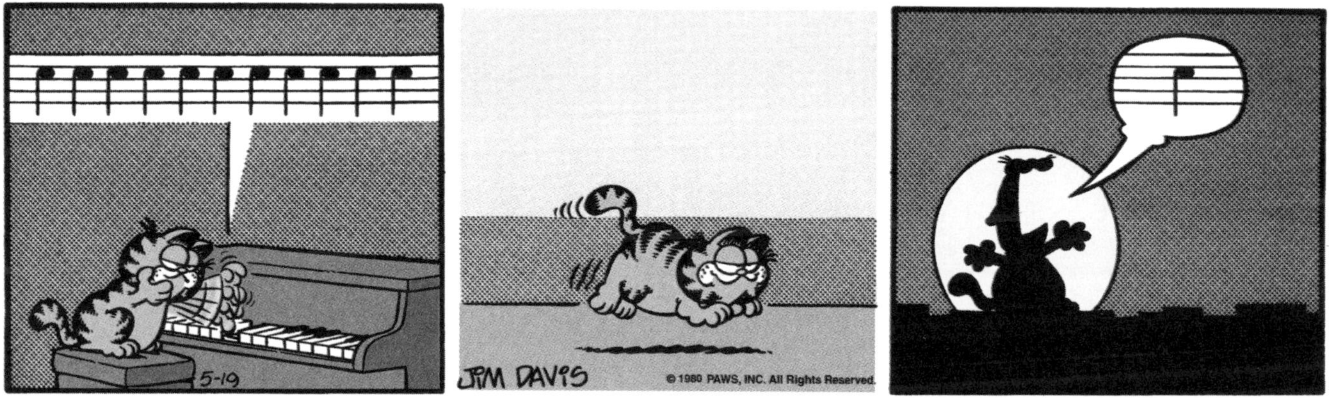
5-19
JIM DAVIS
© 1980 PAWS, INC. All Rights Reserved.

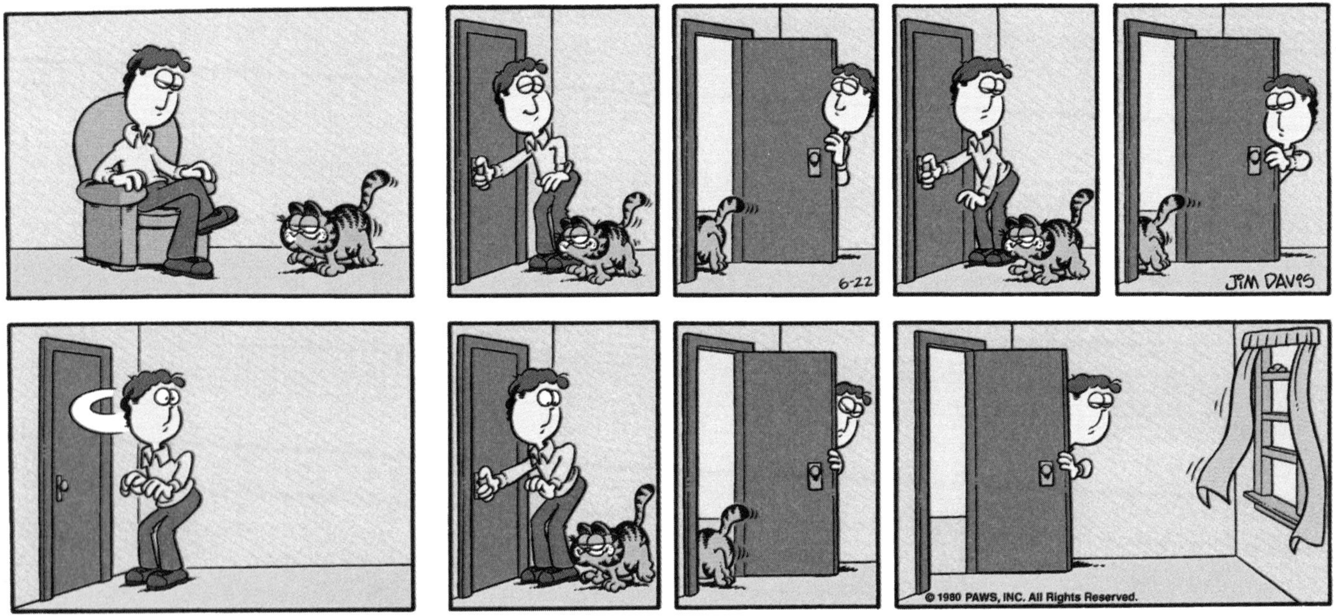
6-22
JIM DAVIS
© 1980 PAWS, INC. All Rights Reserved.

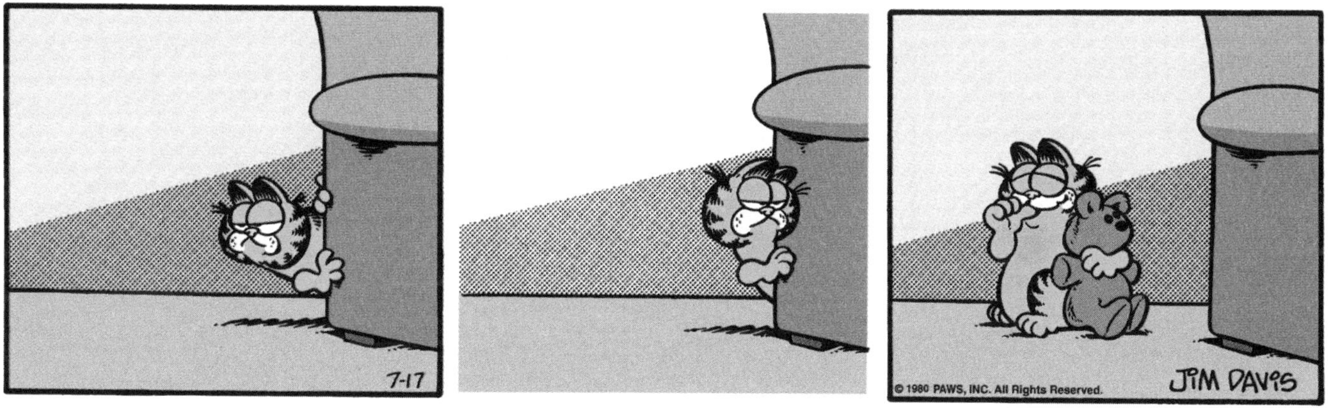
7-17
© 1980 PAWS, INC. All Rights Reserved.
JIM DAVIS

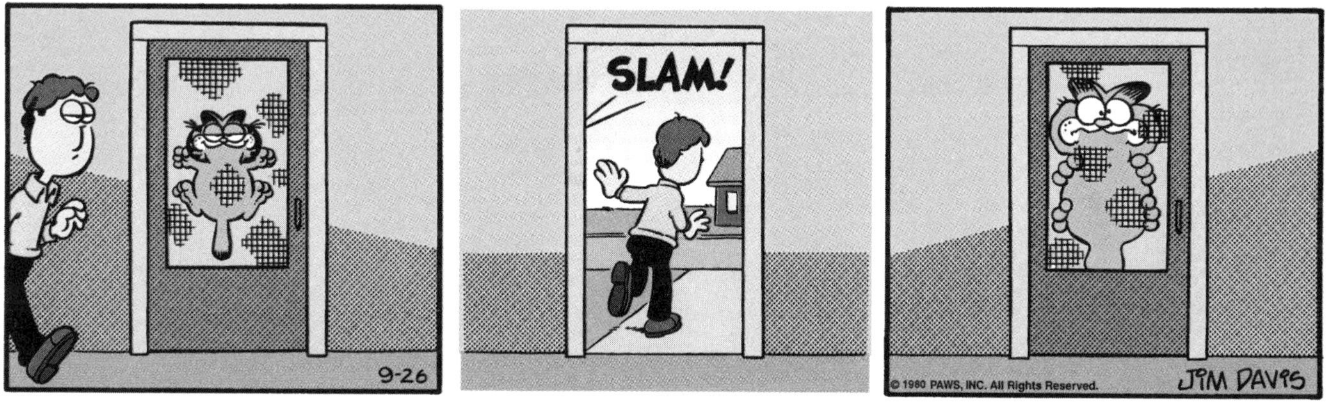
9-26
SLAM!
© 1980 PAWS, INC. All Rights Reserved.
JIM DAVIS

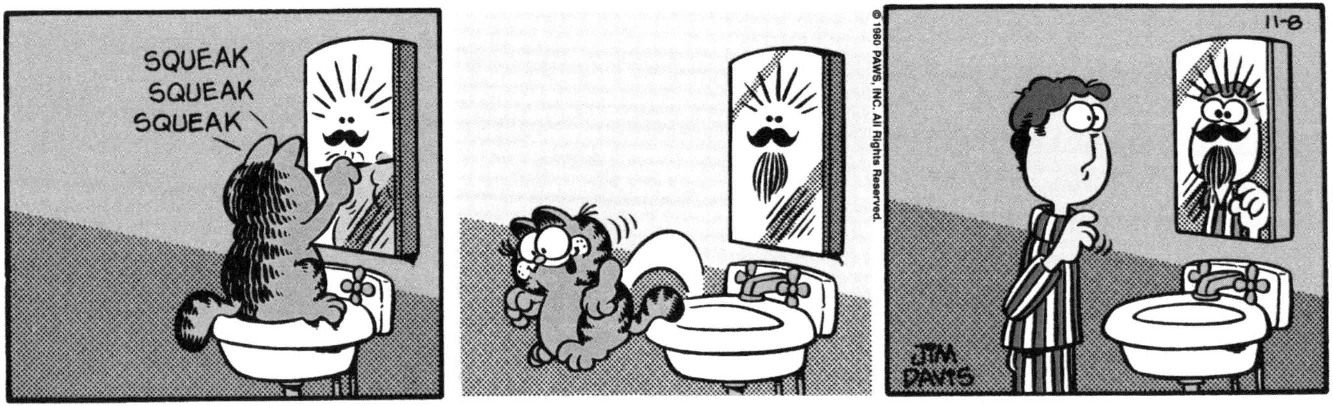
SQUEAK
SQUEAK
SQUEAK
© 1980 PAWS, INC. All Rights Reserved.
11-8
JIM DAVIS

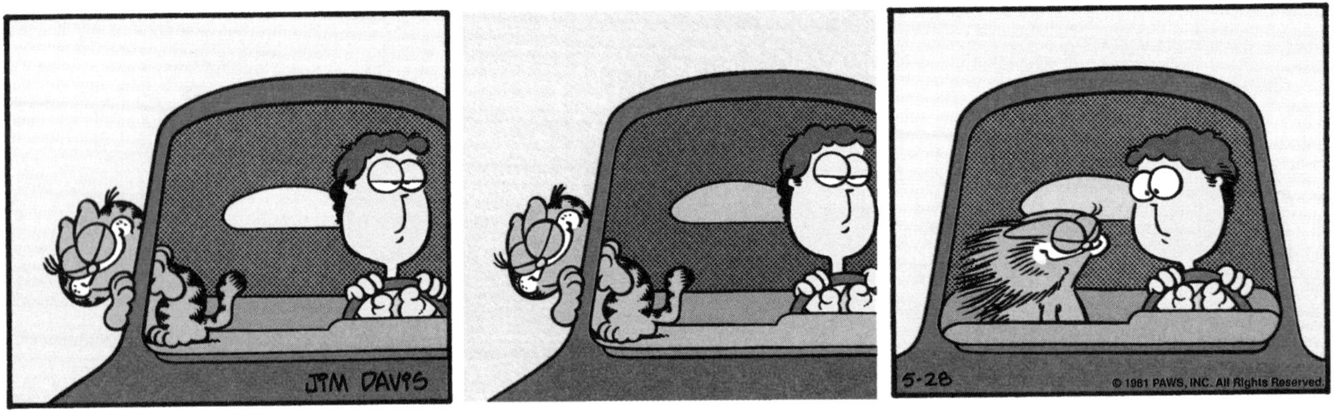
JIM DAVIS
5-28
© 1981 PAWS, INC. All Rights Reserved.

JIM DAVIS
11-1
CHUNG!
© 1981 PAWS, INC. All Rights Reserved.

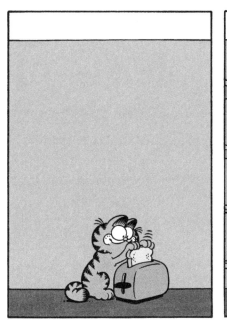

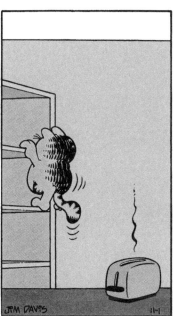

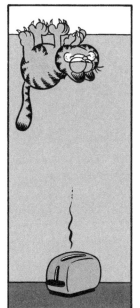

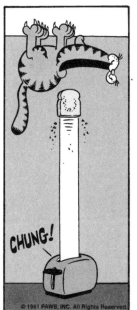

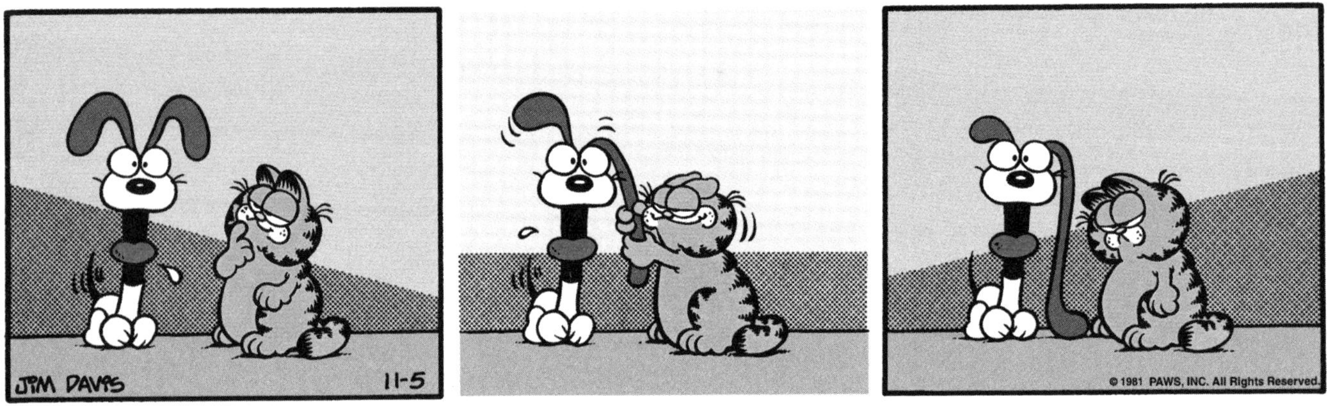
JIM DAVIS
11-5
© 1981 PAWS, INC. All Rights Reserved.

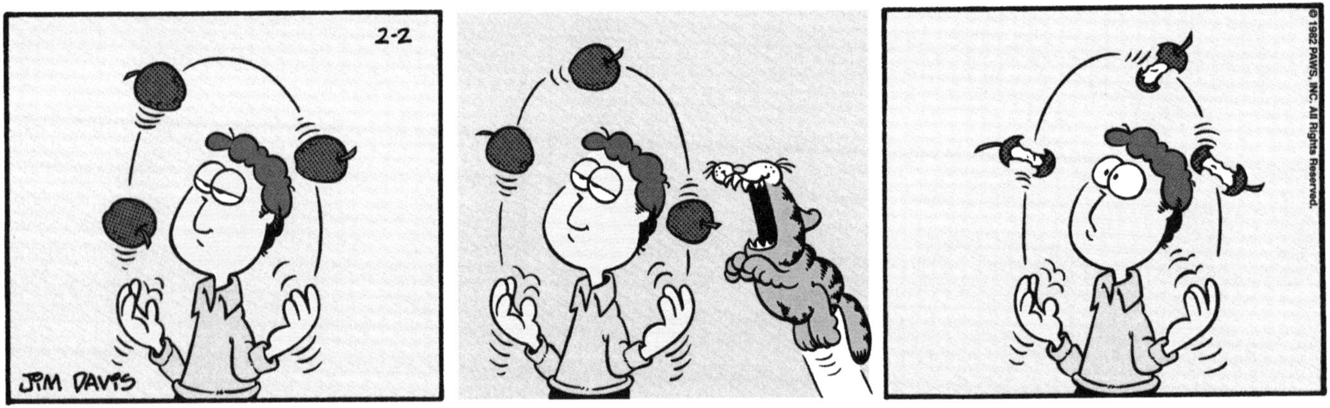
2-2
JIM DAVIS
© 1982 PAWS, INC. All Rights Reserved.

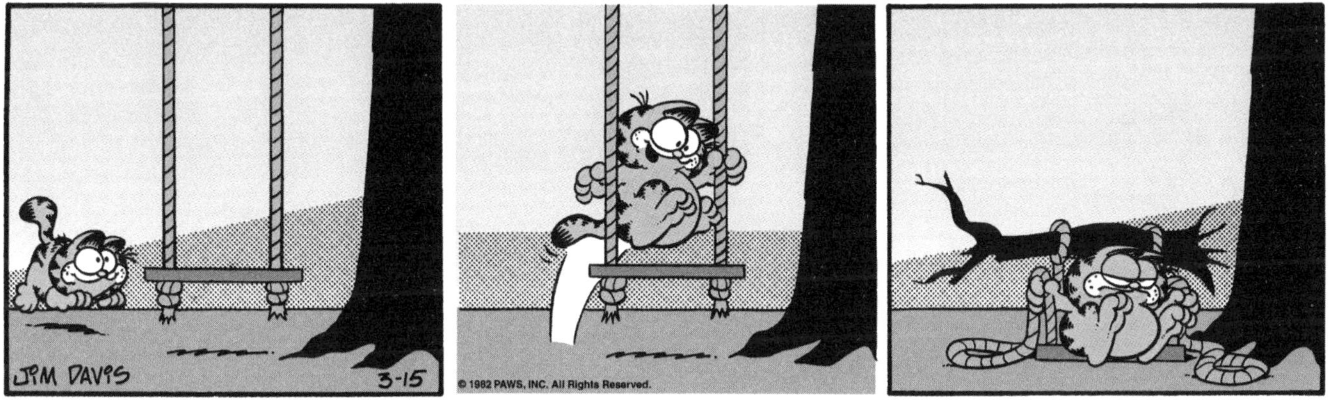
JIM DAVIS
3-15
© 1982 PAWS, INC. All Rights Reserved.

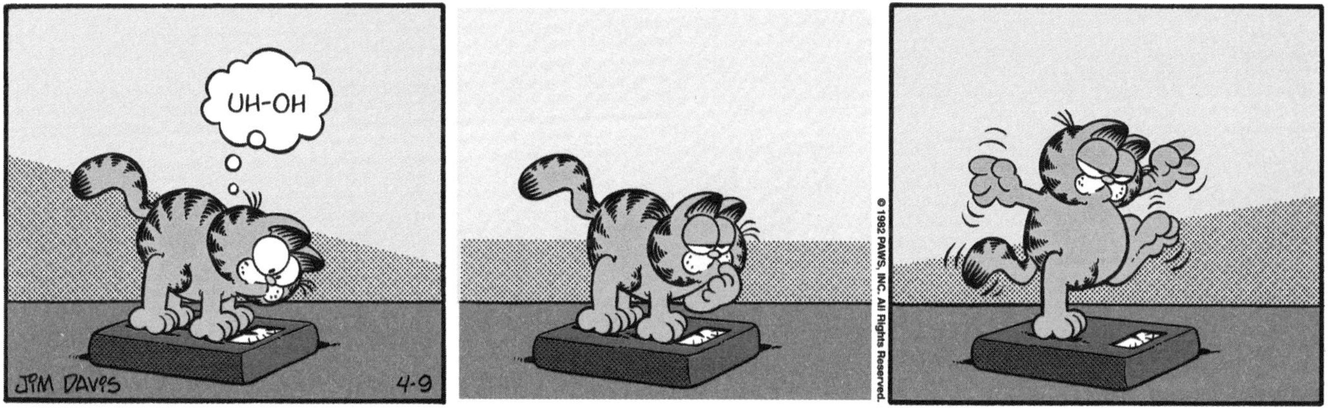
UH-OH
JIM DAVIS
4-9
© 1982 PAWS, INC. All Rights Reserved.

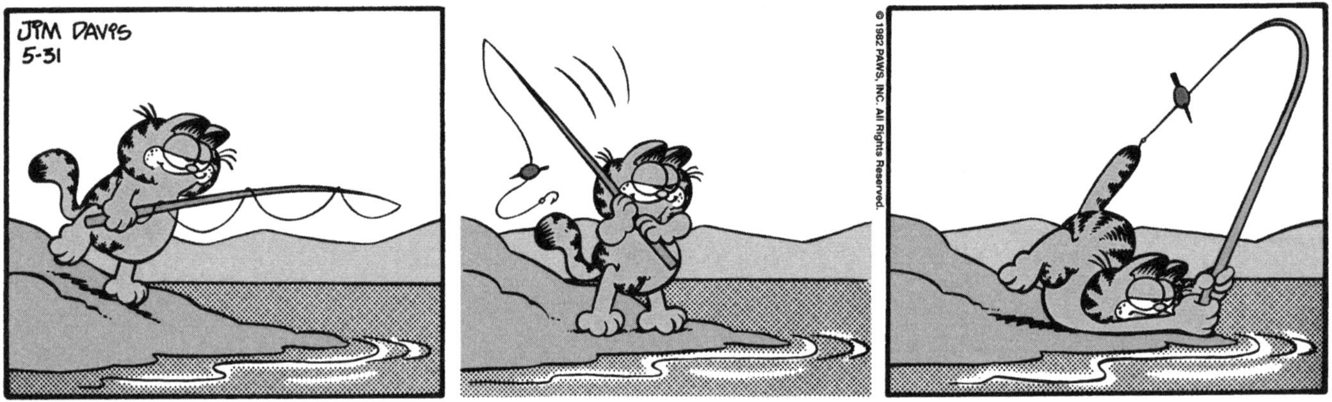
JIM DAVIS
5-31
© 1982 PAWS, INC. All Rights Reserved.

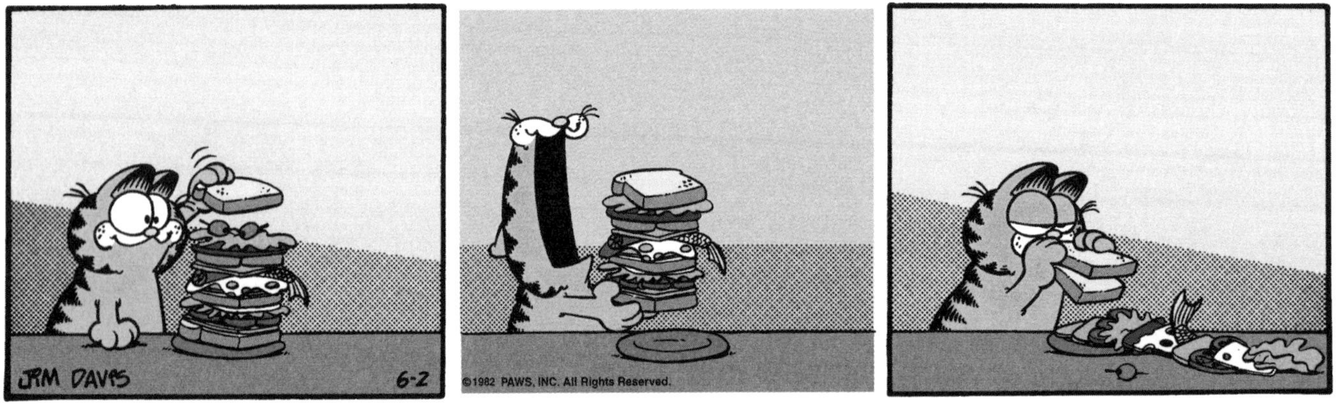
JIM DAVIS
6-2
©1982 PAWS, INC. All Rights Reserved.

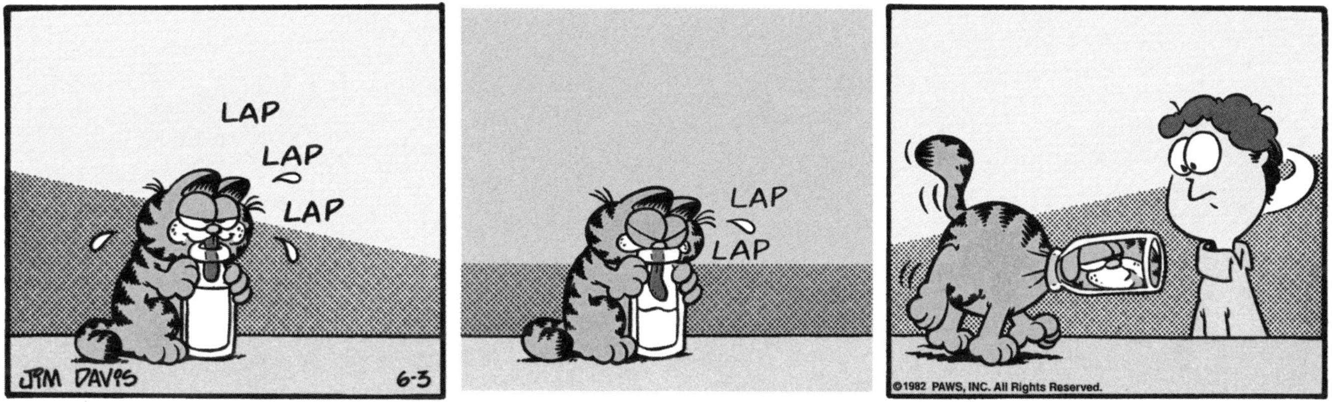
JIM DAVIS
6-3
LAP
LAP
LAP
LAP
LAP
©1982 PAWS, INC. All Rights Reserved.

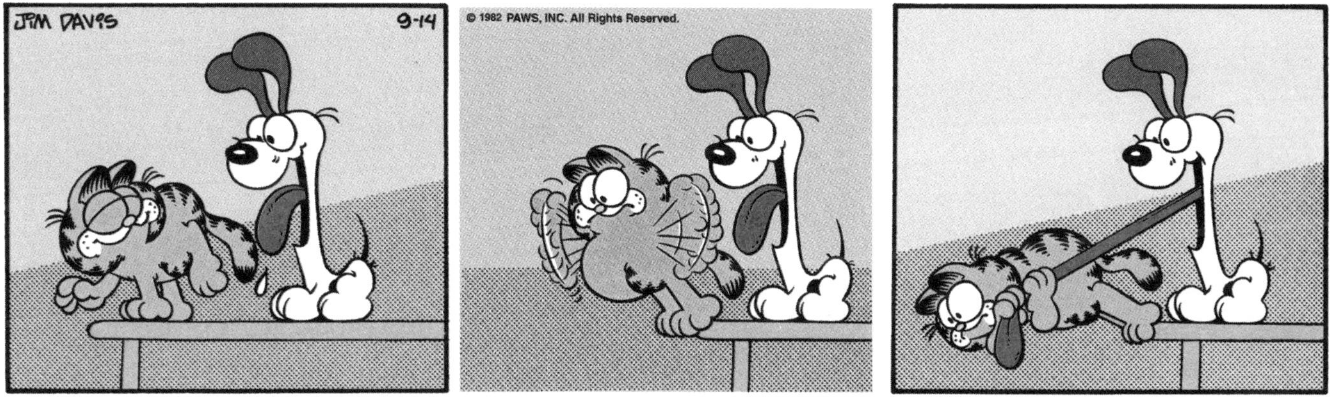
JIM DAVIS
9-14
© 1982 PAWS, INC. All Rights Reserved.

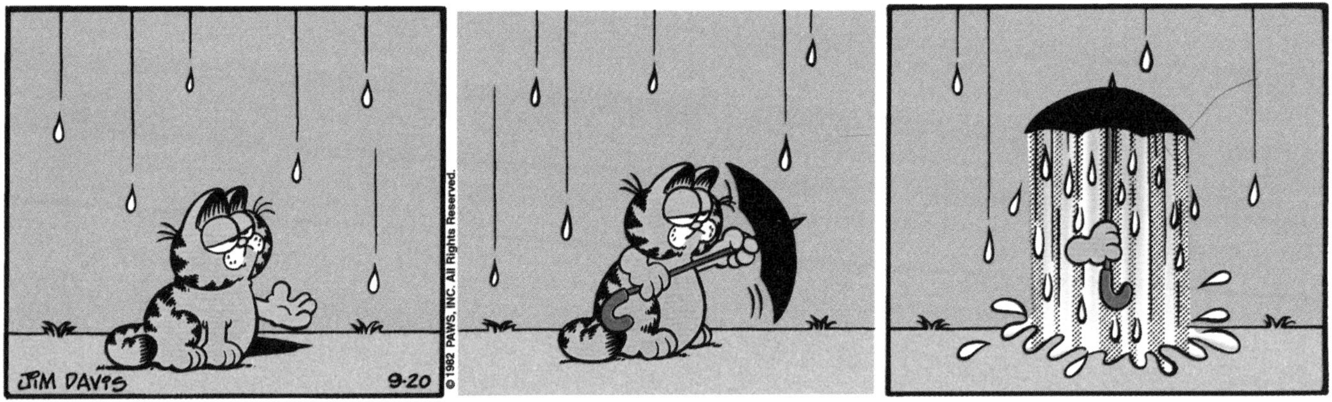
JIM DAVIS
9-20
© 1982 PAWS, INC. All Rights Reserved.

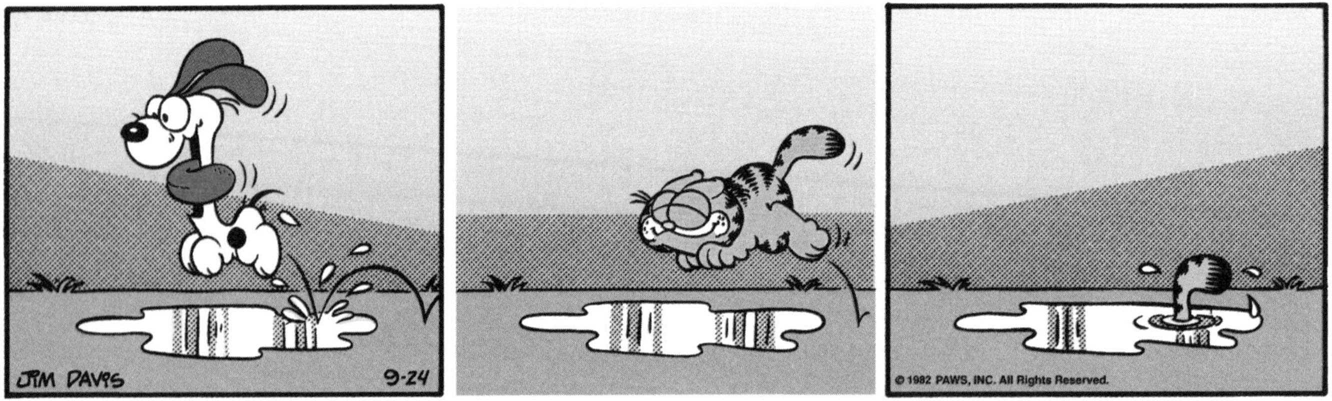
JIM DAVIS
9-24
© 1982 PAWS, INC. All Rights Reserved.

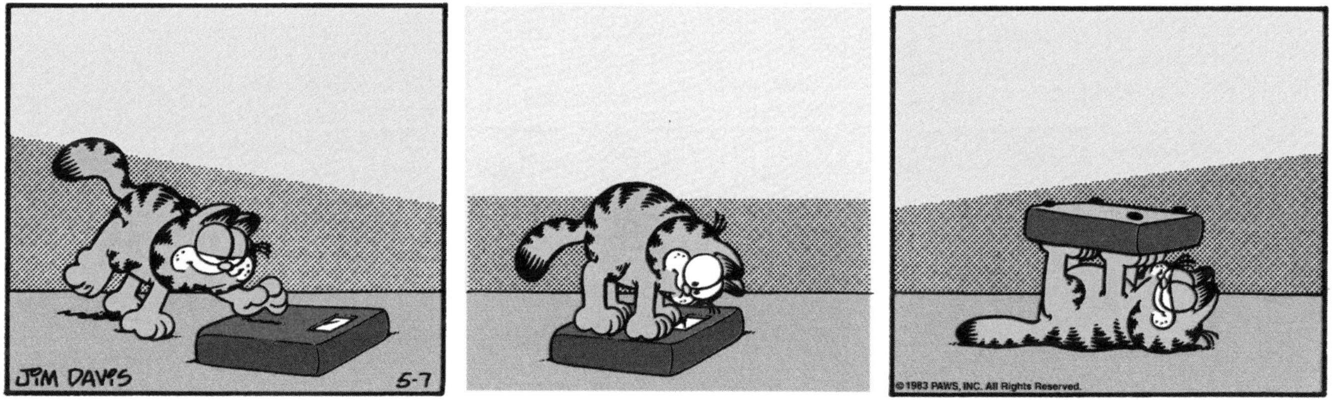
JIM DAVIS
5-7
© 1983 PAWS, INC. All Rights Reserved.

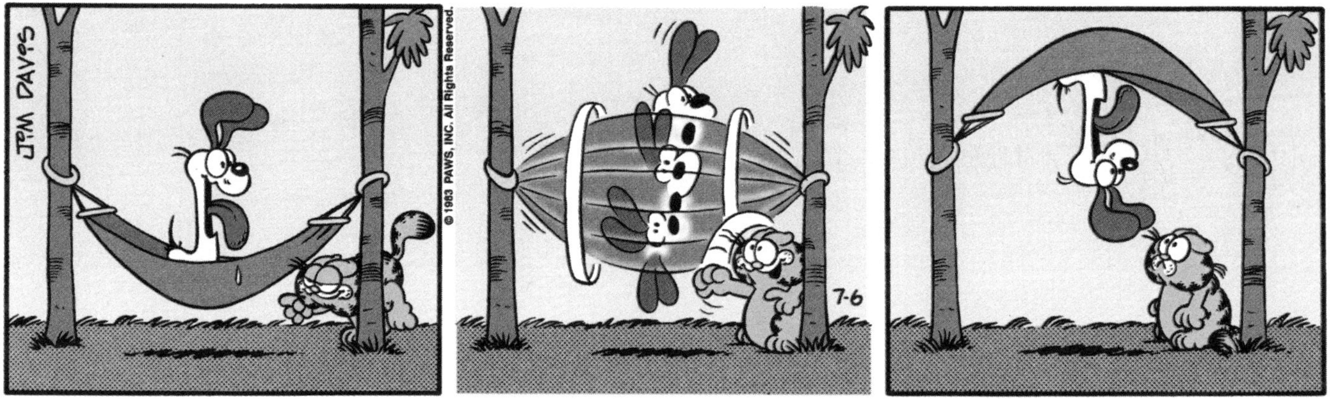
JIM DAVIS
© 1983 PAWS, INC. All Rights Reserved.
7-6

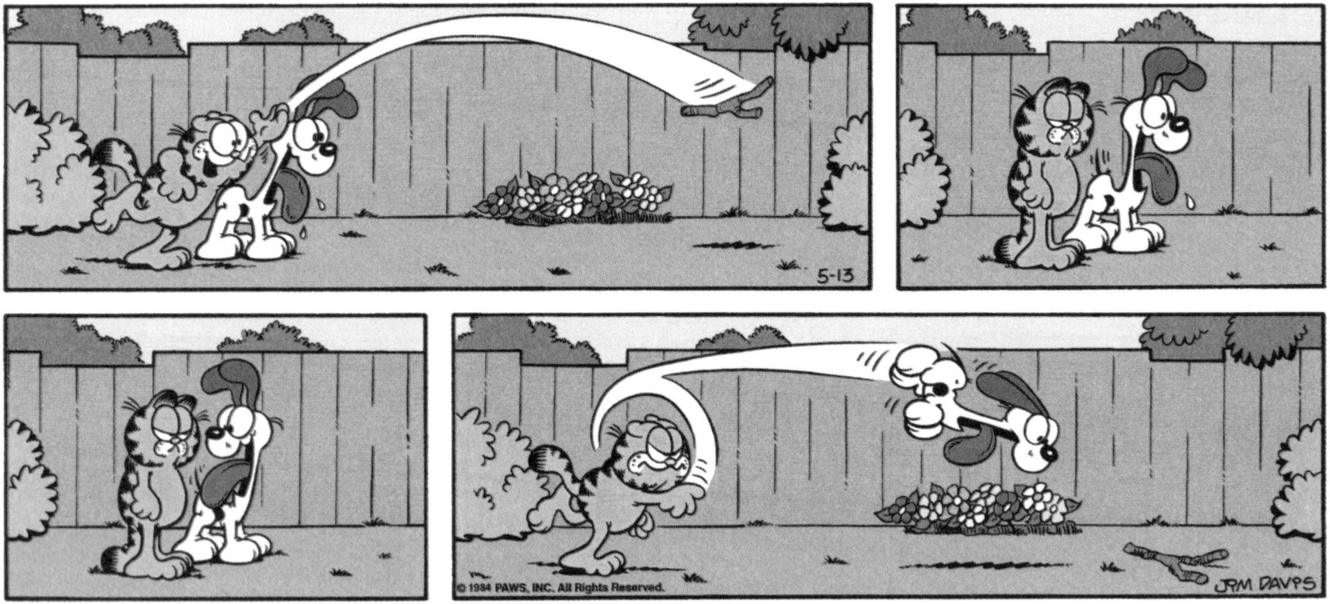
5-13
© 1984 PAWS, INC. All Rights Reserved.
JPM DAVPS

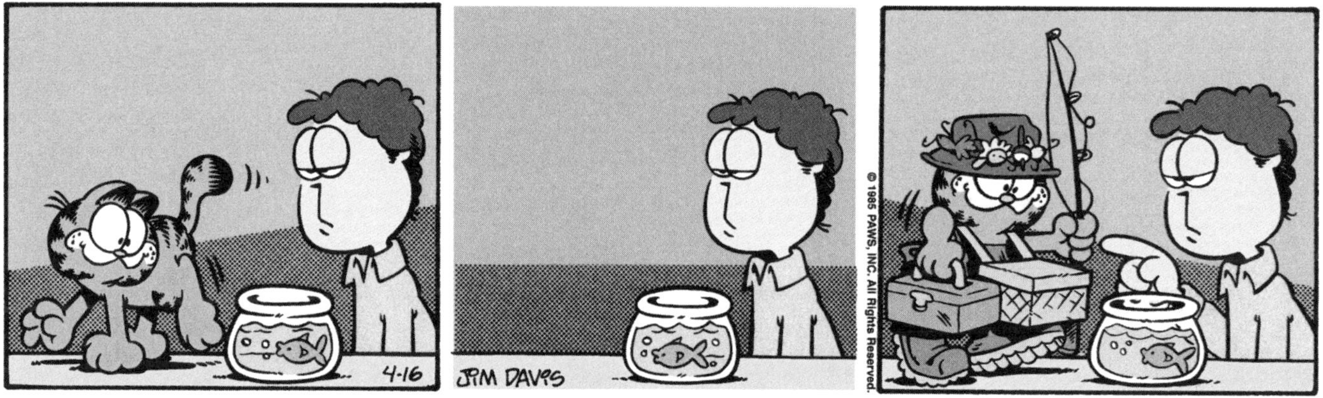
4-16
JIM DAVIS
© 1985 PAWS, INC. All Rights Reserved.

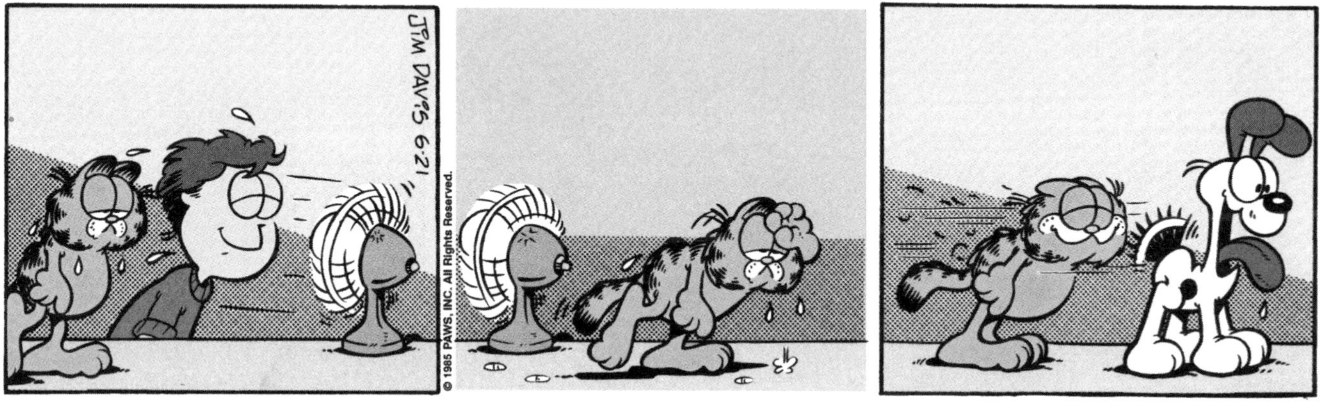
JIM DAVIS 6-21
© 1985 PAWS, INC. All Rights Reserved.

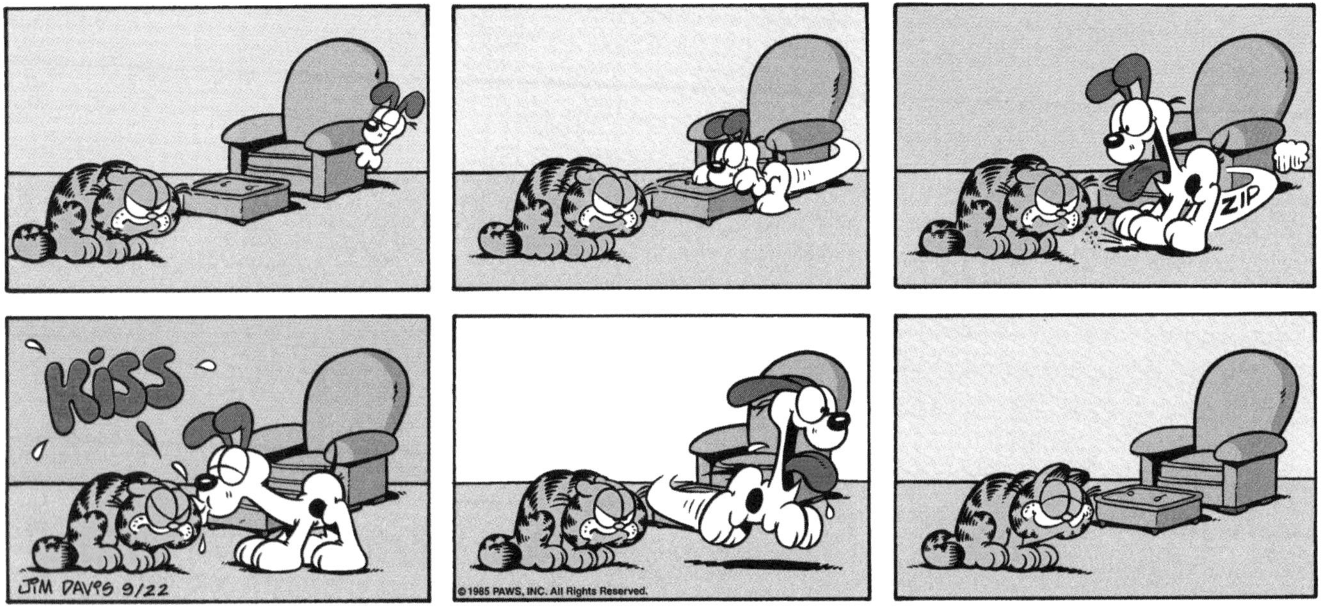
ZIP
KISS
JIM DAVIS 9/22
© 1985 PAWS, INC. All Rights Reserved.

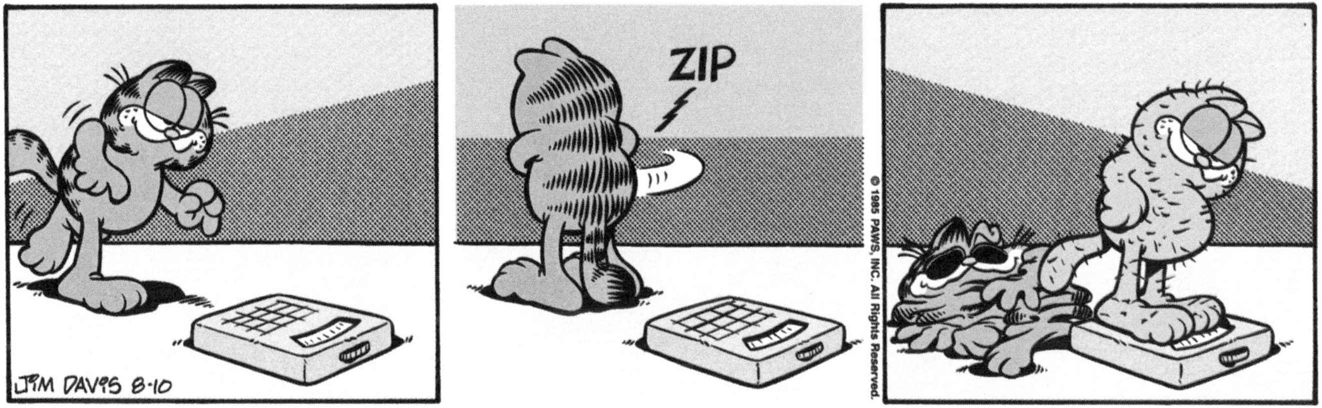
ZIP
JIM DAVIS 8-10
© 1985 PAWS, INC. All Rights Reserved.

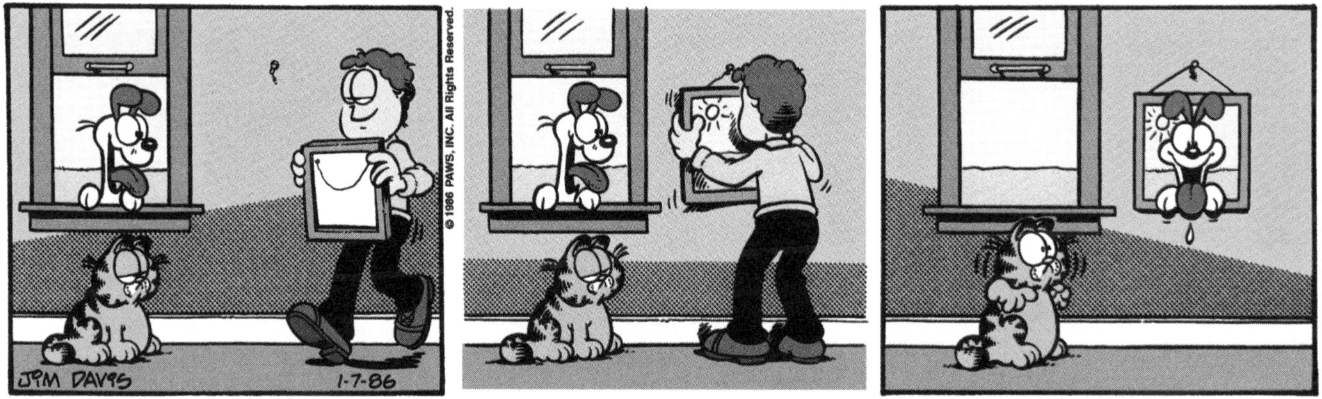
JIM DAVIS
1-7-86
© 1986 PAWS, INC. All Rights Reserved.

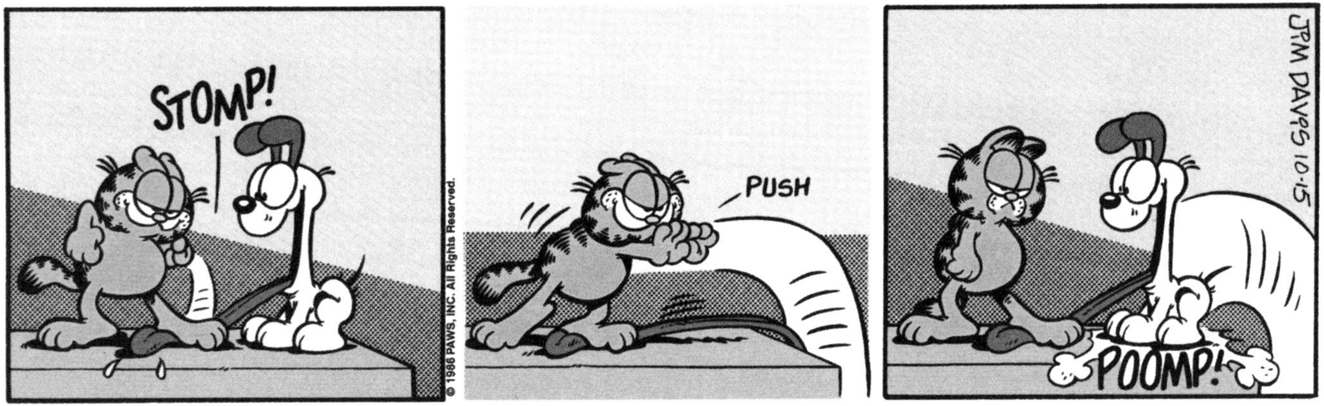
STOMP!
PUSH
POOMP!
JIM DAVIS 10-15
© 1986 PAWS, INC. All Rights Reserved.

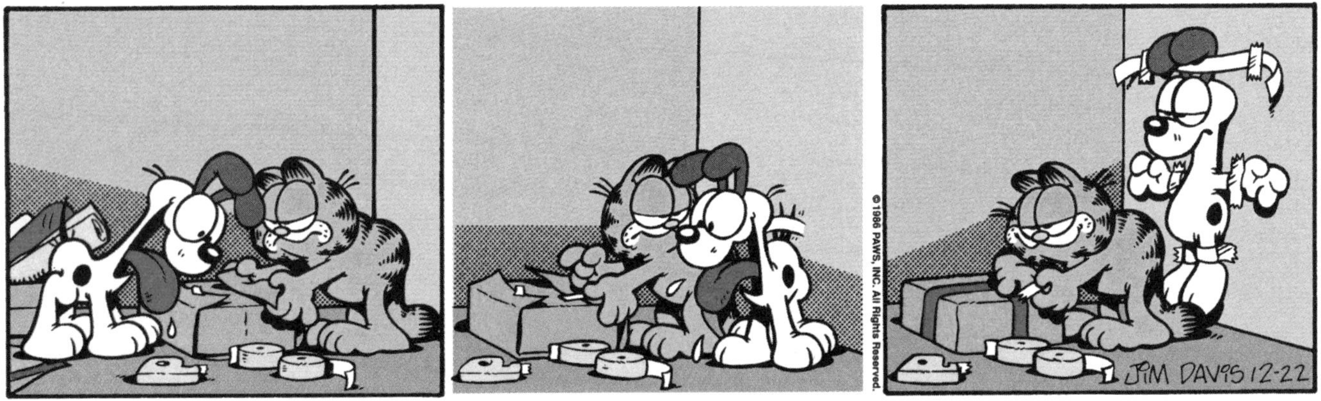
JIM DAVIS 12-22
© 1986 PAWS, INC. All Rights Reserved.

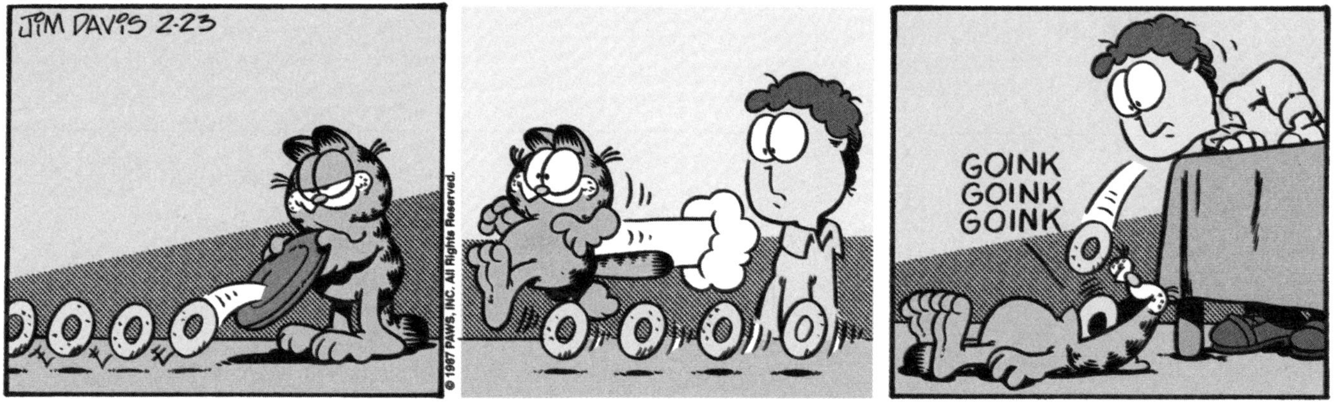

JIM DAVIS 2-23
© 1987 PAWS, INC. All Rights Reserved.
GOINK
GOINK
GOINK

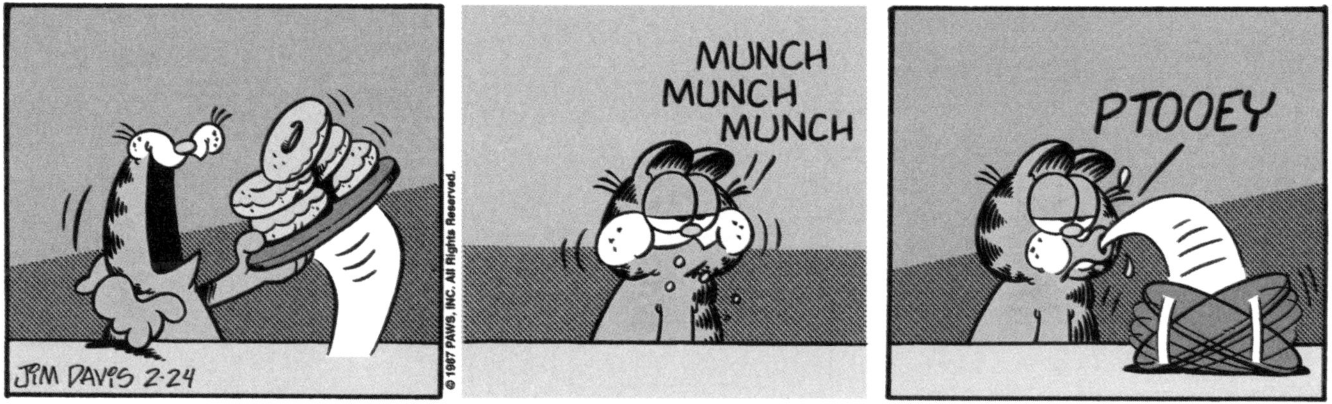

JIM DAVIS 2-24
© 1987 PAWS, INC. All Rights Reserved.
MUNCH
MUNCH
MUNCH
PTOOEY

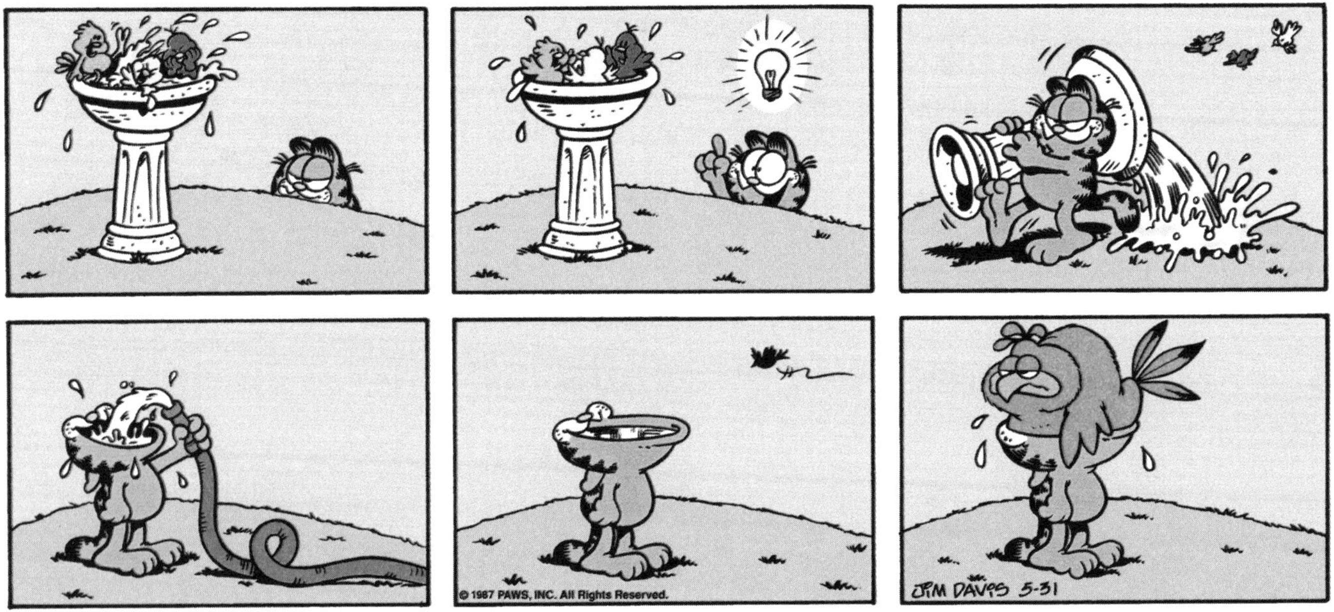
© 1987 PAWS, INC. All Rights Reserved.
JIM DAVIS 5-31

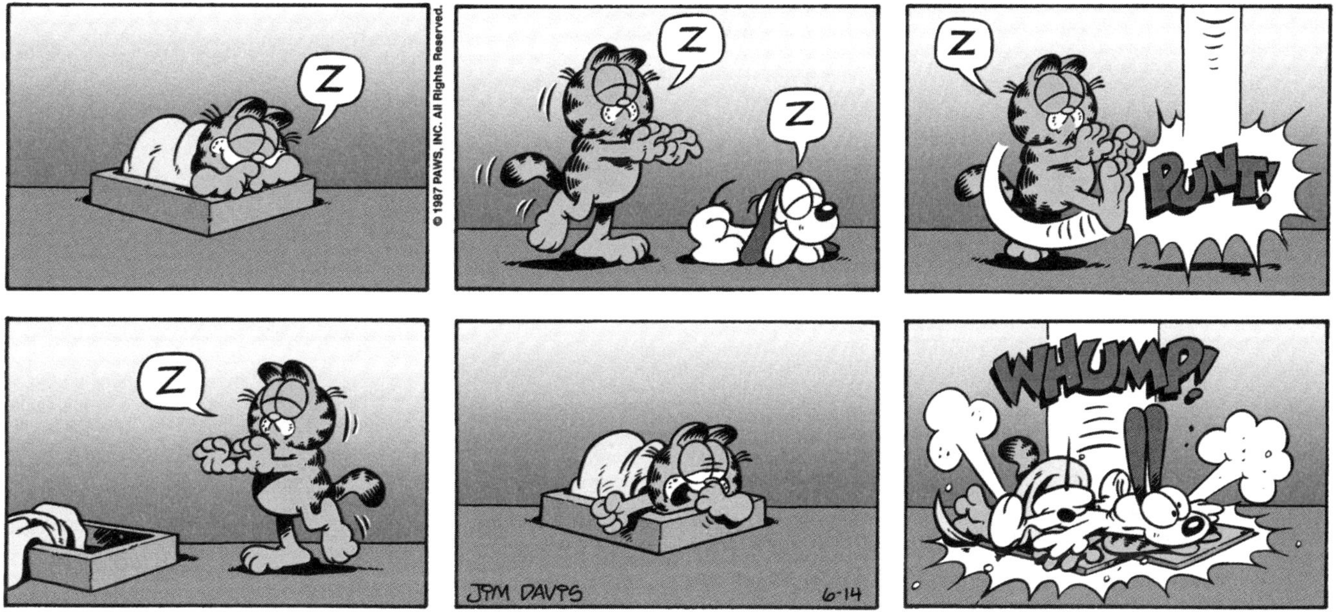
Z
Z
Z
Z
PUNT!
Z
JIM DAVIS
6-14
WHUMP!

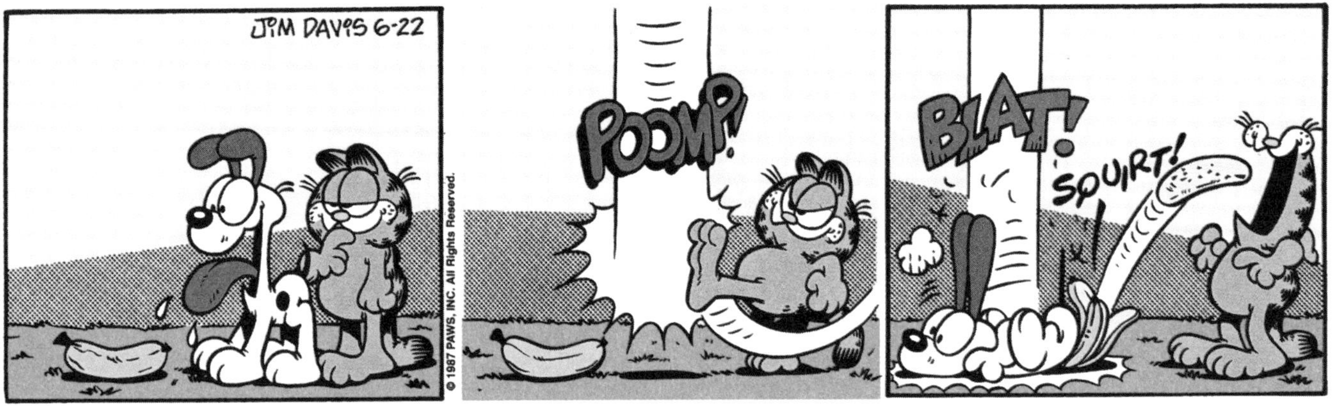
JIM DAVIS 6-22
© 1987 PAWS, INC. All Rights Reserved.
POOMP!
BLAT!
SQUIRT!

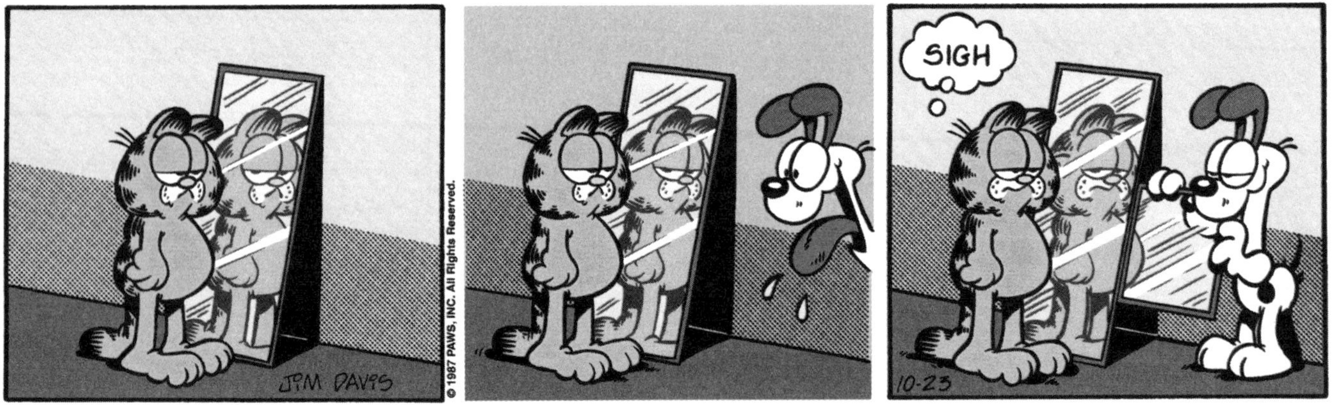
JIM DAVIS
© 1987 PAWS, INC. All Rights Reserved.
SIGH
10-23

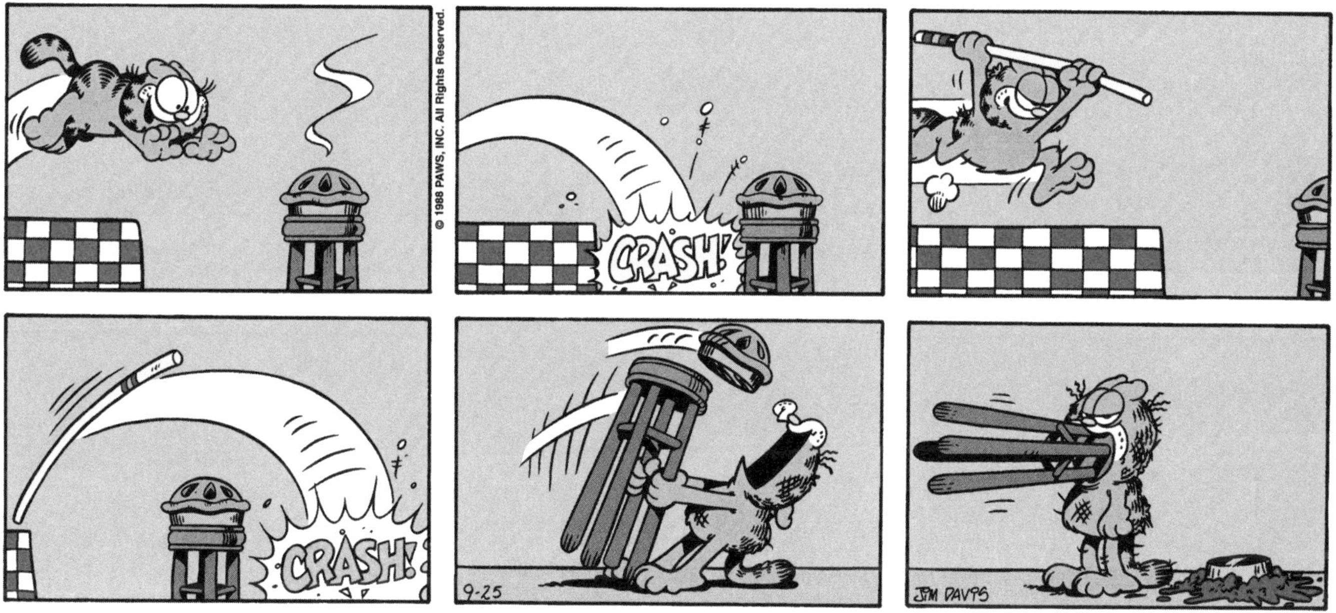
© 1988 PAWS, INC. All Rights Reserved.
CRASH!
CRASH!
9-25
JIM DAVIS

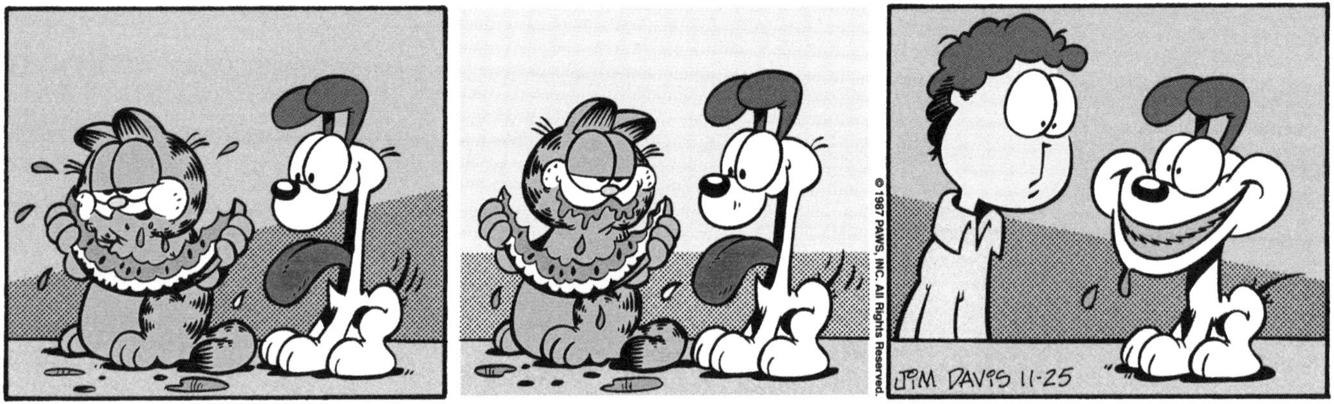
© 1987 PAWS, INC. All Rights Reserved.
JIM DAVIS 11-25

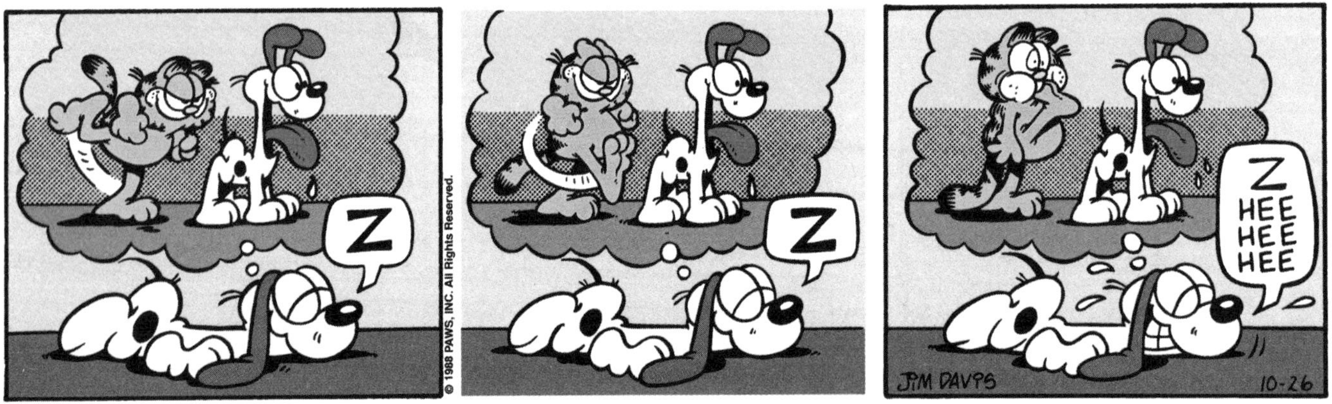
© 1988 PAWS, INC. All Rights Reserved.
Z
Z
Z HEE HEE HEE
JIM DAVIS
10-26

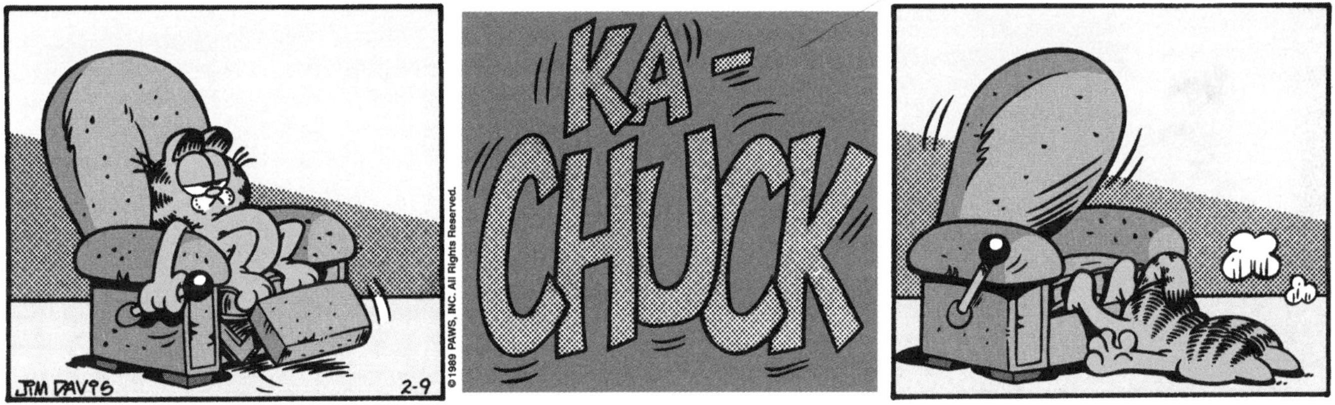
JIM DAVIS
2-9
©1989 PAWS, INC. All Rights Reserved.
KA-CHUCK

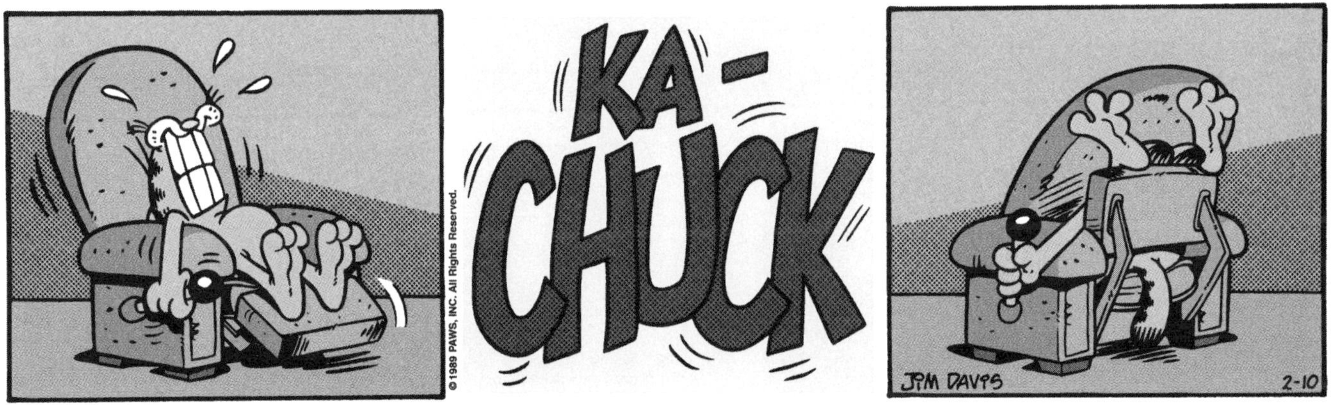
©1989 PAWS, INC. All Rights Reserved.
KA-CHUCK
JIM DAVIS
2-10

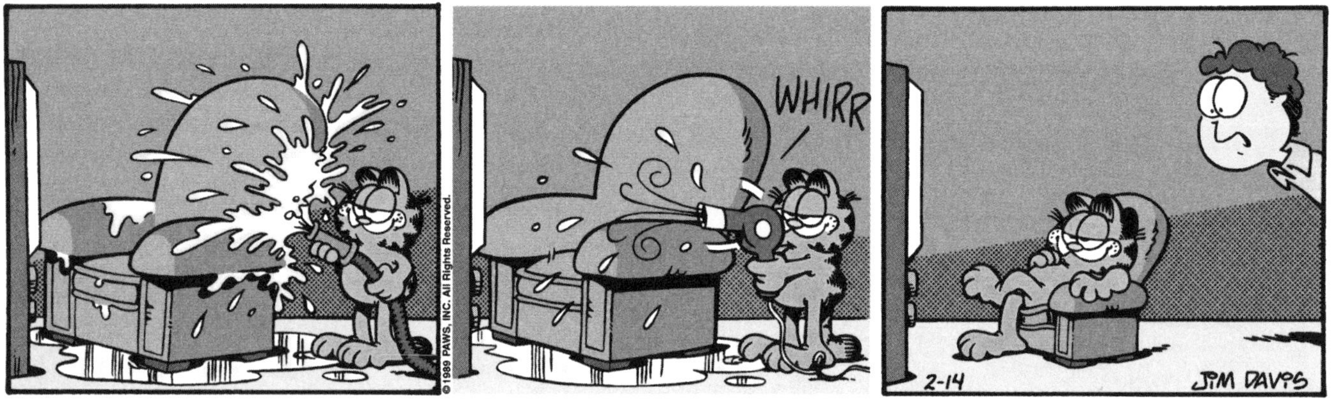
WHIRR
© 1989 PAWS, INC. All Rights Reserved.
2-14
JIM DAVIS

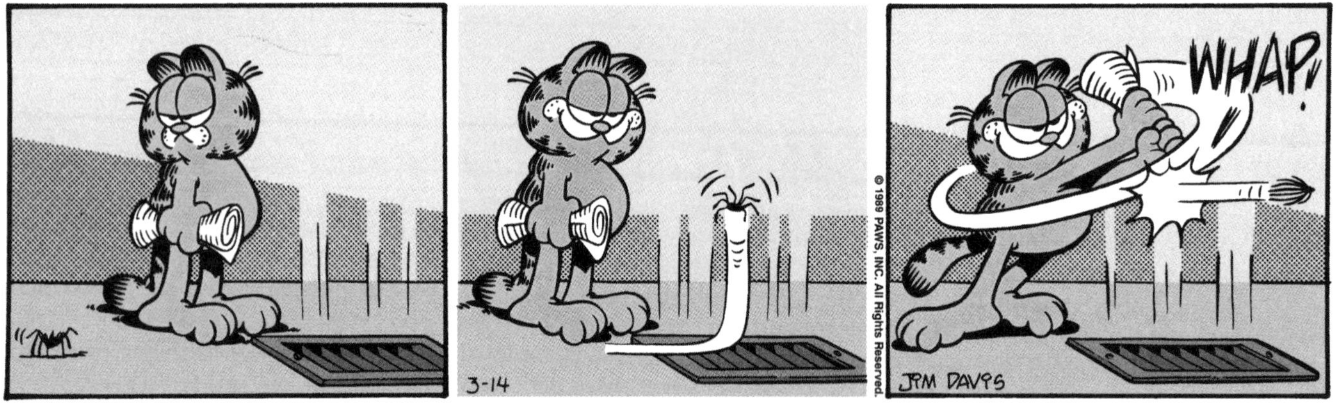
3-14
© 1989 PAWS, INC. All Rights Reserved.
WHAP!
JIM DAVIS

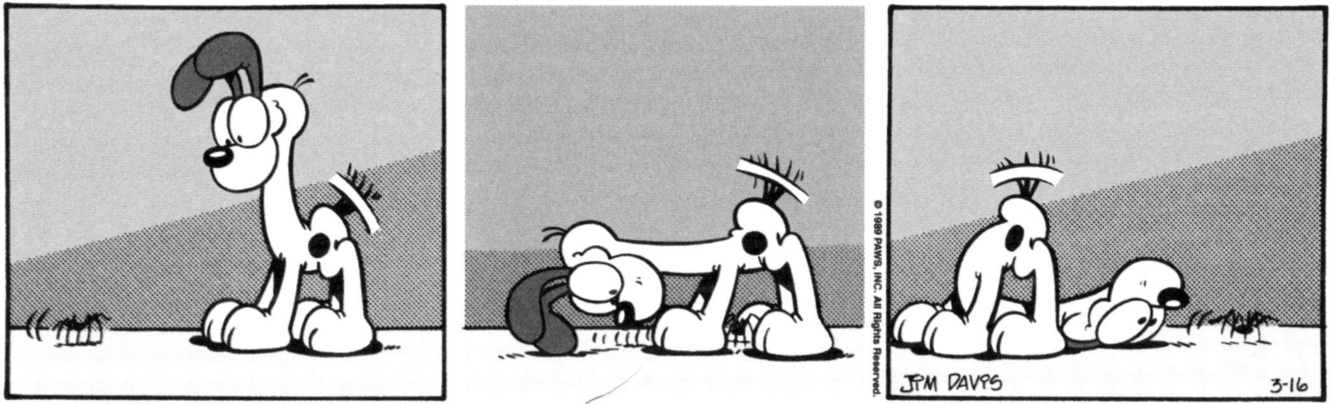
© 1989 PAWS, INC. All Rights Reserved.
JIM DAVIS
3-16

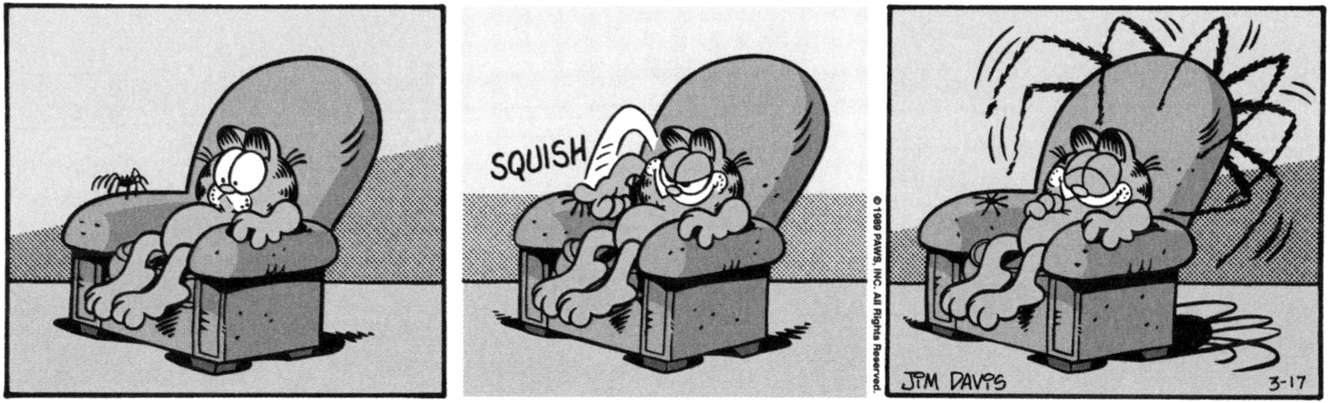
SQUISH
© 1989 PAWS, INC. All Rights Reserved.
JIM DAVIS
3-17

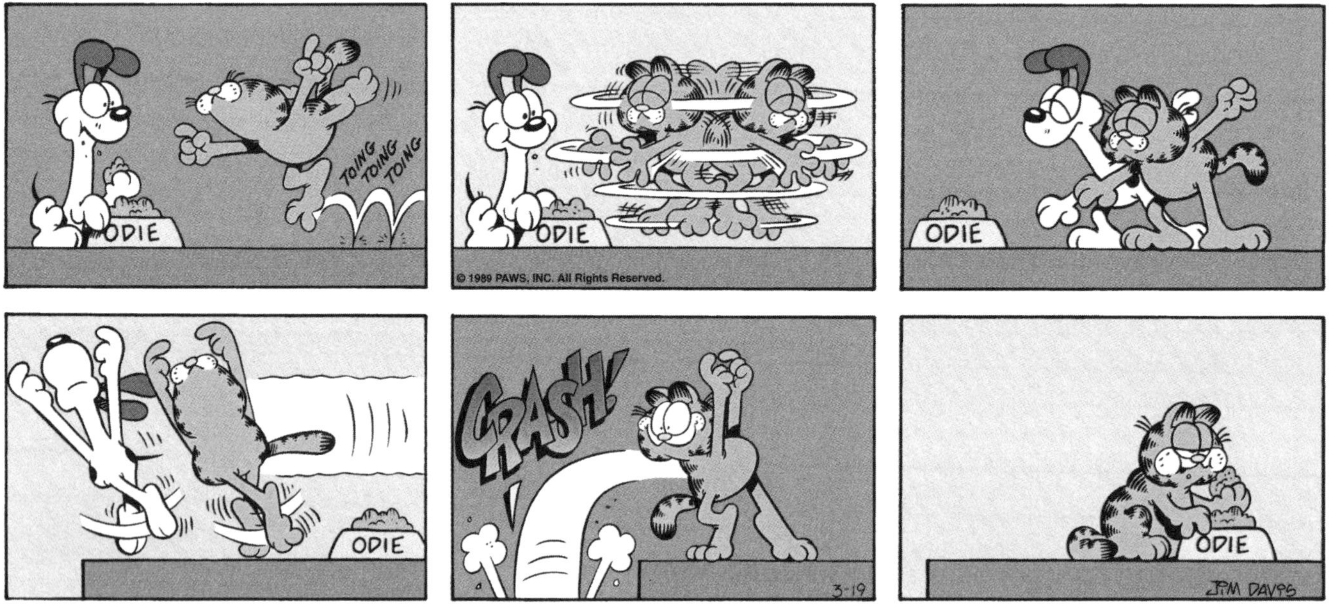

ODIE
TOING TOING TOING
ODIE
© 1989 PAWS, INC. All Rights Reserved.
ODIE
ODIE
CRASH!
3-19
ODIE
JIM DAVIS

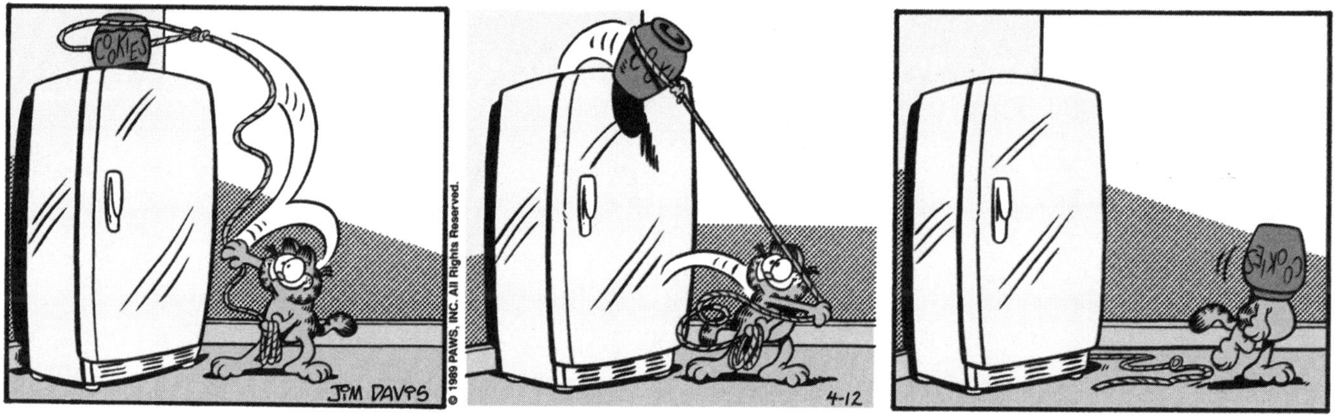
COOKIES
JIM DAVIS
© 1989 PAWS, INC. All Rights Reserved.
4-12
COOKIES

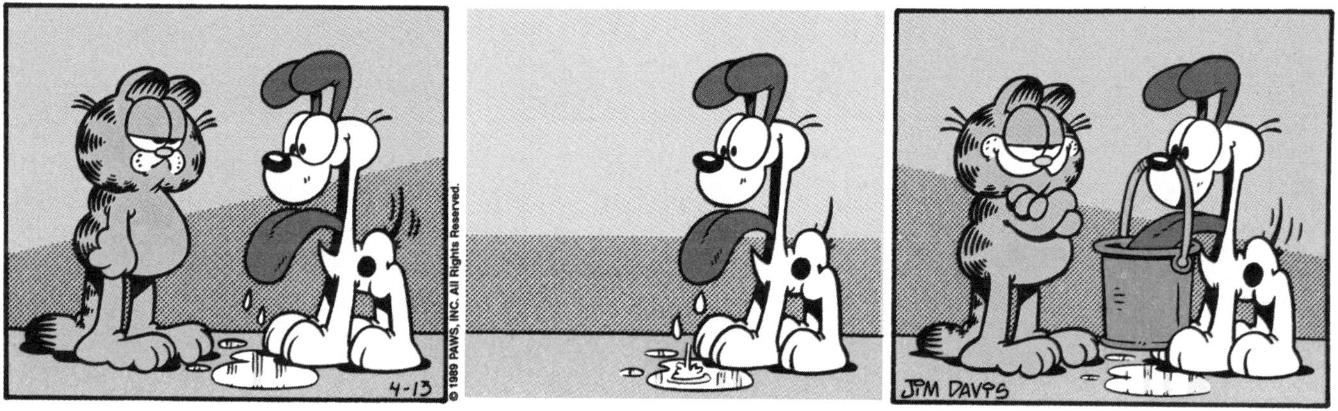
4-13
© 1989 PAWS, INC. All Rights Reserved.
JIM DAVIS

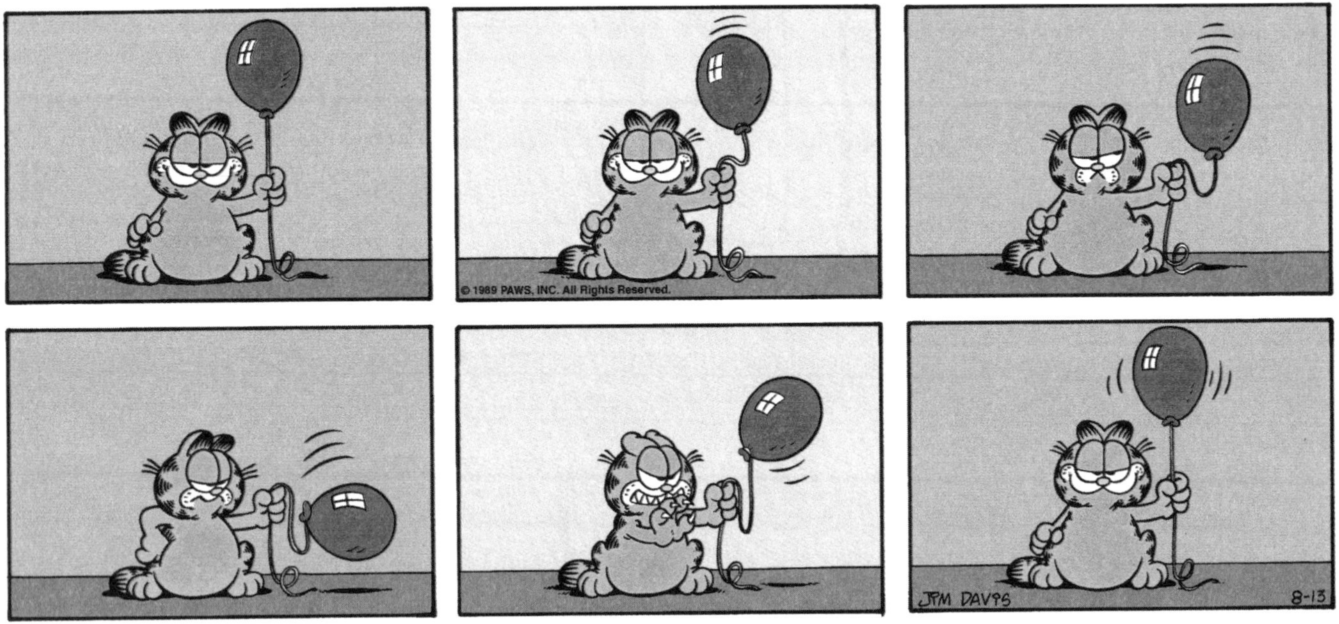
© 1989 PAWS, INC. All Rights Reserved.
JPM DAVPS
8-13

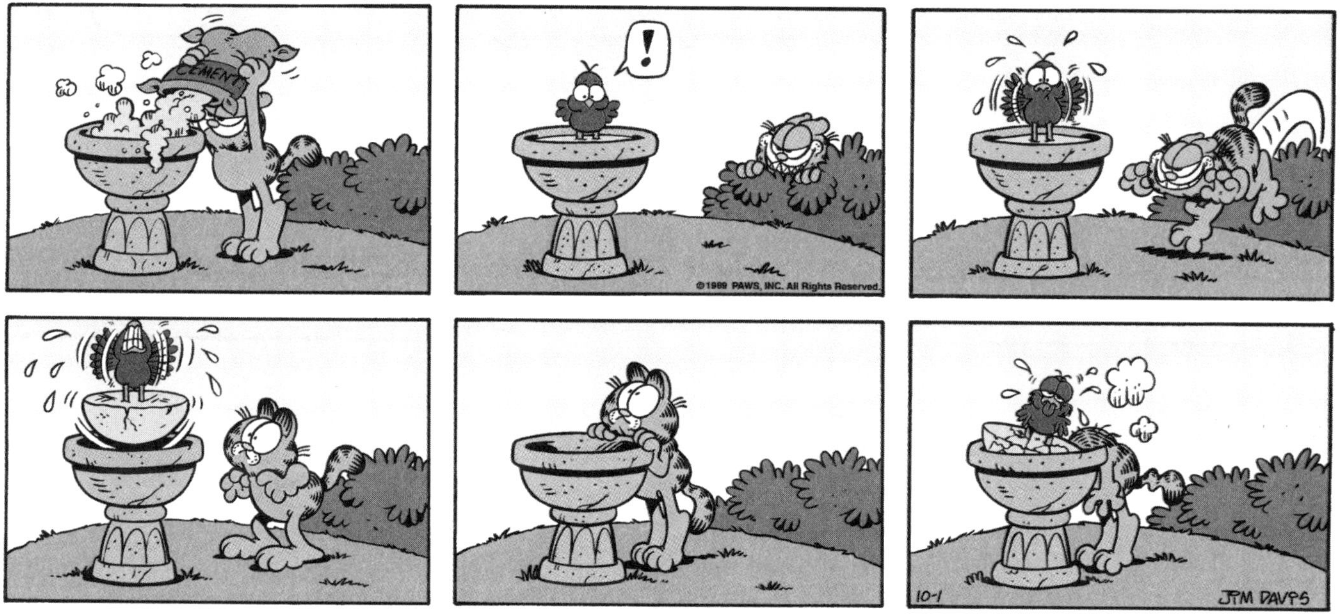
CEMENT
!
©1989 PAWS, INC. All Rights Reserved.
10-1
JIM DAVIS

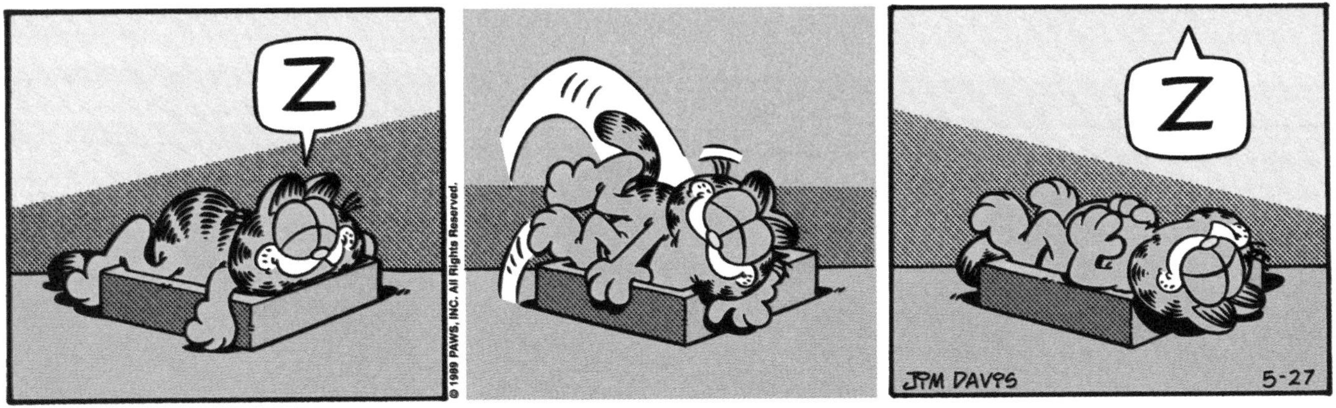
Z
Z
© 1989 PAWS, INC. All Rights Reserved.
JIM DAVIS
5-27

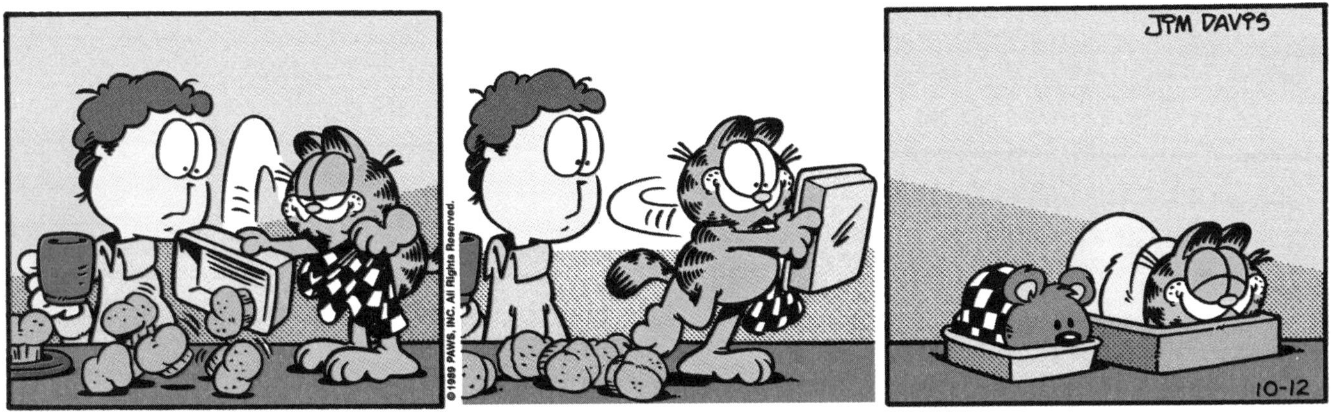
© 1989 PAWS, INC. All Rights Reserved.
JIM DAVIS
10-12

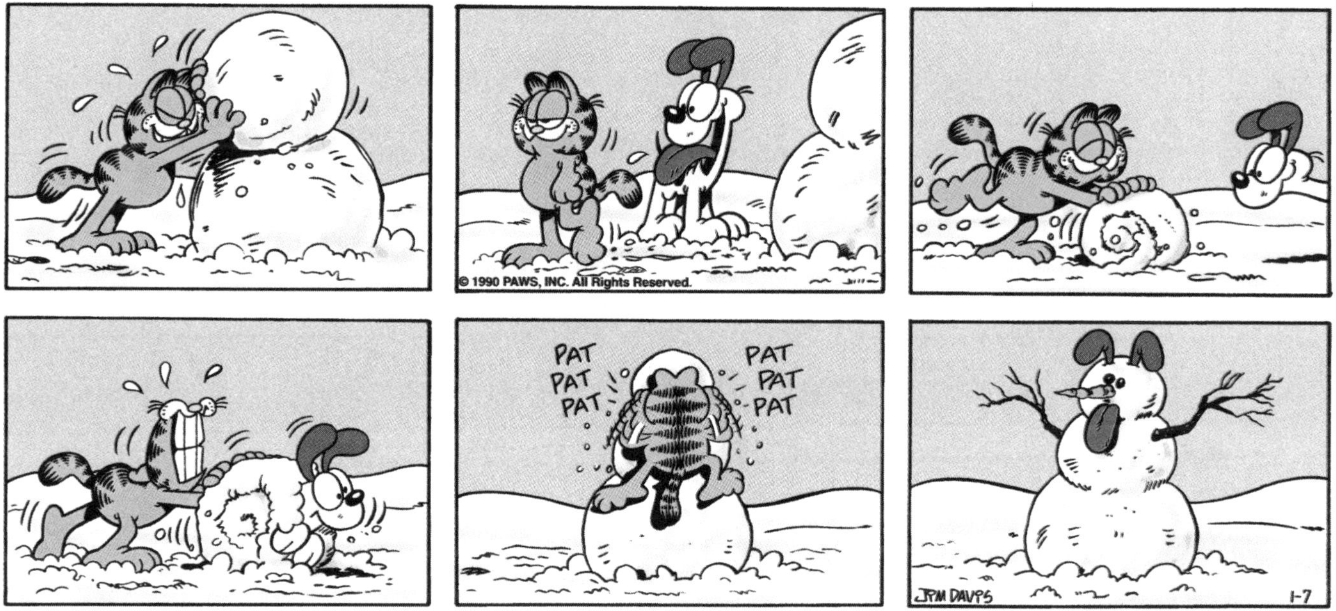
© 1990 PAWS, INC. All Rights Reserved.
PAT PAT PAT
PAT PAT PAT
JPM DAVIS
1-7

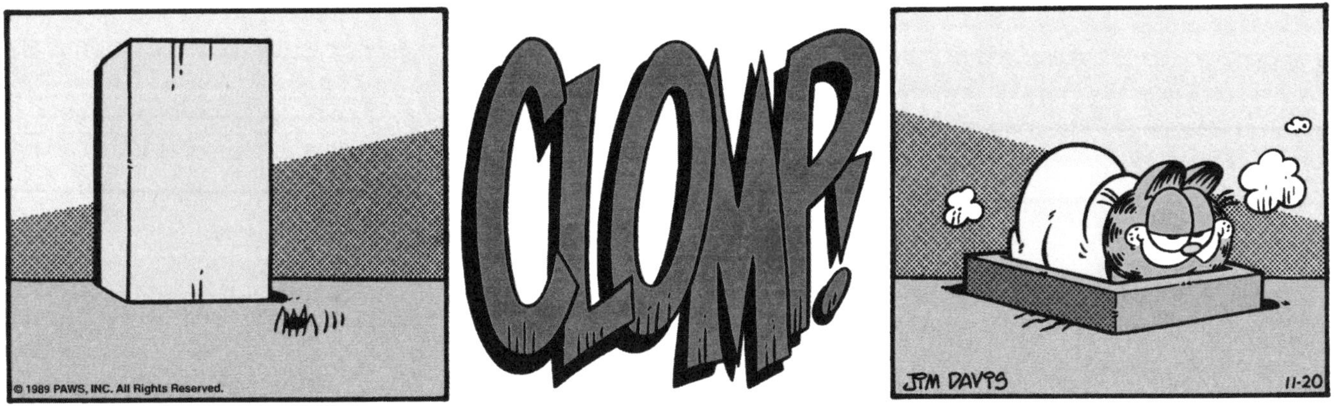
© 1989 PAWS, INC. All Rights Reserved.
CLOMP!
JIM DAVIS
11-20

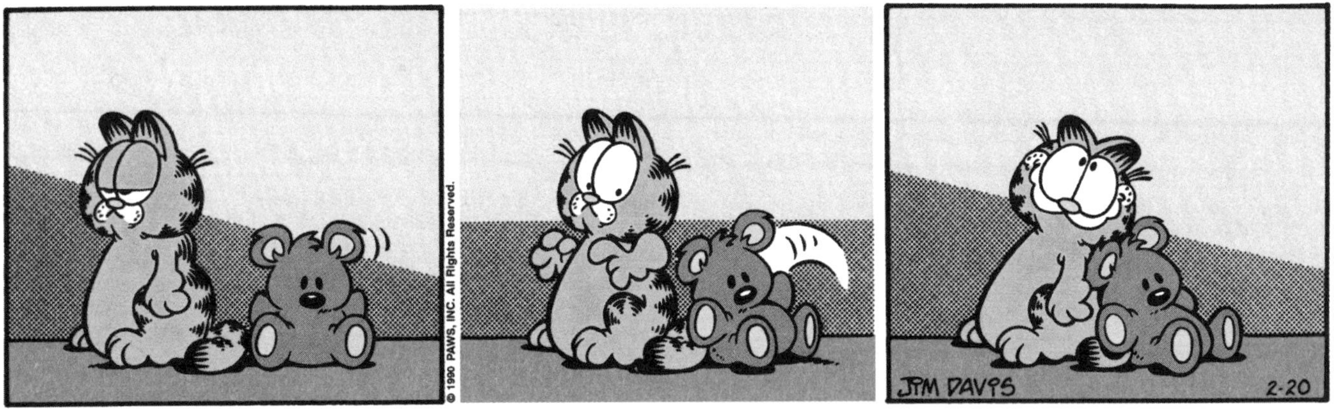
© 1990 PAWS, INC. All Rights Reserved.
JIM DAVIS
2-20

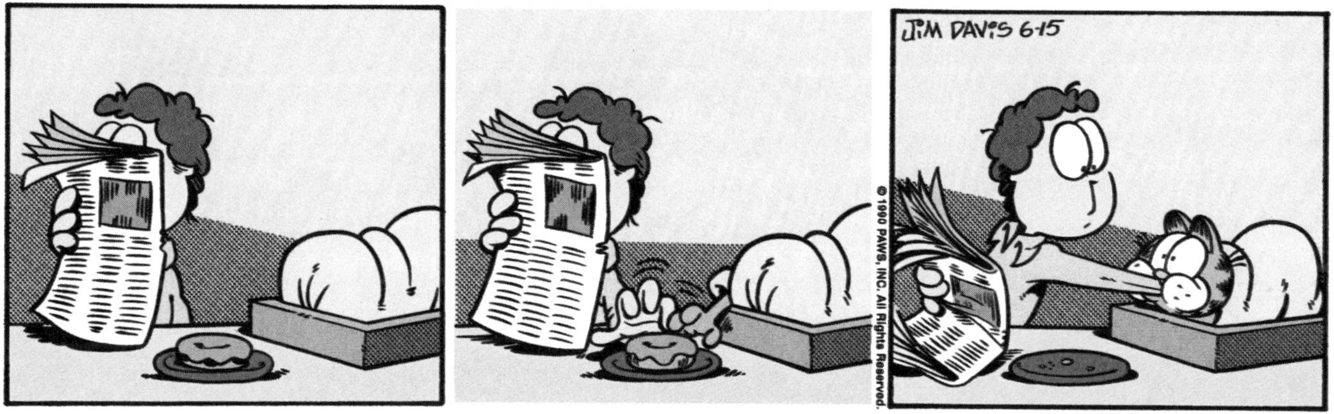
JIM DAVIS 6-15
© 1990 PAWS, INC. All Rights Reserved.

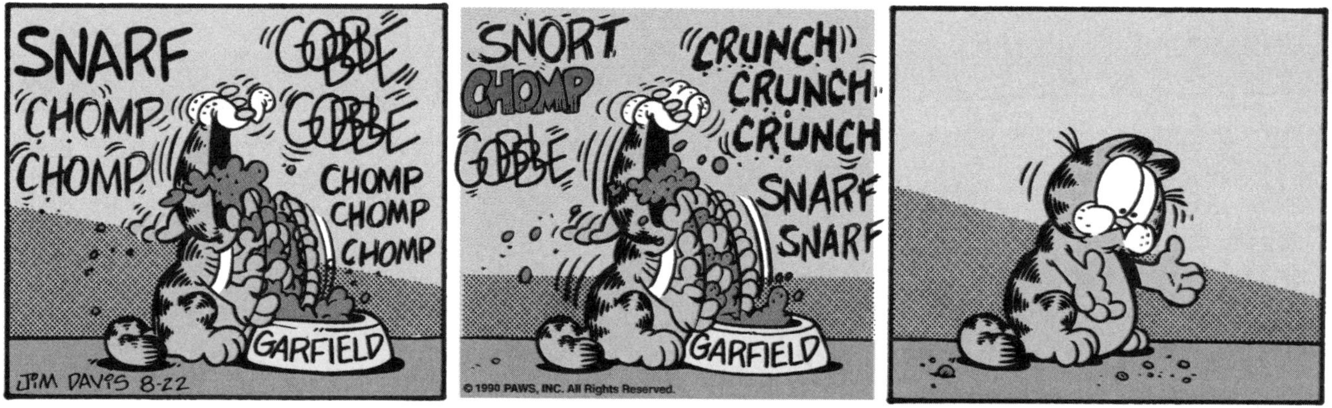
SNARF
CHOMP
CHOMP
GOBBLE
GOBBLE
CHOMP
CHOMP
CHOMP
GARFIELD
JIM DAVIS 8-22
SNORT
CHOMP
GOBBLE
CRUNCH
CRUNCH
CRUNCH
SNARF
SNARF
GARFIELD
© 1990 PAWS, INC. All Rights Reserved.

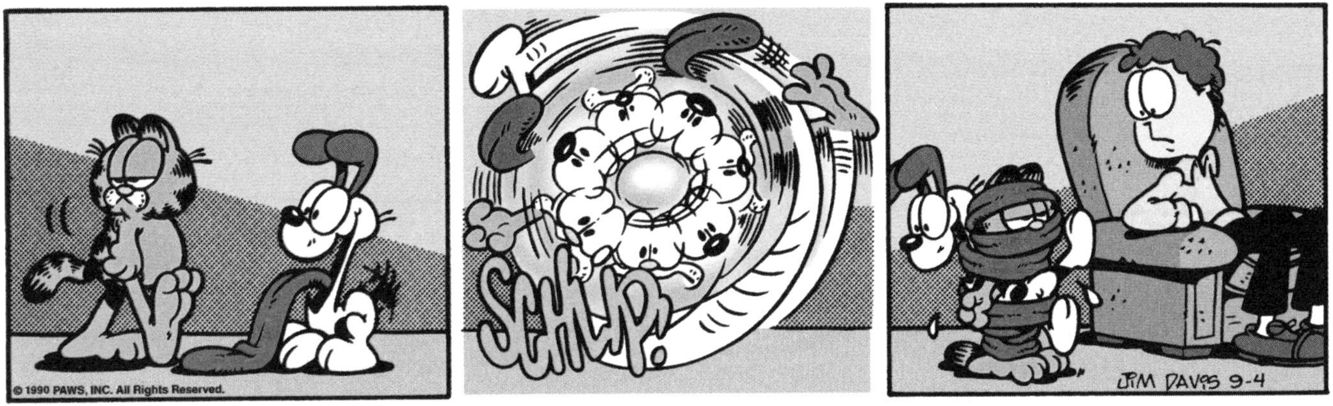
© 1990 PAWS, INC. All Rights Reserved.
SCHLUP!
JIM DAVIS 9-4

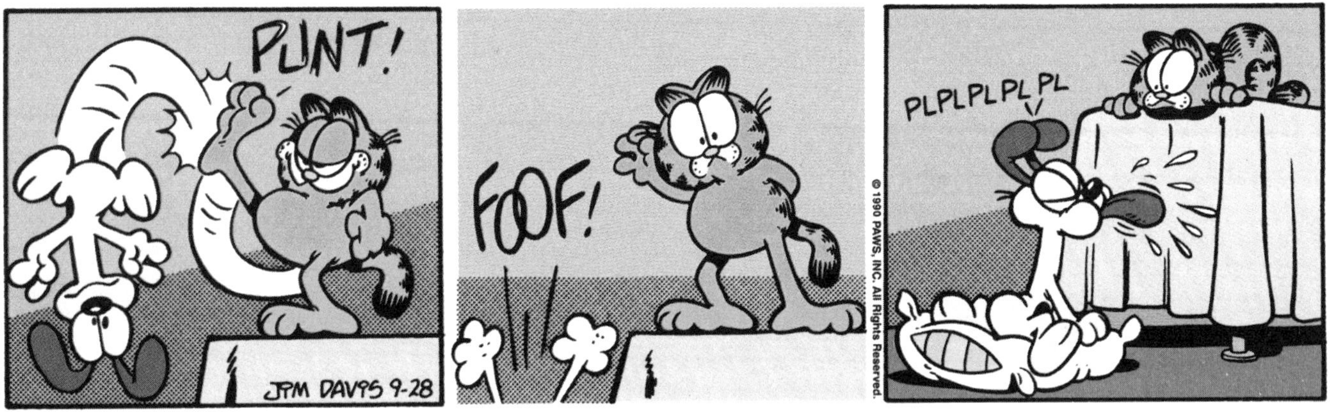
PUNT!
JIM DAVIS 9-28
FOOF!
© 1990 PAWS, INC. All Rights Reserved.
PLPLPLPLPL

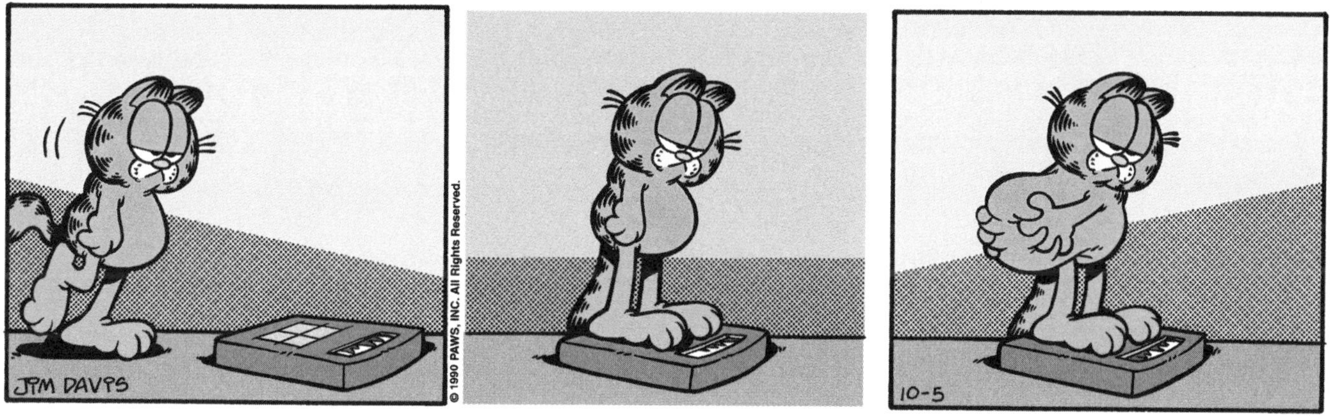
JIM DAVIS
© 1990 PAWS, INC. All Rights Reserved.
10-5

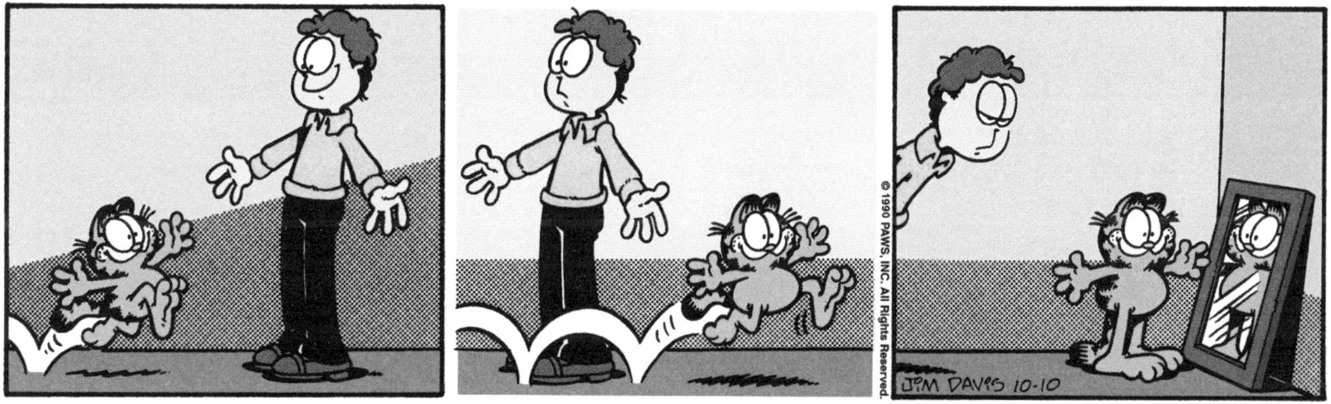
© 1990 PAWS, INC. All Rights Reserved.
JIM DAVIS 10-10

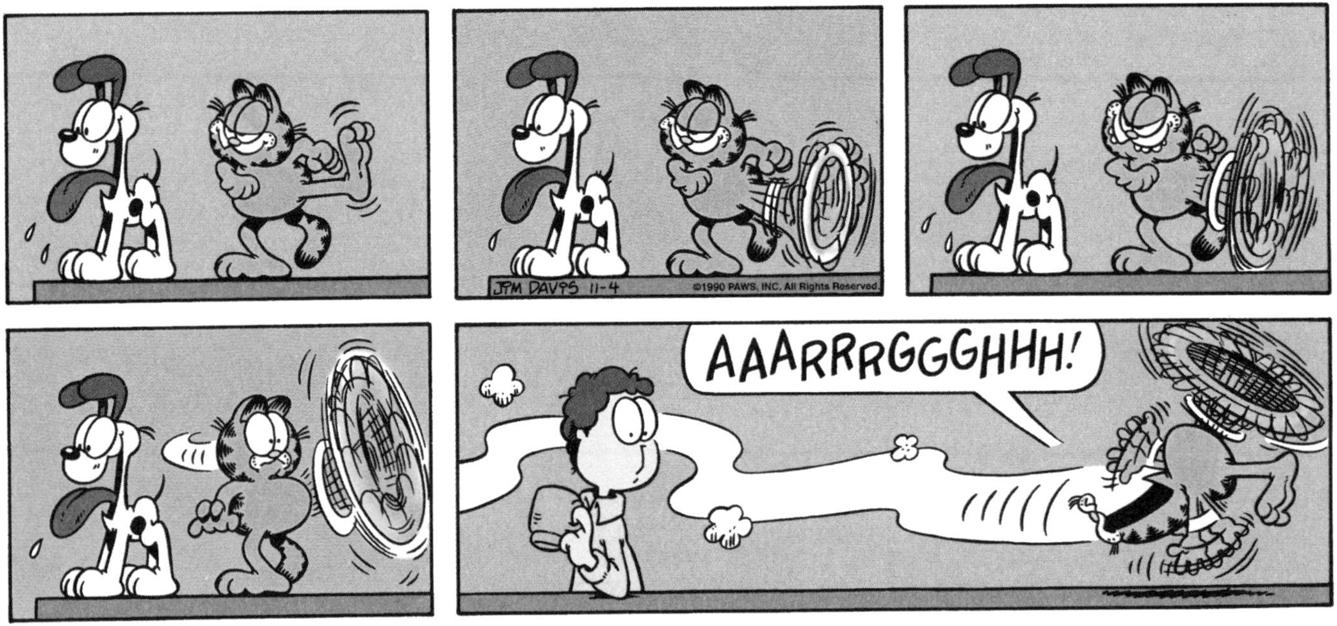
JIM DAVIS 11-4
©1990 PAWS, INC. All Rights Reserved.
AAARRRRGGGHHH!

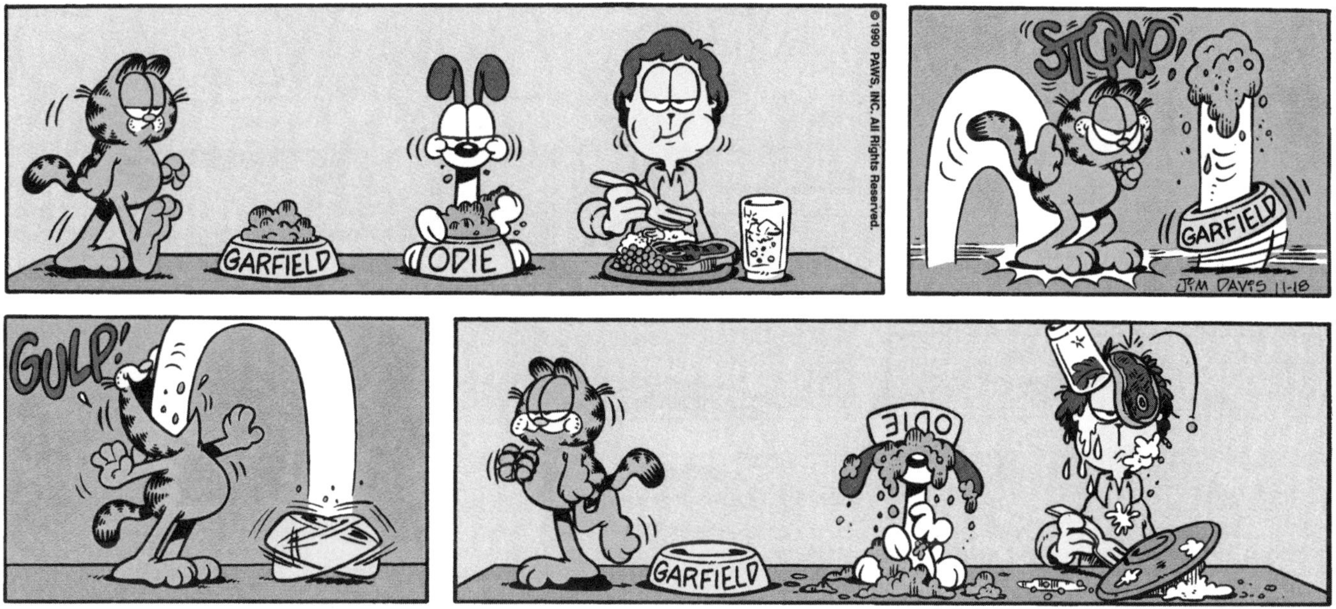
© 1990 PAWS, INC. All Rights Reserved.
GARFIELD
ODIE
STOMP!
GARFIELD
JIM DAVIS 11-18
GULP!
GARFIELD
ODIE

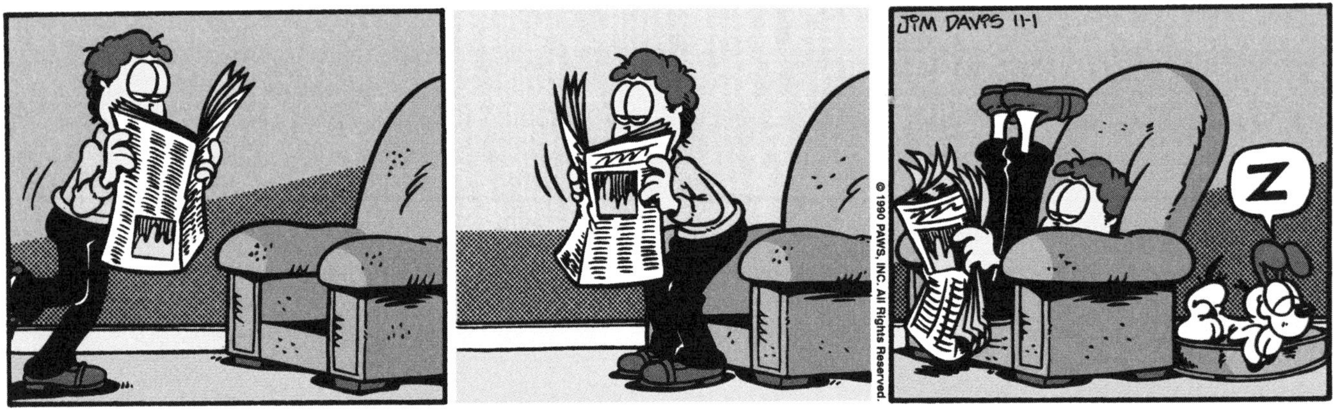
JIM DAVIS 11-1
© 1990 PAWS, INC. All Rights Reserved.
Z

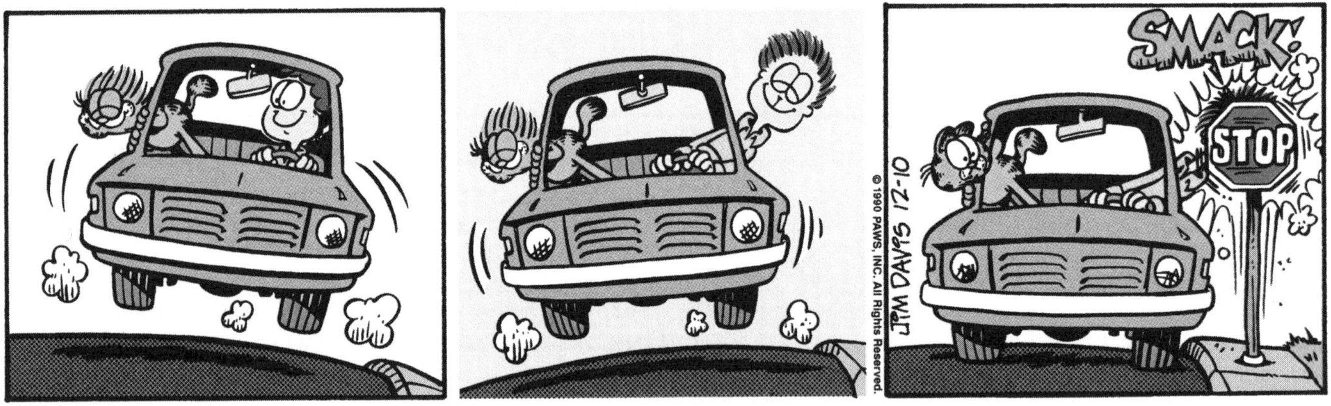
© 1990 PAWS, INC. All Rights Reserved.
JIM DAVIS 12-10
SMACK!
STOP

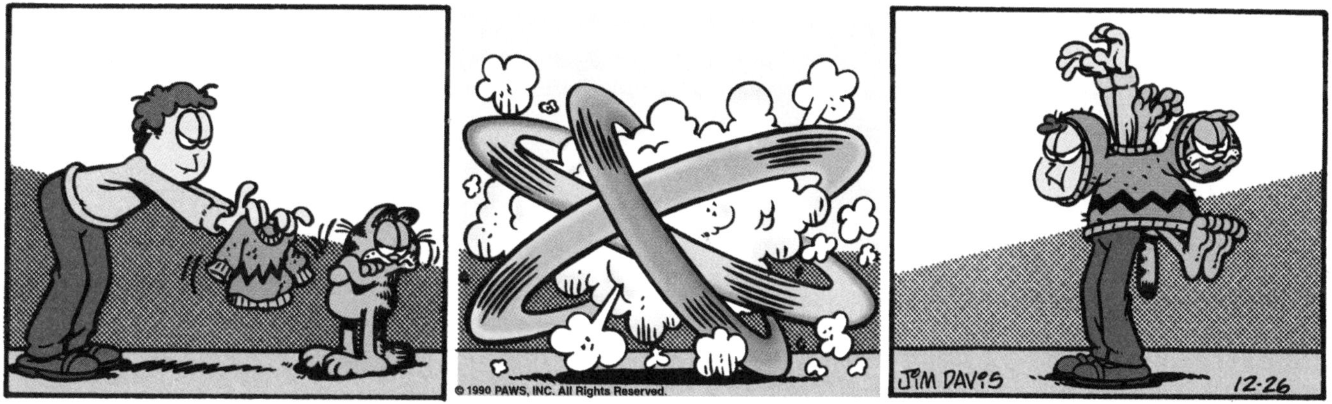
© 1990 PAWS, INC. All Rights Reserved.
JIM DAVIS
12-26

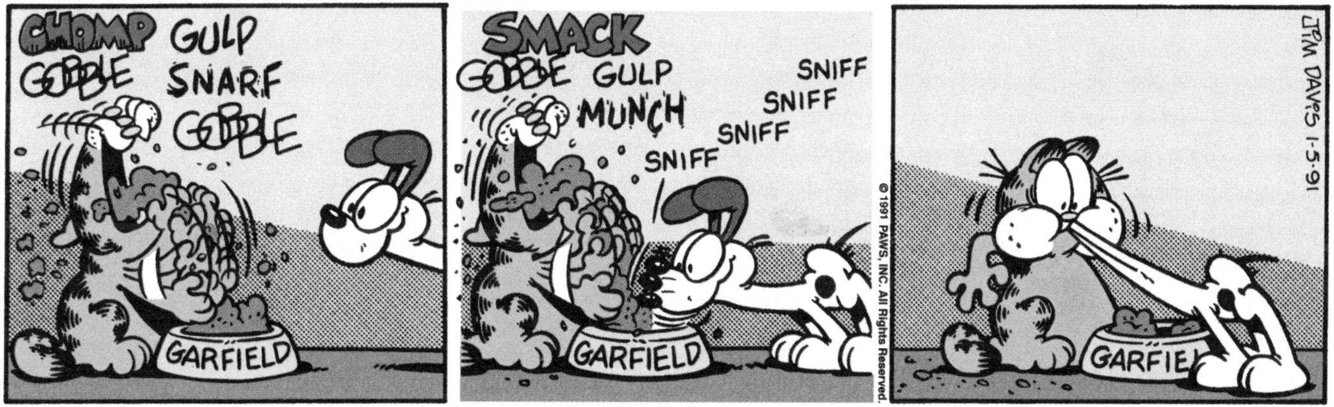
CHOMP
GULP
GOBBLE
SNARF
GOBBLE
GARFIELD
SMACK
GOBBLE
GULP
MUNCH
SNIFF
SNIFF
SNIFF
SNIFF
GARFIELD
© 1991 PAWS, INC. All Rights Reserved.
JIM DAVIS 1-5-91
GARFIE

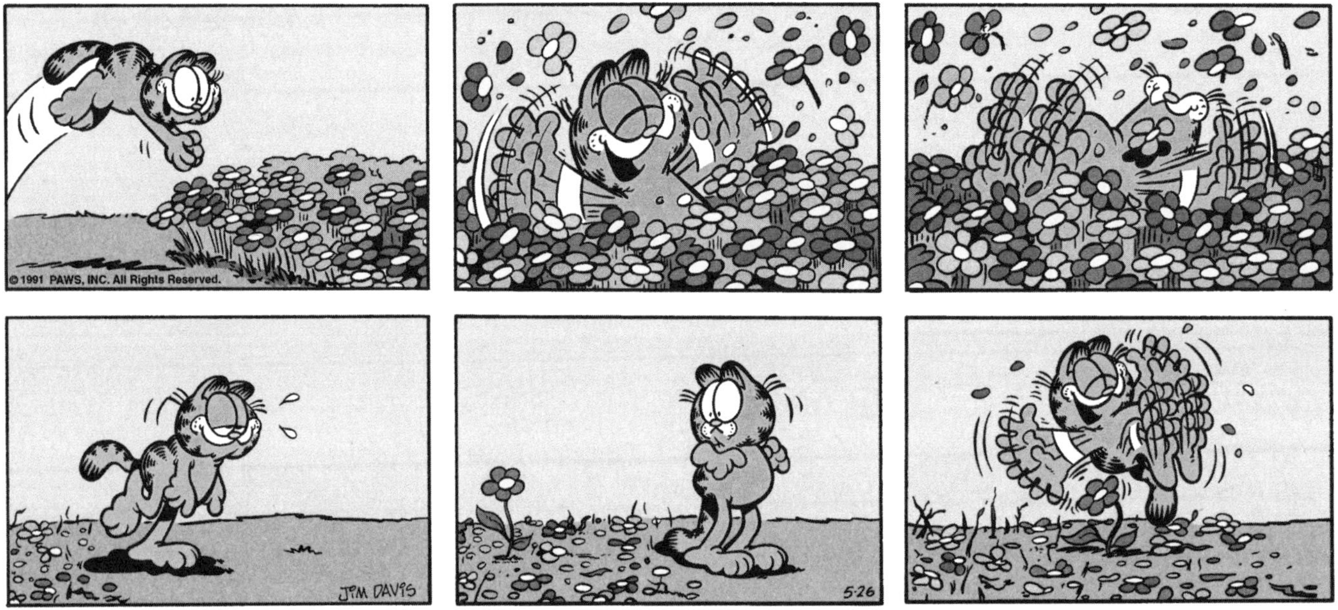
© 1991 PAWS, INC. All Rights Reserved.
JIM DAVIS
5·26

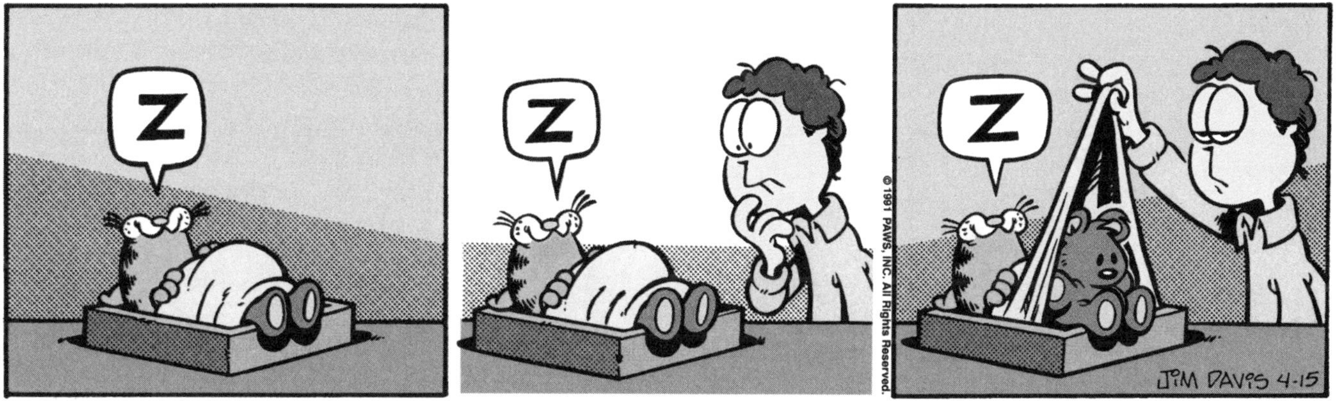
Z
Z
Z
© 1991 PAWS, INC. All Rights Reserved.
JIM DAVIS 4-15

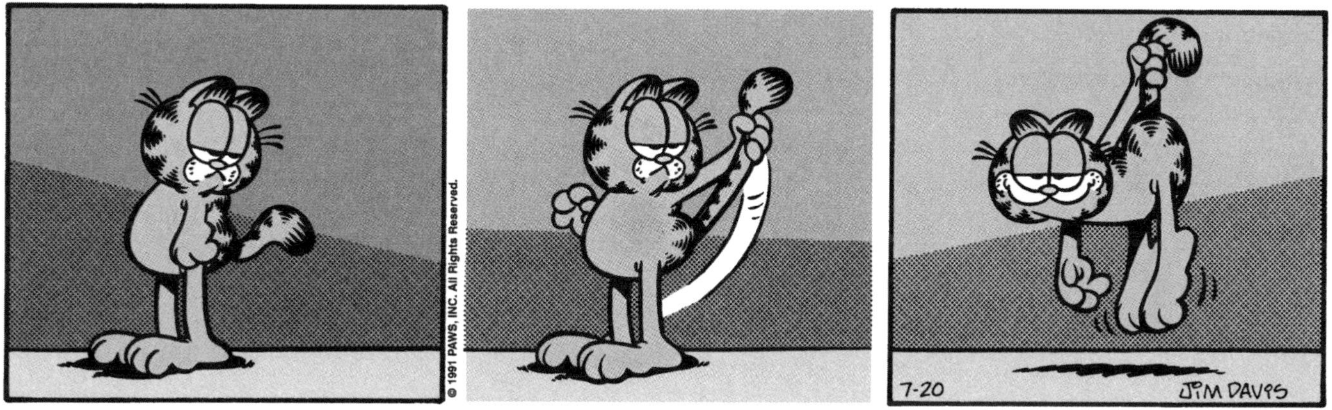
© 1991 PAWS, INC. All Rights Reserved.
7-20
JIM DAVIS

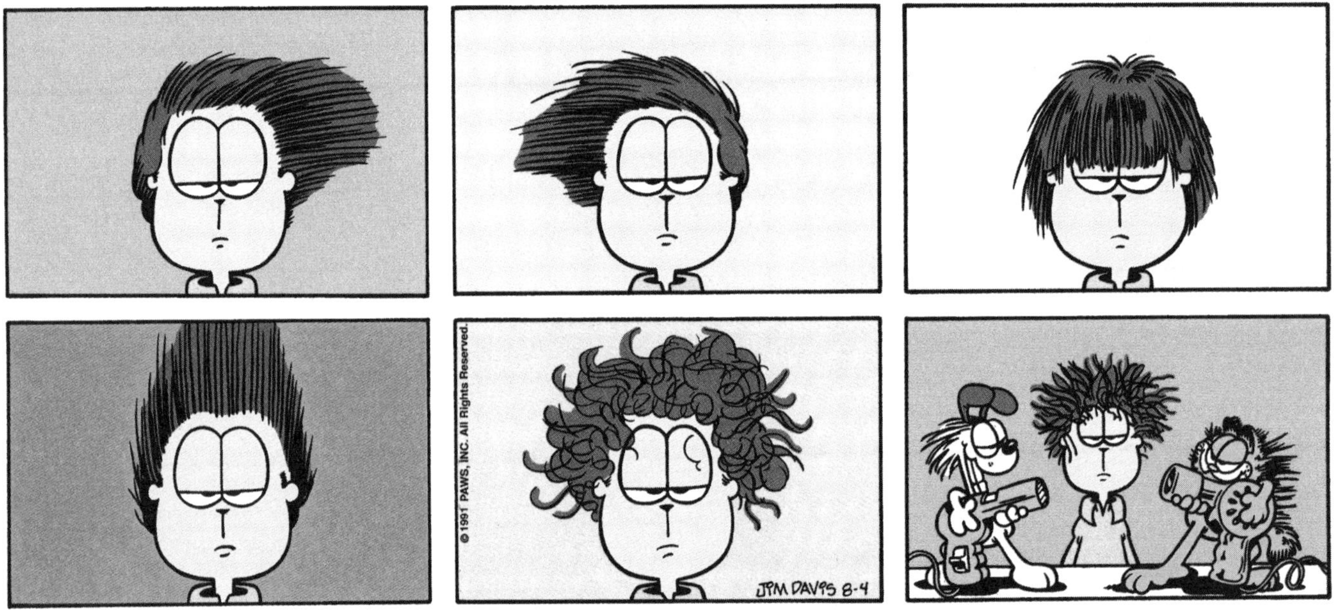

© 1991 PAWS, INC. All Rights Reserved.
JIM DAVIS 8-4

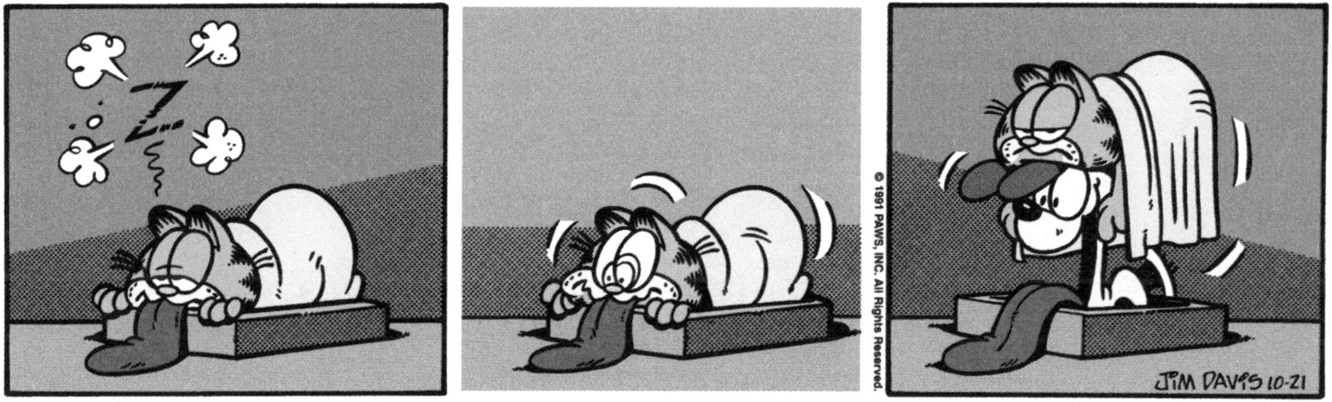
© 1991 PAWS, INC. All Rights Reserved.
JIM DAVIS 10-21

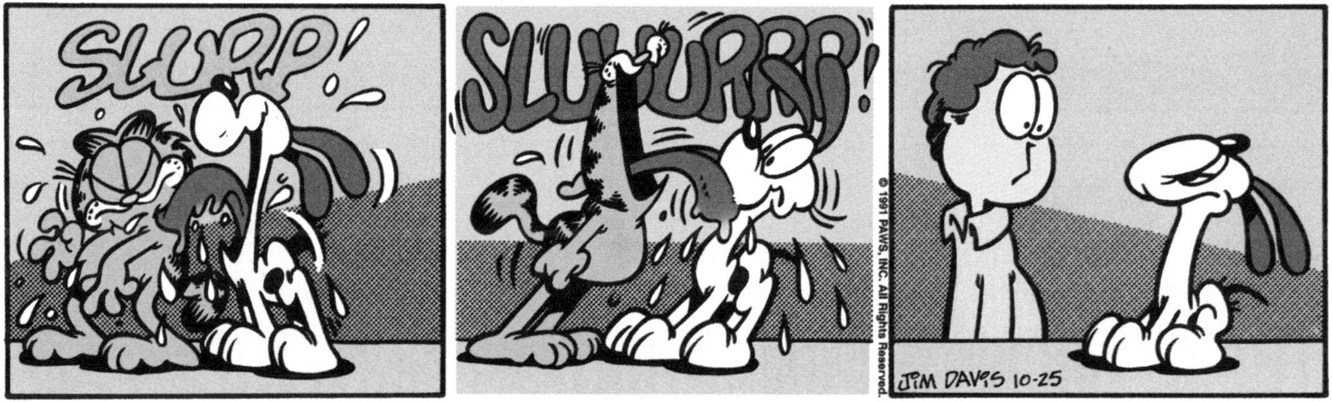
SLURP!
SLUUURRP!
© 1991 PAWS, INC. All Rights Reserved.
JIM DAVIS 10-25

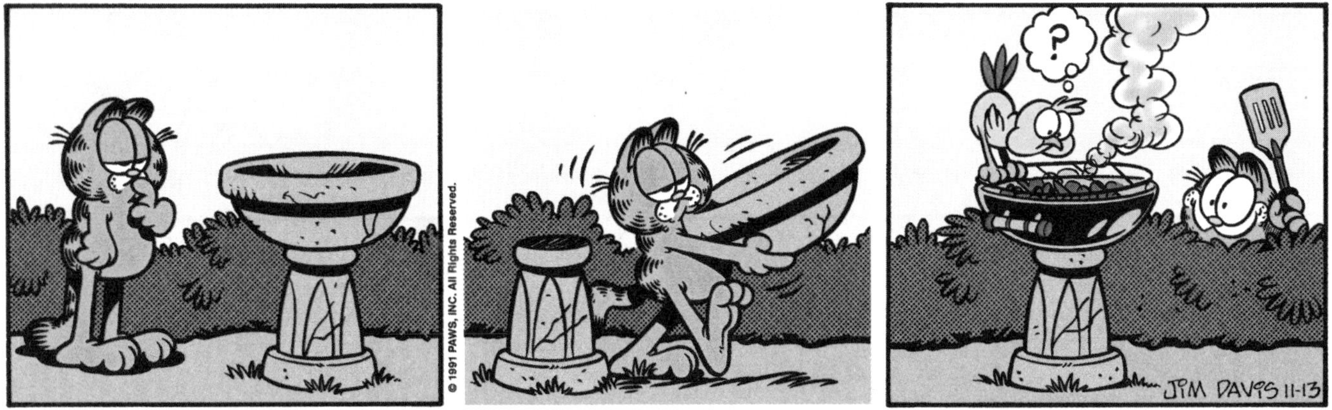
© 1991 PAWS, INC. All Rights Reserved.
?
JIM DAVIS 11-13

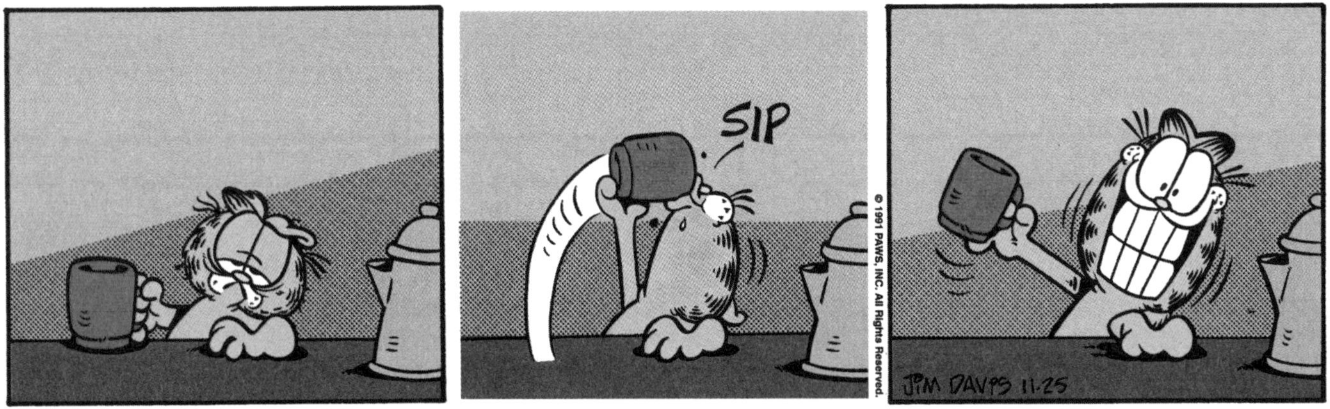
SIP
© 1991 PAWS, INC. All Rights Reserved.
JIM DAVIS 11-25

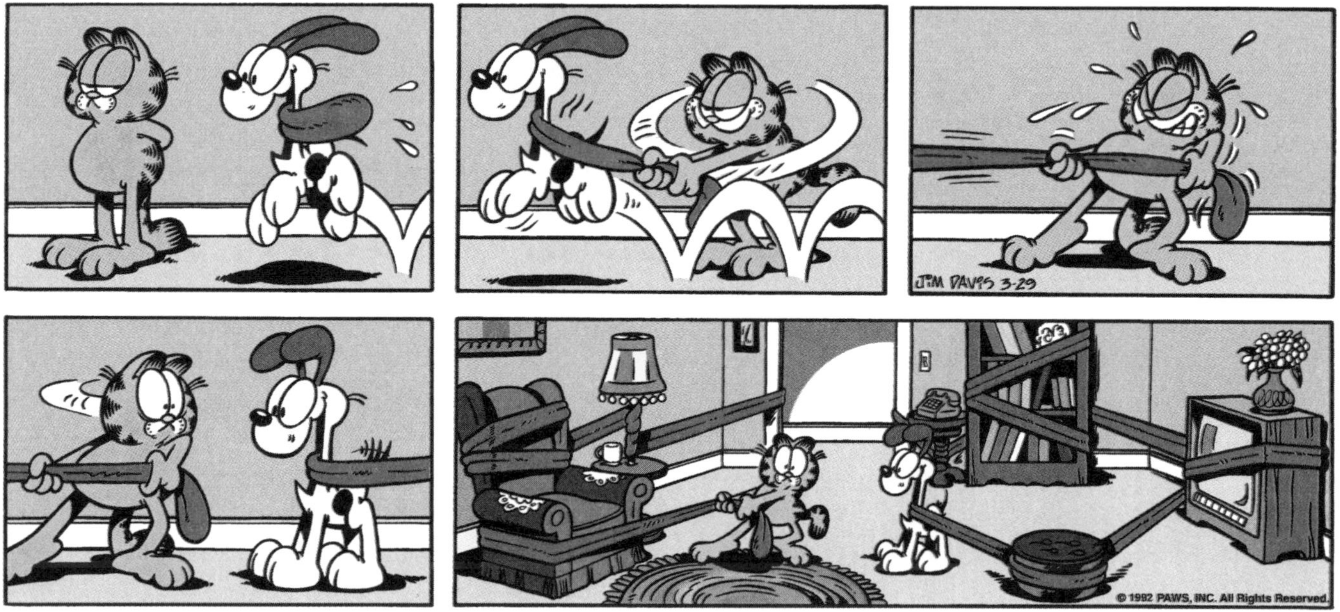
JIM DAVIS 3-29
© 1992 PAWS, INC. All Rights Reserved.

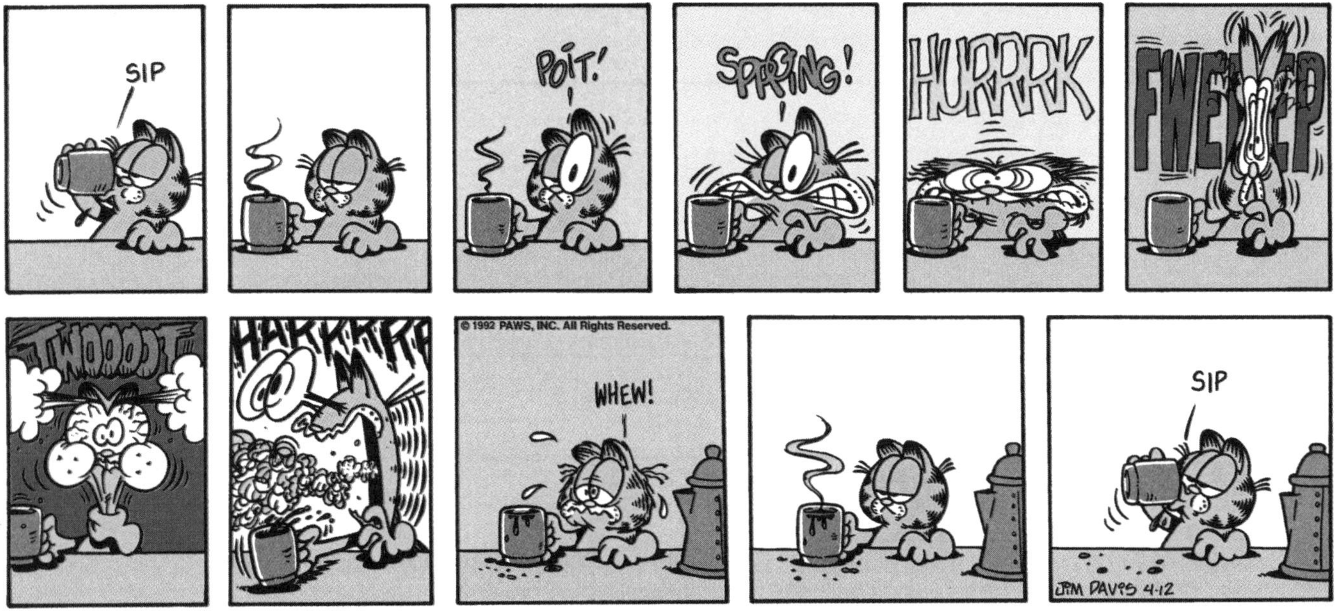
SIP
POIT!
SPROING!
HURRRRK
TWOOOOT
HARRRRRR
WHEW!
SIP
JIM DAVIS 4-12

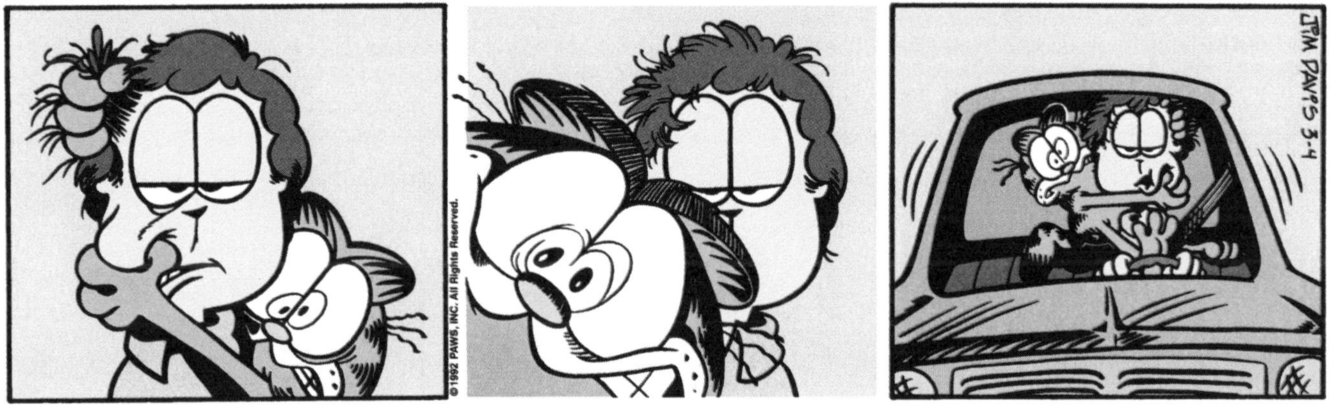
© 1992 PAWS, INC. All Rights Reserved.
JIM DAVIS 3-4

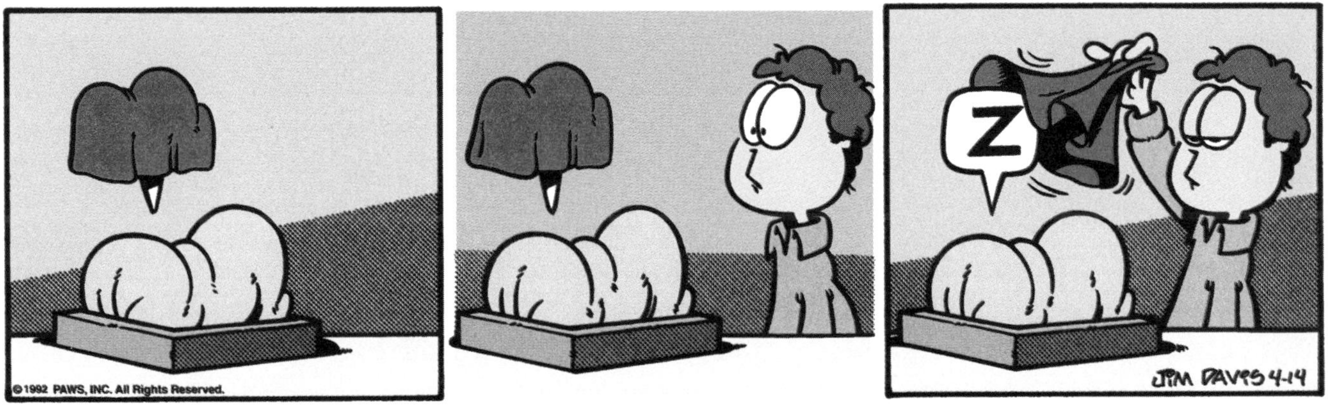
Z
© 1992 PAWS, INC. All Rights Reserved.
JIM DAVIS 4-14

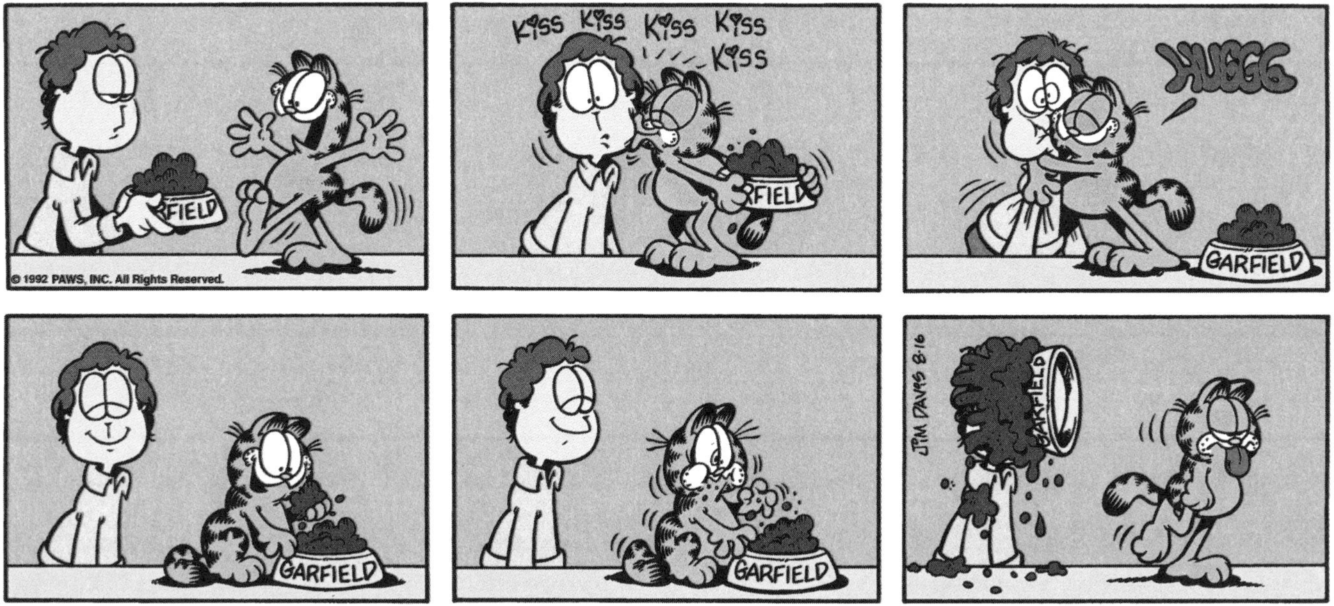

© 1992 PAWS, INC. All Rights Reserved.
FIELD
KISS KISS KISS KISS
KISS
FIELD
HUGGG
GARFIELD
GARFIELD
GARFIELD
JIM DAVIS 8-16
GARFIELD

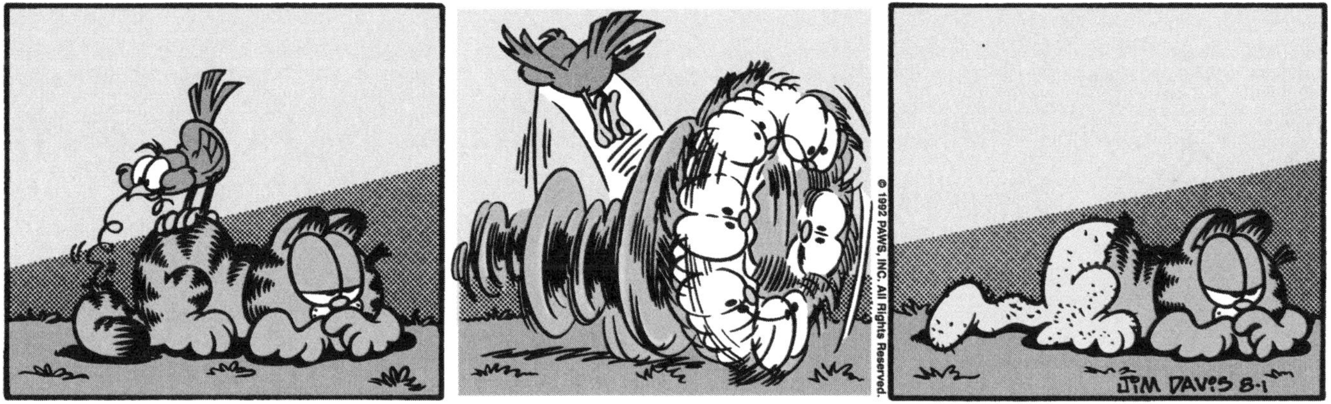
© 1992 PAWS, INC. All Rights Reserved.
JIM DAVIS 8-1

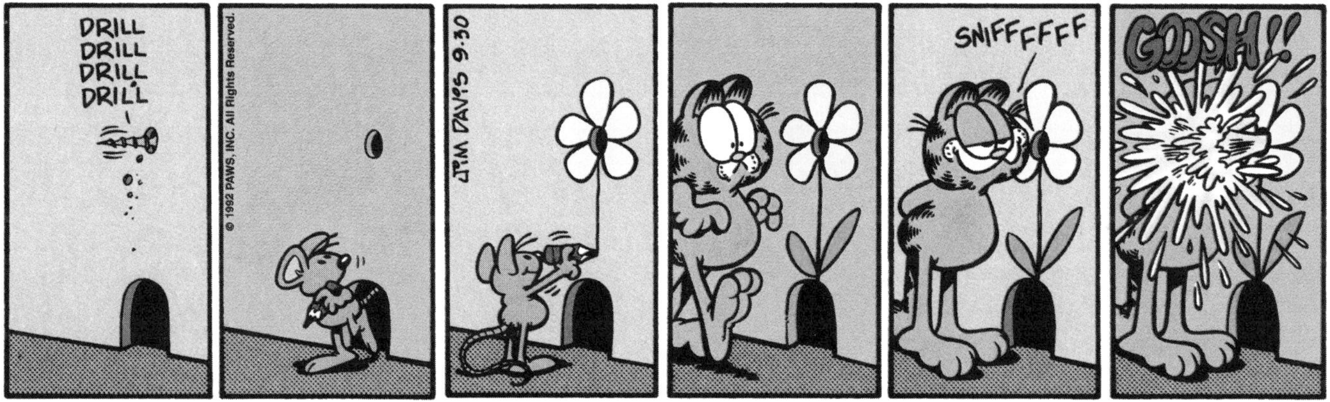
DRILL
DRILL
DRILL
DRILL
© 1992 PAWS, INC. All Rights Reserved.
JIM DAVIS 9-30
SNIFFFFFF
GOOSH!!

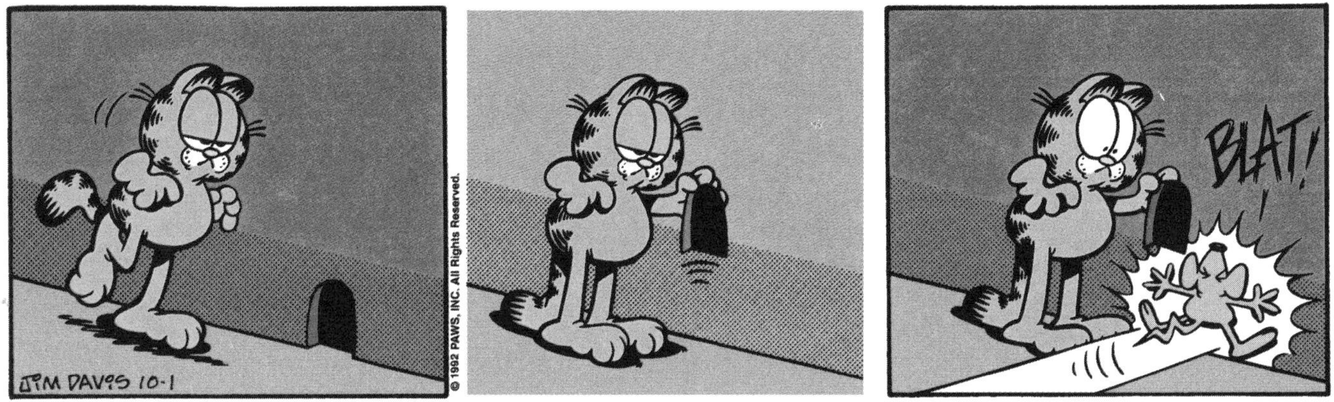
JIM DAVIS 10-1
© 1992 PAWS, INC. All Rights Reserved.
BLAT!

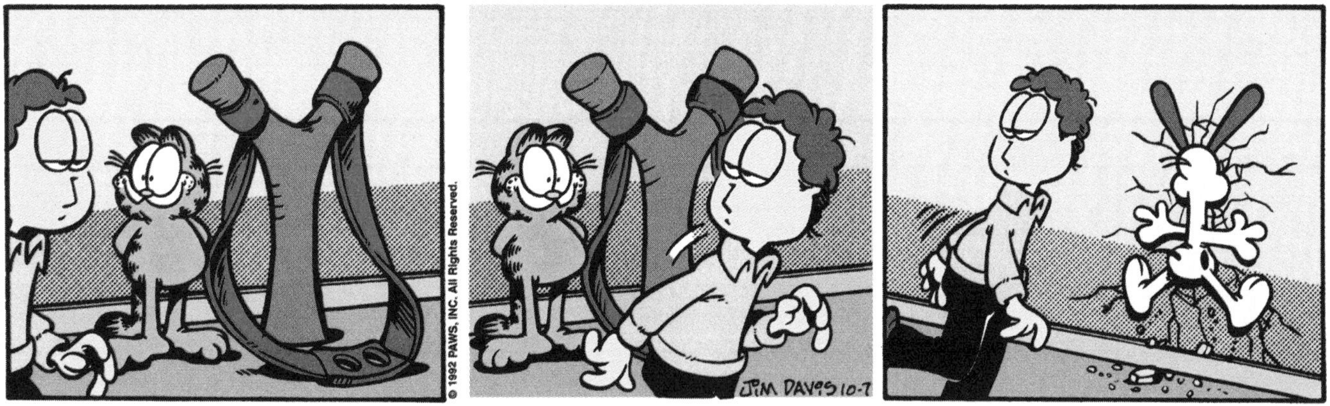
© 1992 PAWS, INC. All Rights Reserved.
JIM DAVIS 10-7

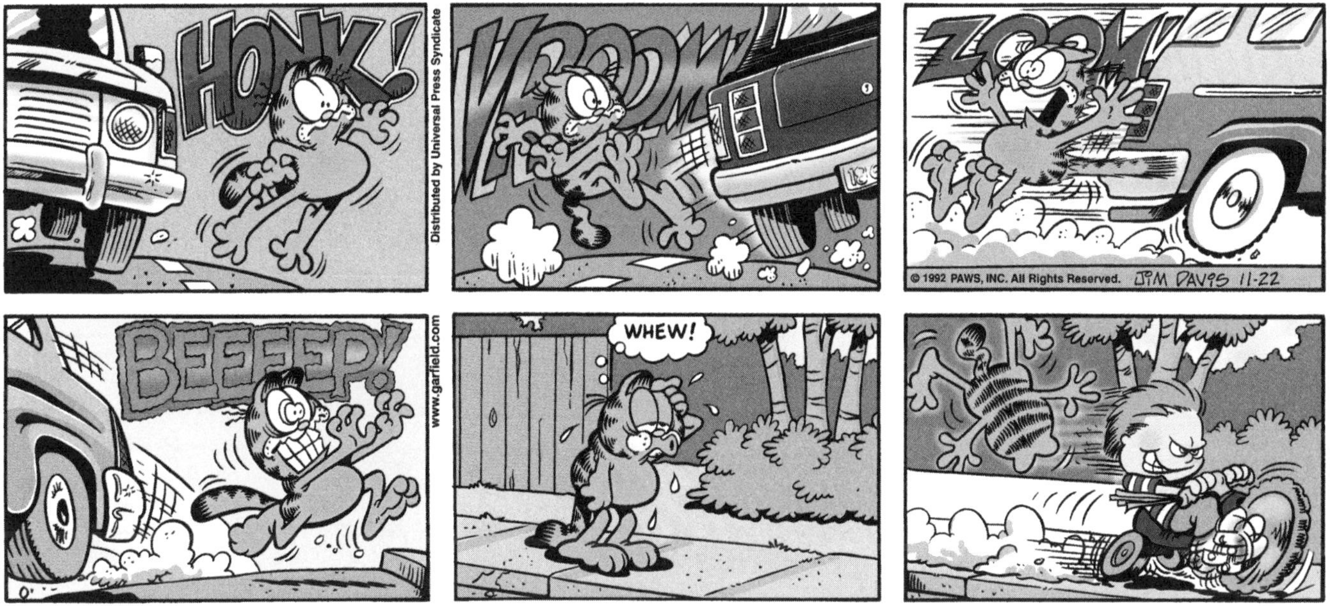
HONK!
Distributed by Universal Press Syndicate
VROOOM!
ZOOM!
© 1992 PAWS, INC. All Rights Reserved.
JIM DAVIS 11-22
BEEEEP!
www.garfield.com
WHEW!

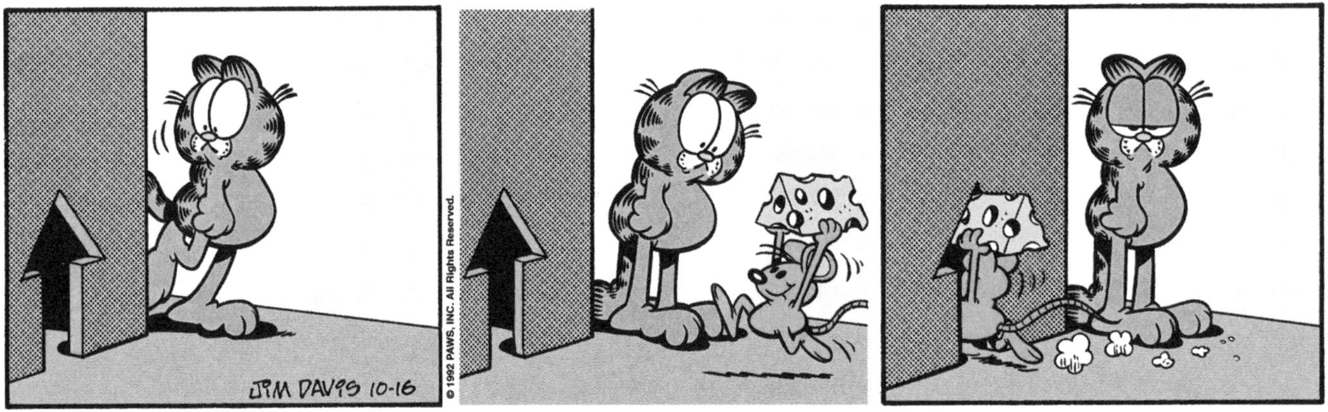
JIM DAVIS 10-16
© 1992 PAWS, INC. All Rights Reserved.

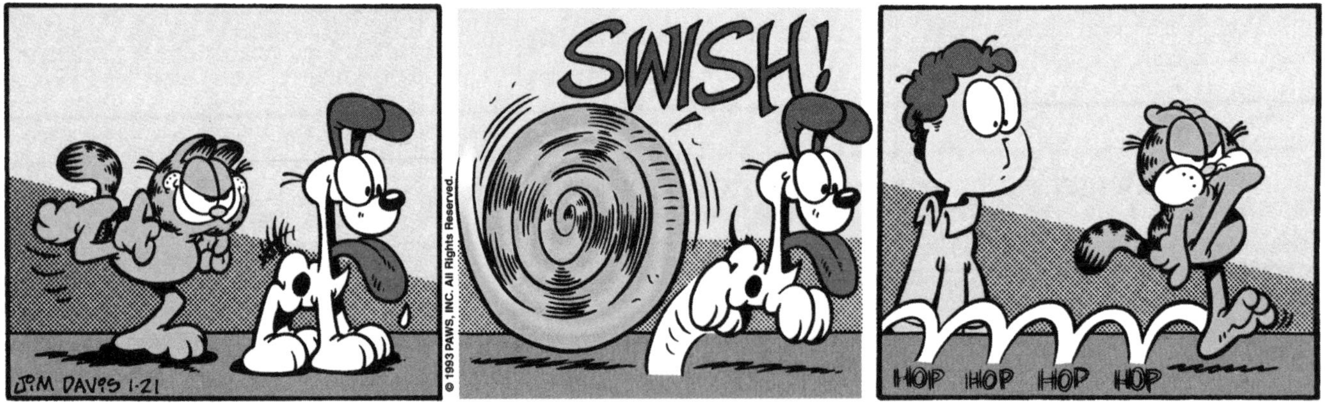
JIM DAVIS 1-21
© 1993 PAWS, INC. All Rights Reserved.
SWISH!
HOP HOP HOP HOP

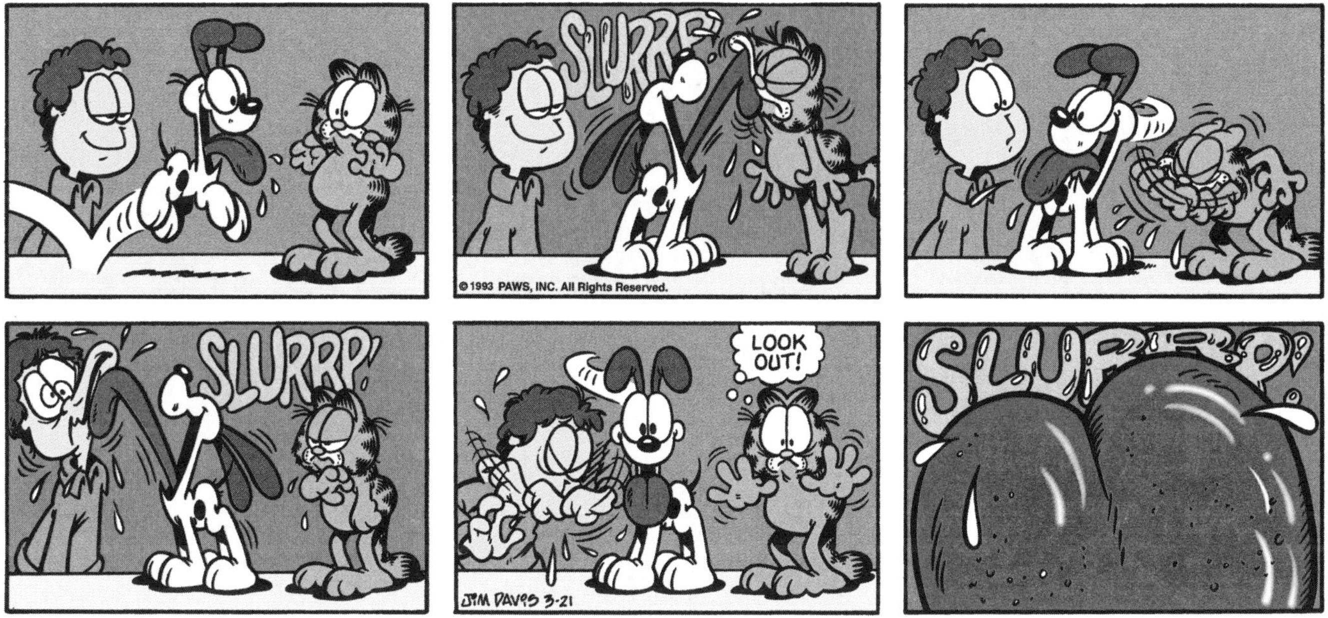
SLURRP!
© 1993 PAWS, INC. All Rights Reserved.
SLURRP!
LOOK OUT!
JIM DAVIS 3-21
SLURRP!

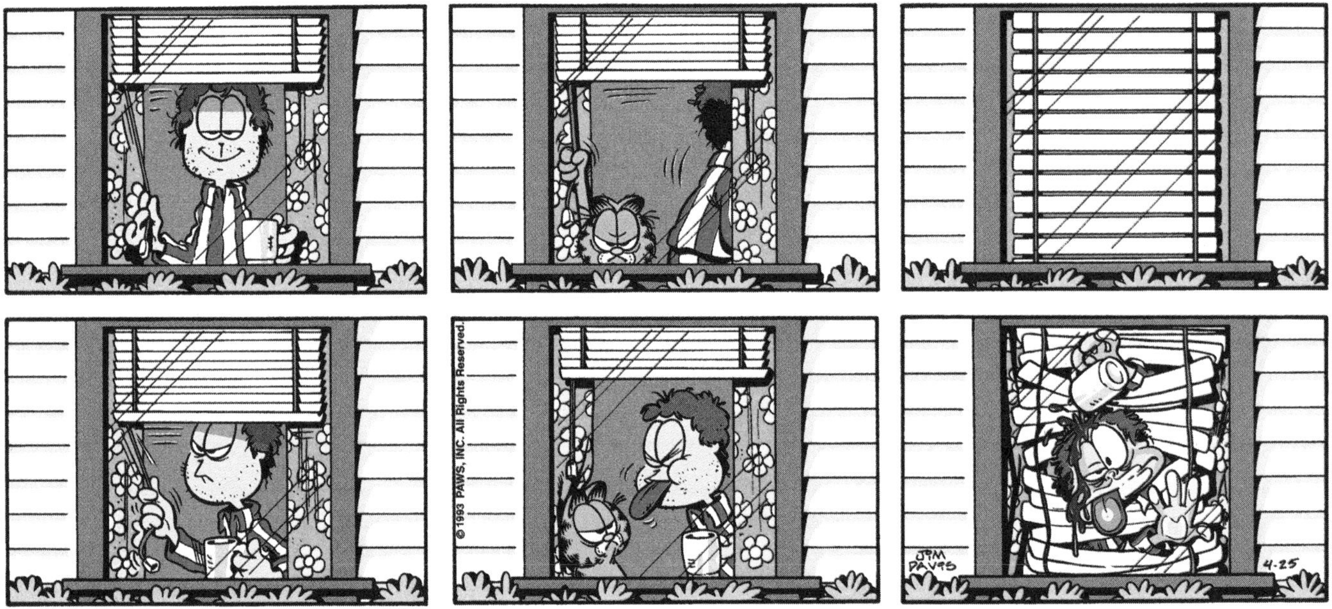
© 1993 PAWS, INC. All Rights Reserved.
JIM DAVIS
4-25

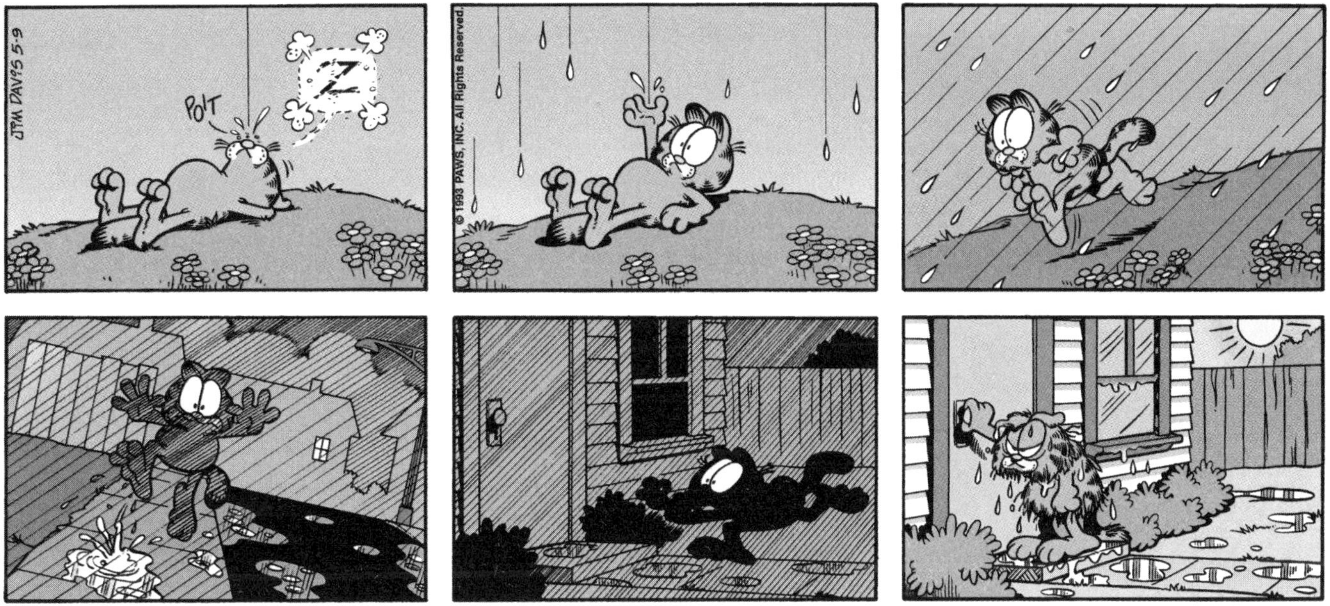
JIM DAVIS 5-9
POIT
Z
© 1993 PAWS, INC. All Rights Reserved.

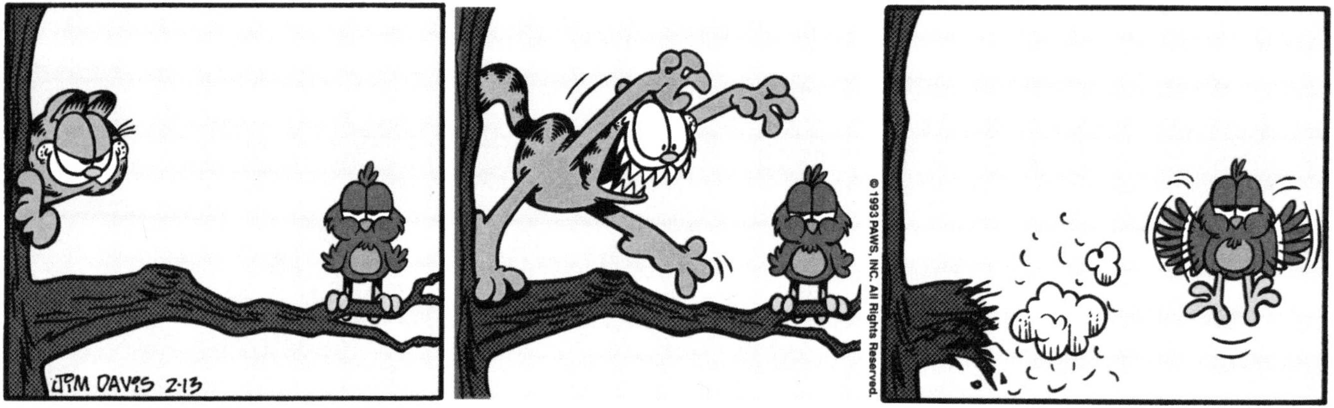
JIM DAVIS 2-13
© 1993 PAWS, INC. All Rights Reserved.

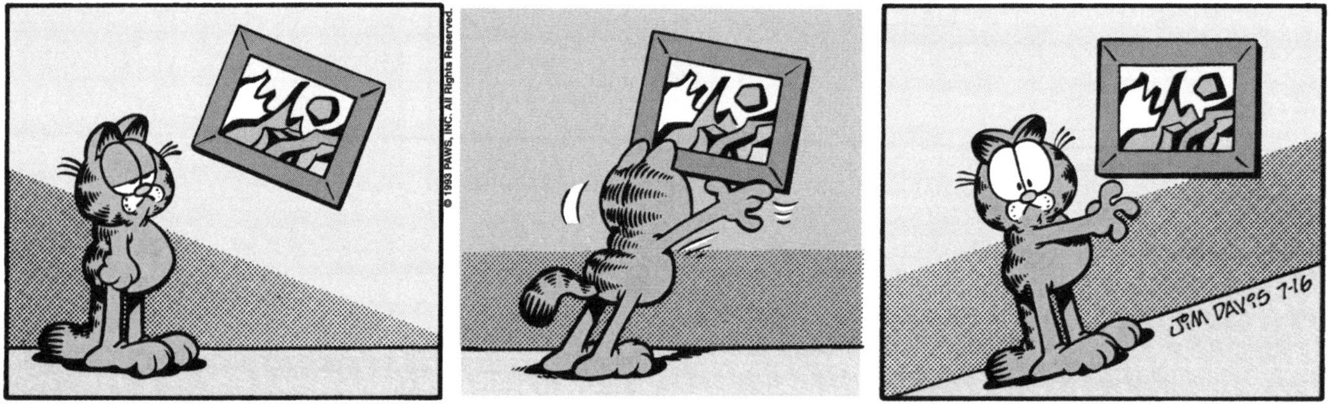
© 1993 PAWS, INC. All Rights Reserved.
JIM DAVIS 7-16

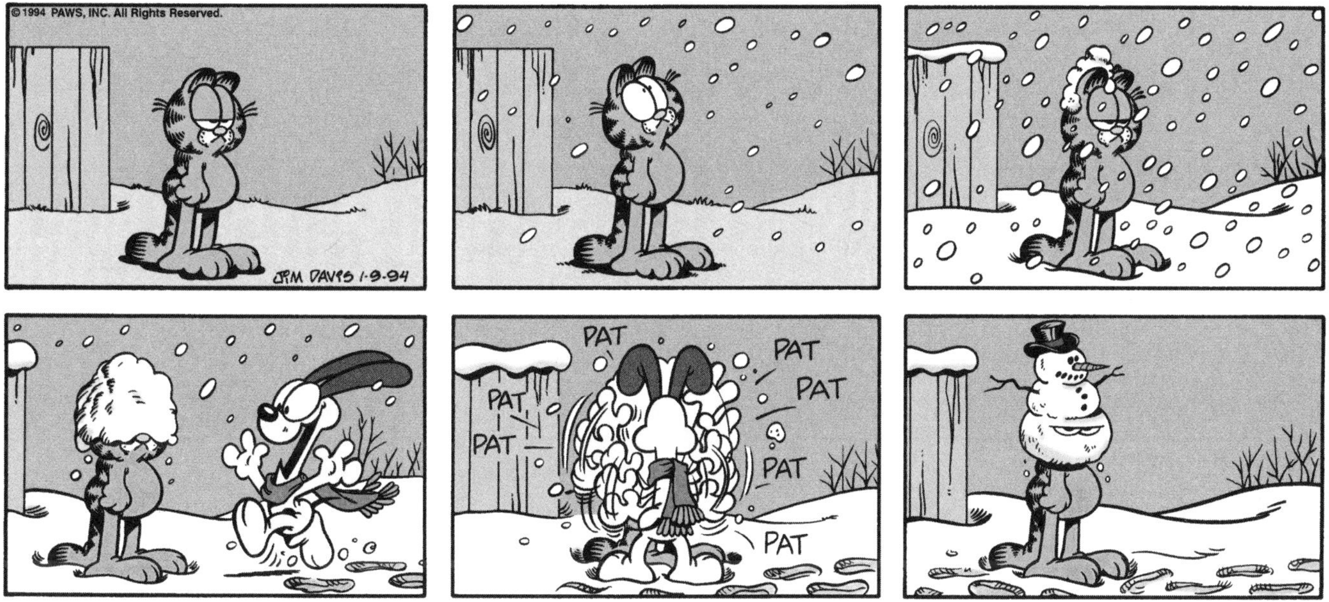

© 1994 PAWS, INC. All Rights Reserved.
JIM DAVIS 1-9-94
PAT
PAT
PAT
PAT
PAT
PAT
PAT

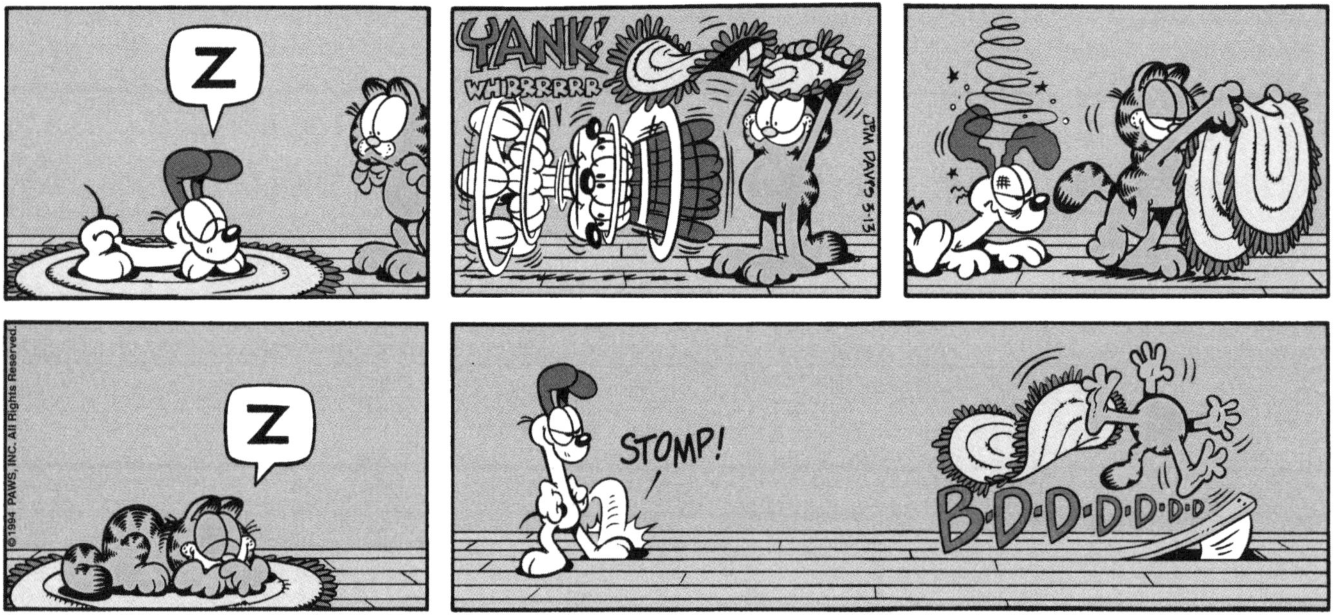
Z
YANK!
WHIRRRRRR
JIM DAVIS 3-13
Z
STOMP!
B-D-D-D-D-D-D

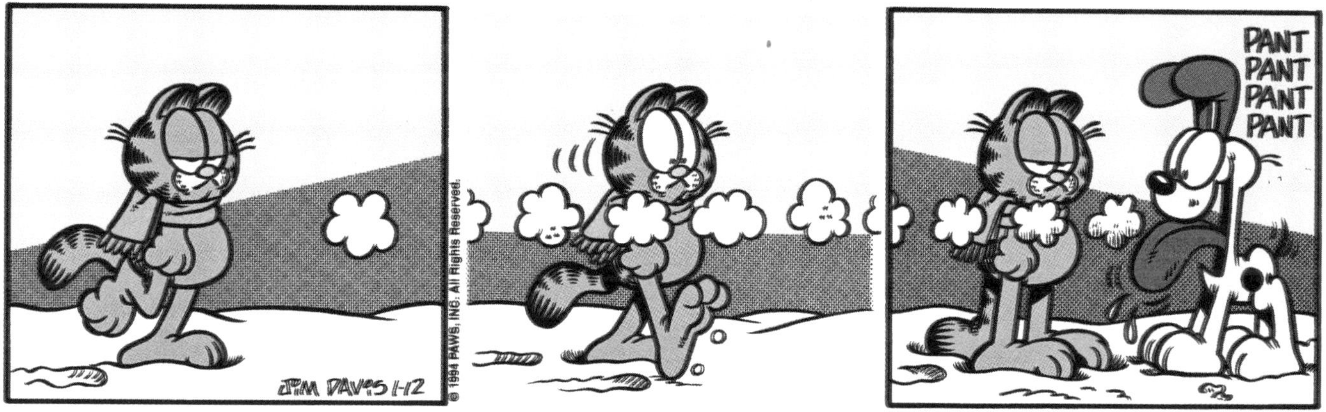
PANT
PANT
PANT
PANT
JIM DAVIS 1-12
© 1994 PAWS, INC. All Rights Reserved.

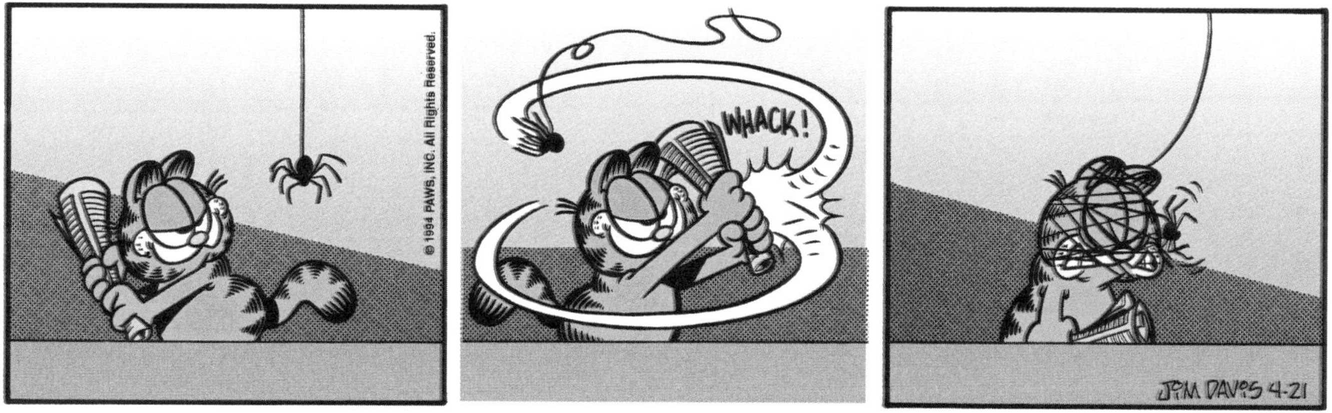
© 1994 PAWS, INC. All Rights Reserved.
WHACK!
JIM DAVIS 4-21

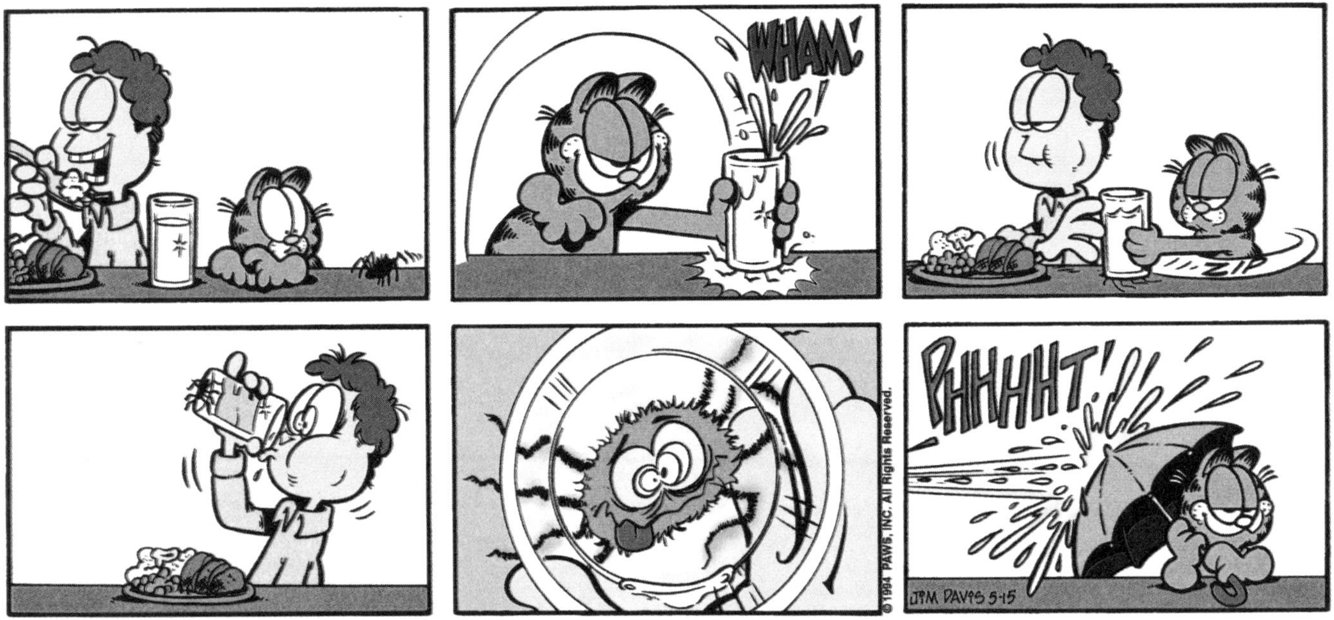
WHAM!
ZIP
PHHHHT!
JIM DAVIS 5-15
© 1994 PAWS, INC. All Rights Reserved.

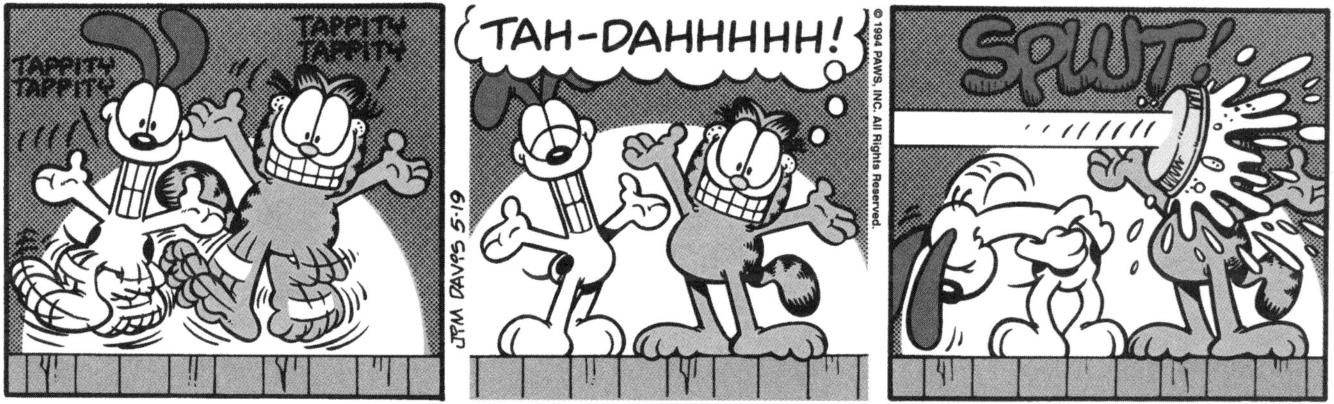
TAPPITY TAPPITY
TAPPITY TAPPITY
TAH-DAHHHHH!
JIM DAVIS 5-19
© 1994 PAWS, INC. All Rights Reserved.
SPLUT!

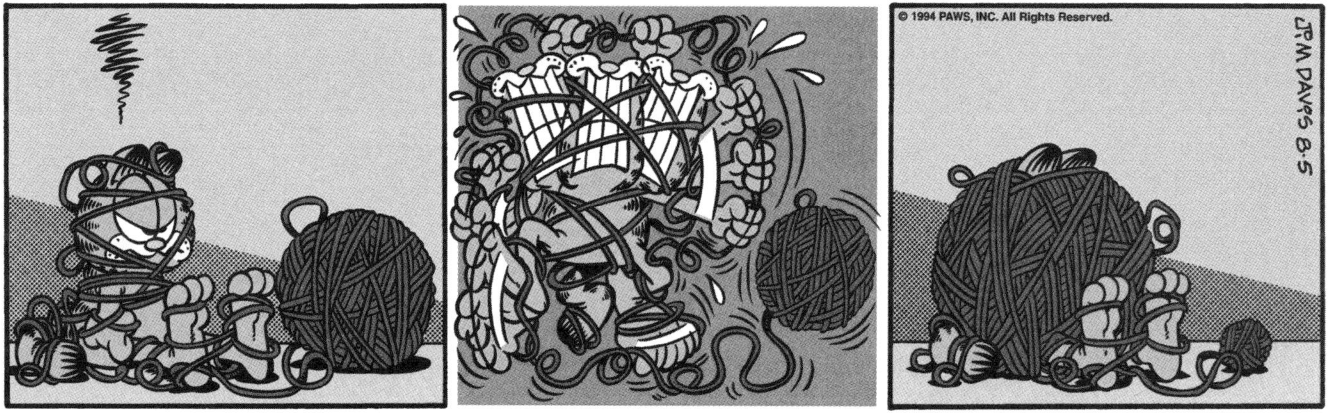
© 1994 PAWS, INC. All Rights Reserved.
JIM DAVIS 8-5

JIM DAVIS 8-14

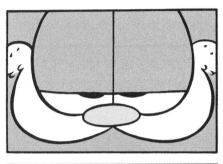

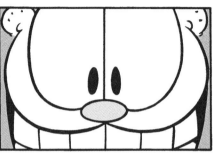

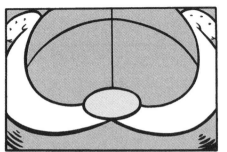

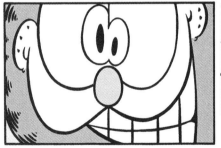

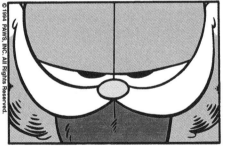

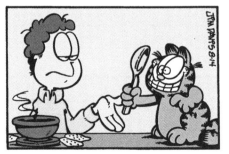

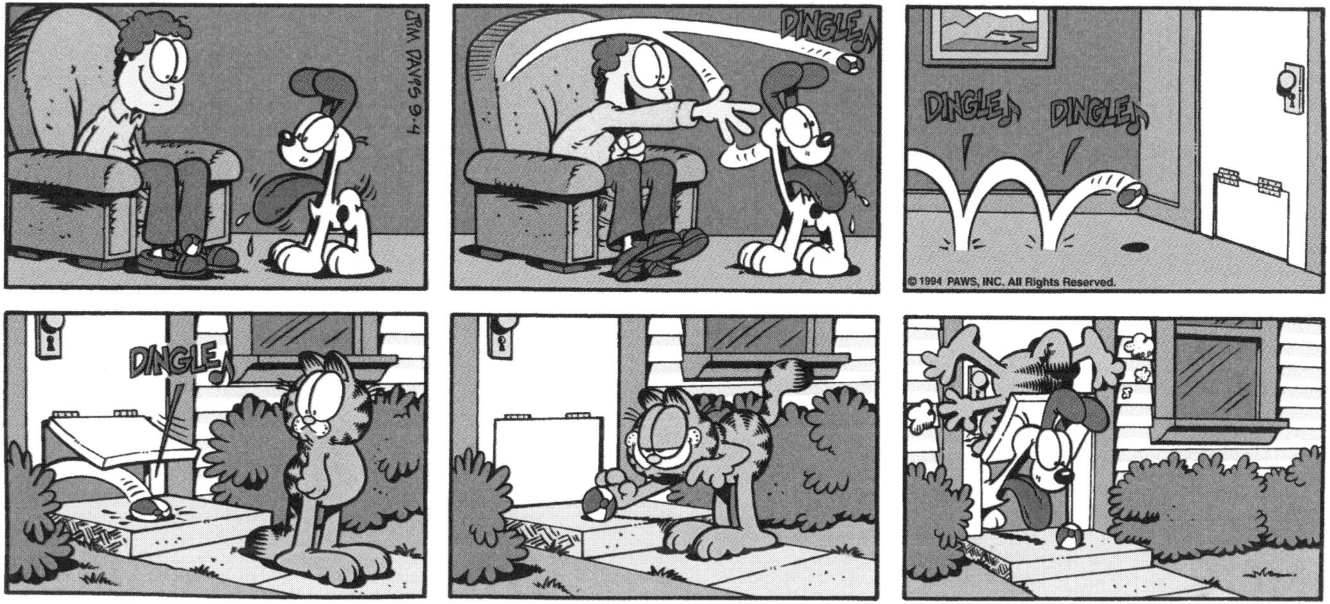
JIM DAVIS 9-4
DINGLE
DINGLE
DINGLE
© 1994 PAWS, INC. All Rights Reserved.
DINGLE

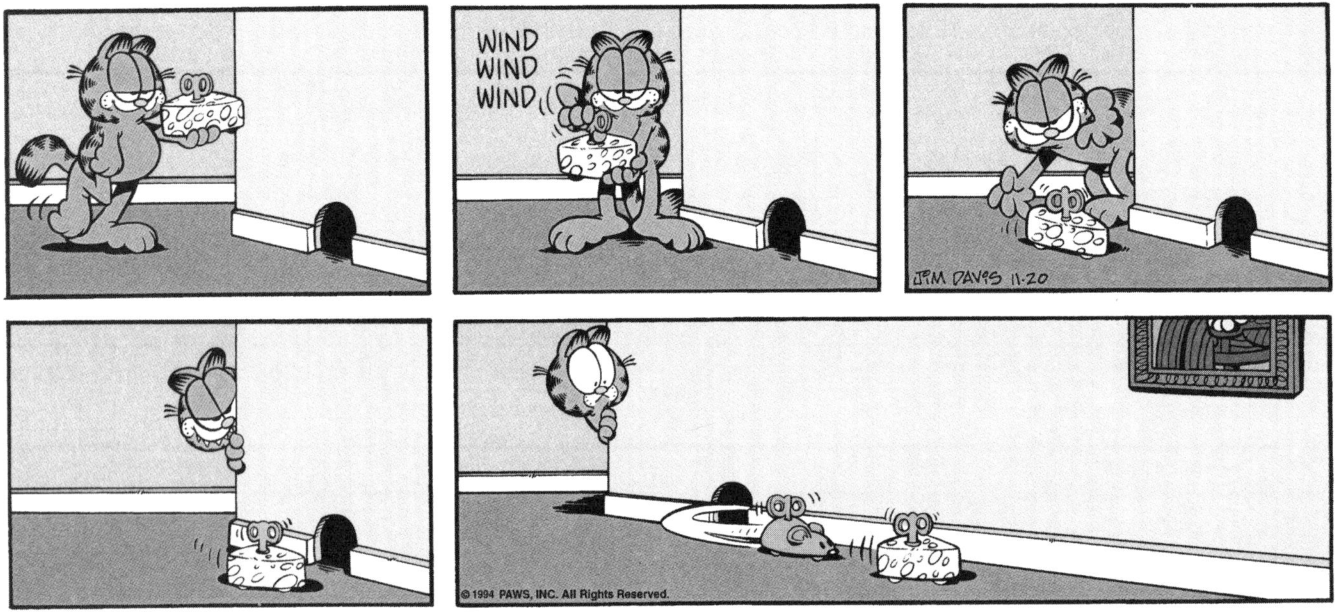
WIND
WIND
WIND
JIM DAVIS 11-20
© 1994 PAWS, INC. All Rights Reserved.

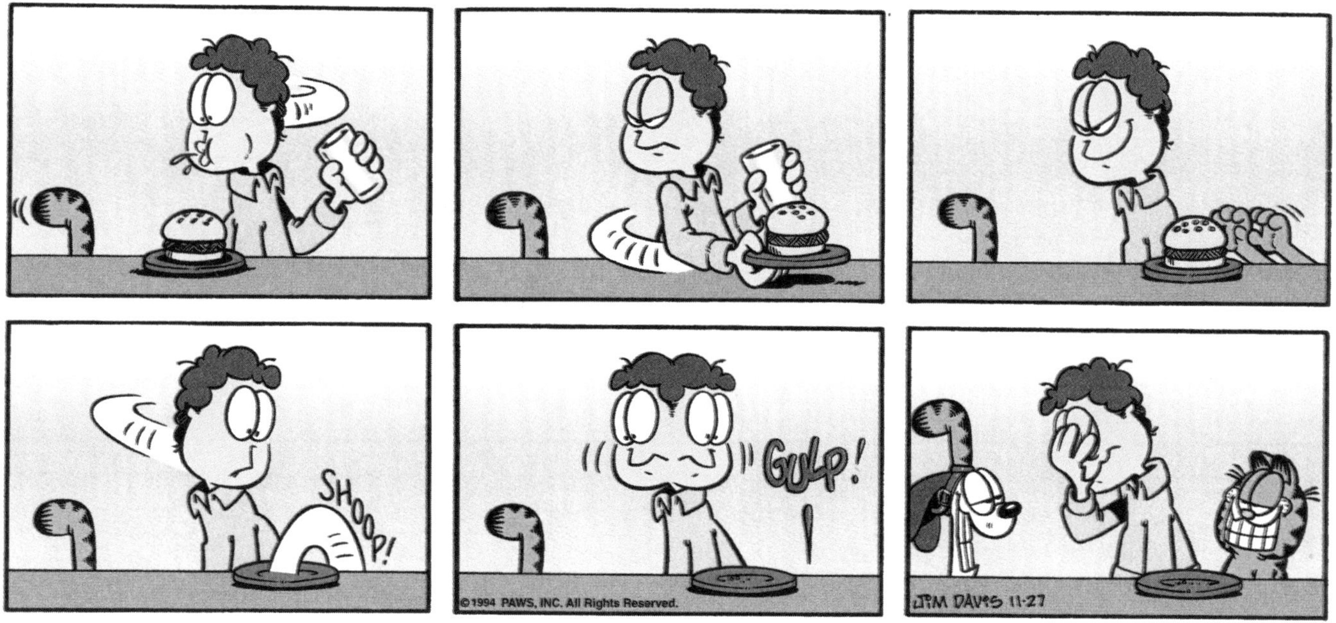
SHOOOP!
GULP!
©1994 PAWS, INC. All Rights Reserved.
JIM DAVIS 11-27

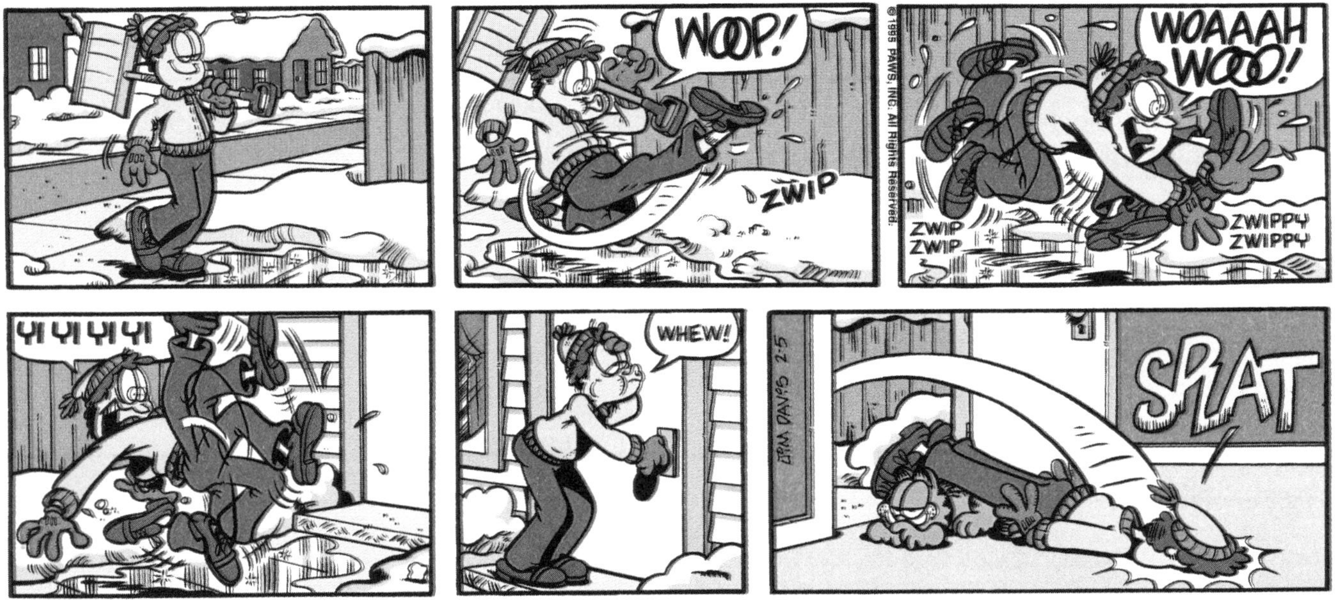
WOOP!
ZWIP
WOAAAH WOOO!
ZWIP ZWIP
ZWIPPY ZWIPPY
YI YI YI YI
WHEW!
SPLAT
JPM DAVIS 2-5

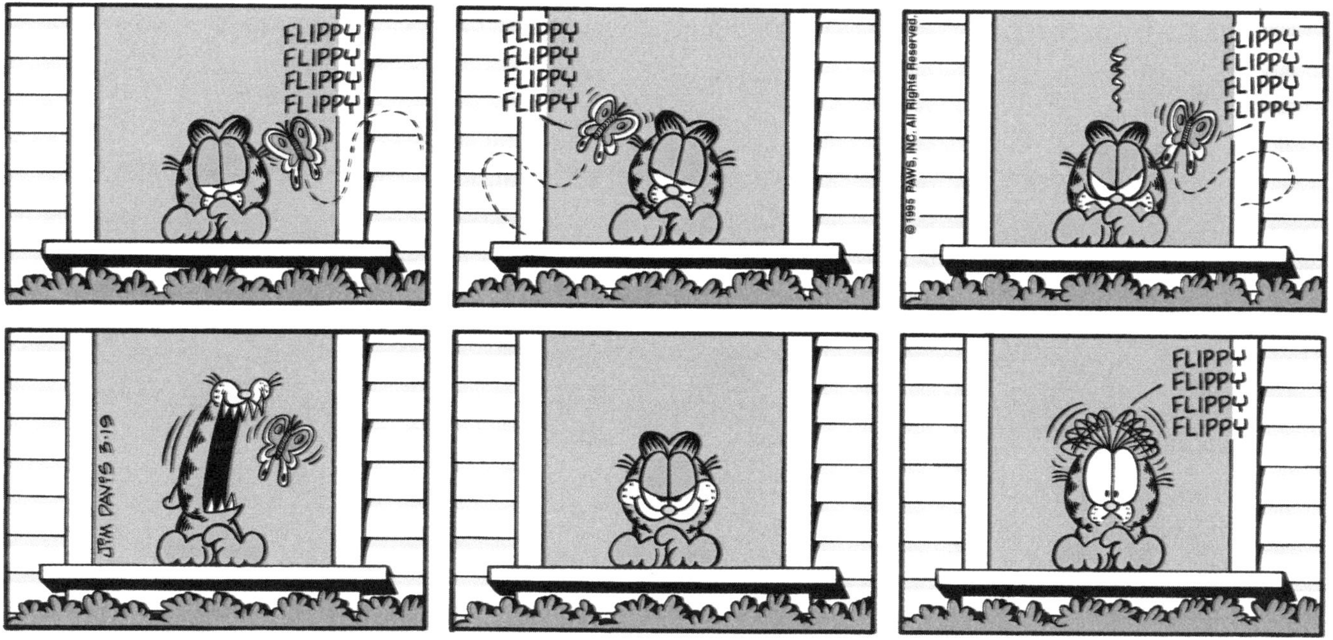
FLIPPY FLIPPY FLIPPY FLIPPY
FLIPPY FLIPPY FLIPPY FLIPPY
© 1995 PAWS, INC. All Rights Reserved.
FLIPPY FLIPPY FLIPPY FLIPPY
JIM DAVIS 3·19
FLIPPY FLIPPY FLIPPY FLIPPY

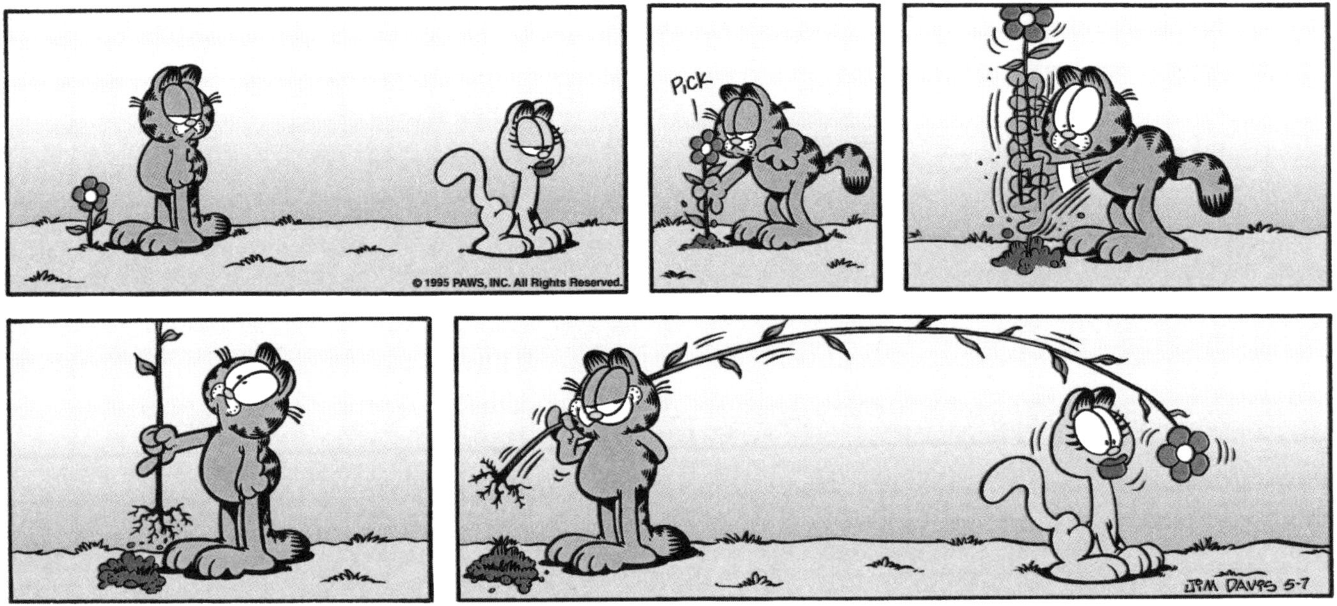
PICK
© 1995 PAWS, INC. All Rights Reserved.
JIM DAVIS 5-7

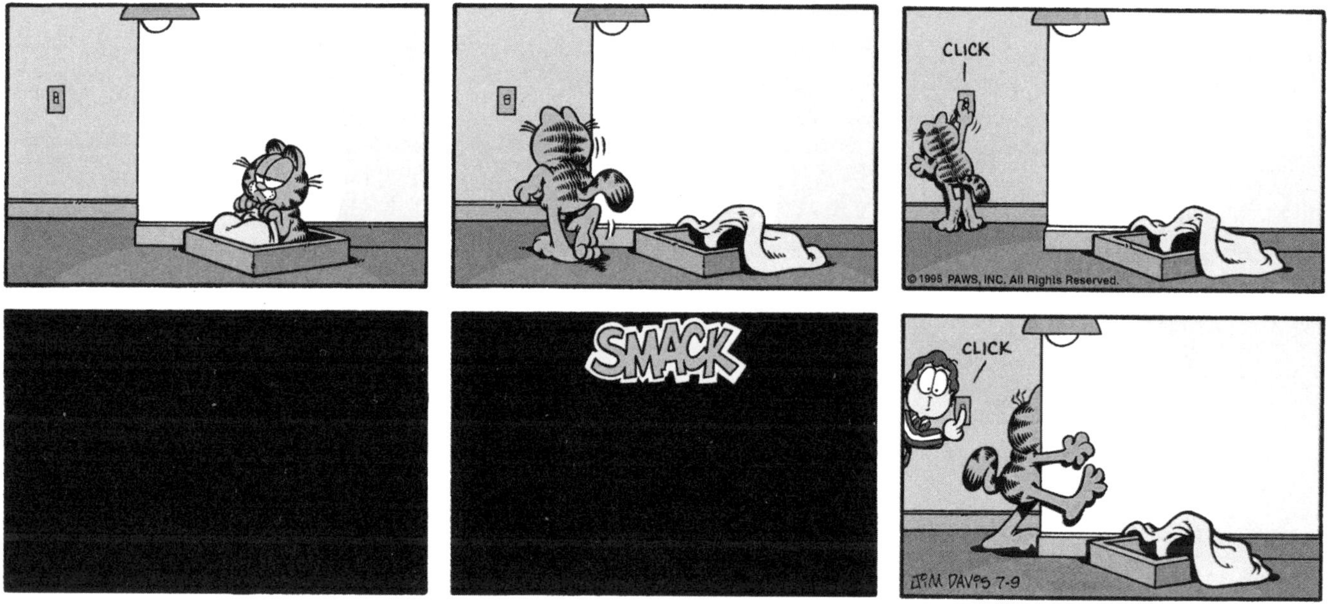
CLICK
© 1995 PAWS, INC. All Rights Reserved.
SMACK
CLICK
JIM DAVIS 7-9

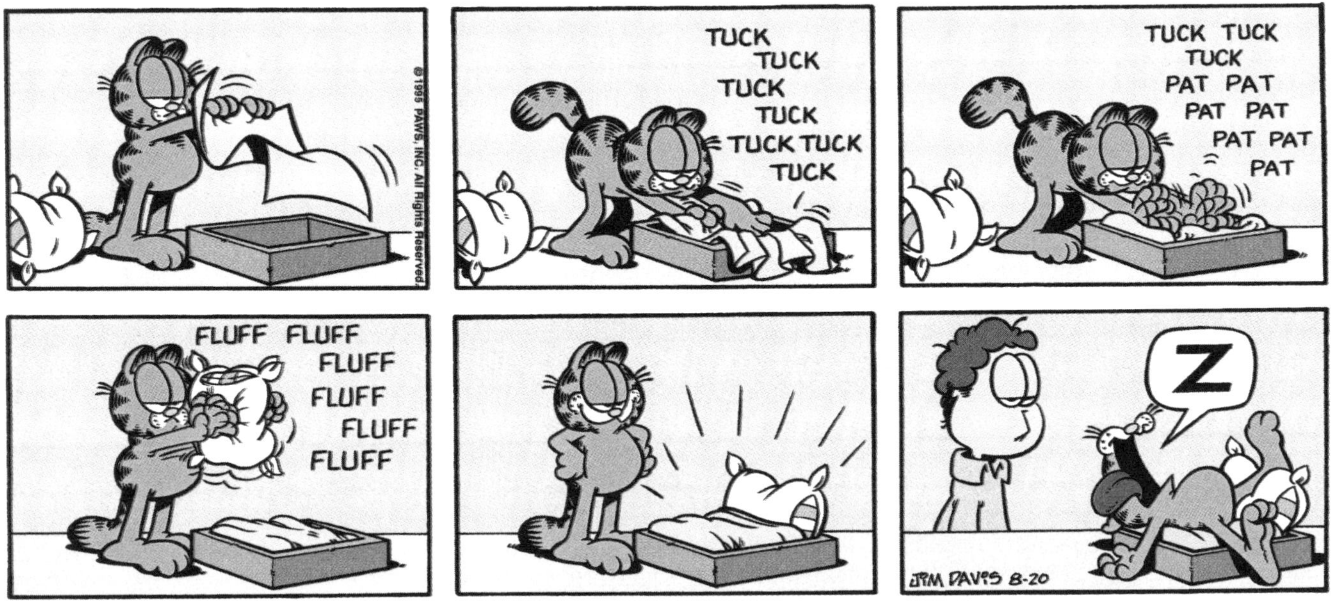
© 1995 PAWS, INC. All Rights Reserved.
TUCK
TUCK
TUCK
TUCK
TUCK TUCK
TUCK
TUCK TUCK
TUCK
PAT PAT
PAT PAT
PAT PAT
PAT
FLUFF FLUFF
FLUFF
FLUFF
FLUFF
FLUFF
Z
JIM DAVIS 8-20

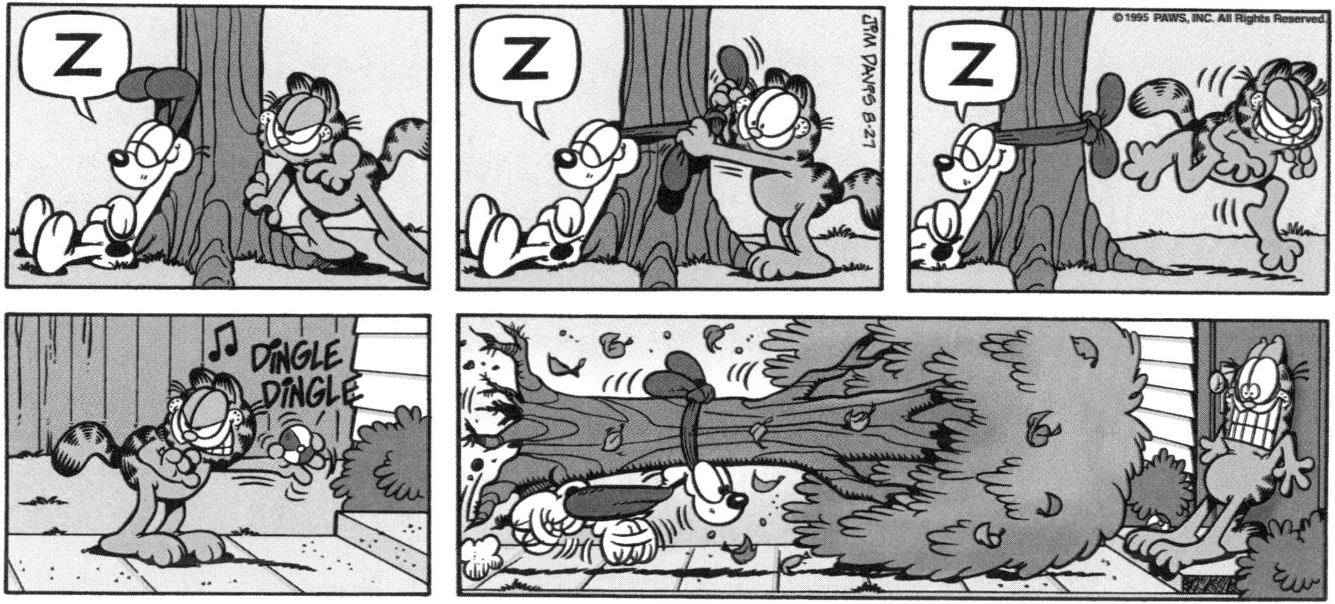

Z
Z
JIM DAVIS 8-27
© 1995 PAWS, INC. All Rights Reserved.
Z
DINGLE DINGLE

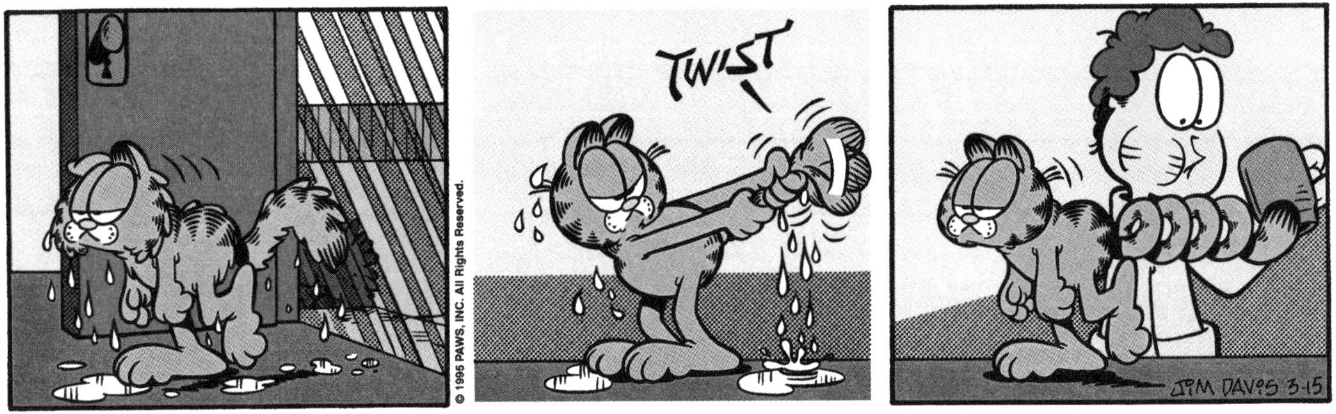
© 1995 PAWS, INC. All Rights Reserved.
TWIST
JIM DAVIS 3-15

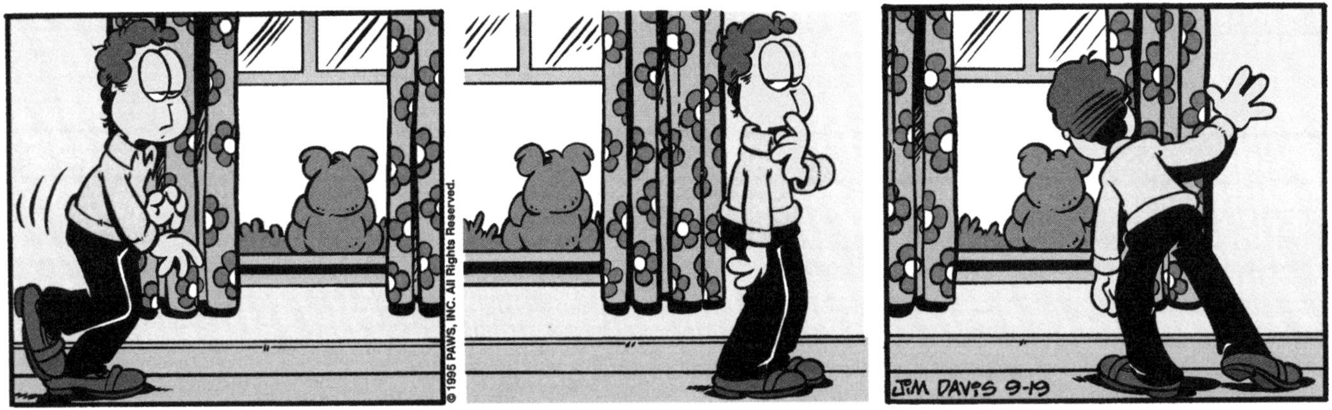
© 1995 PAWS, INC. All Rights Reserved.
JIM DAVIS 9-19

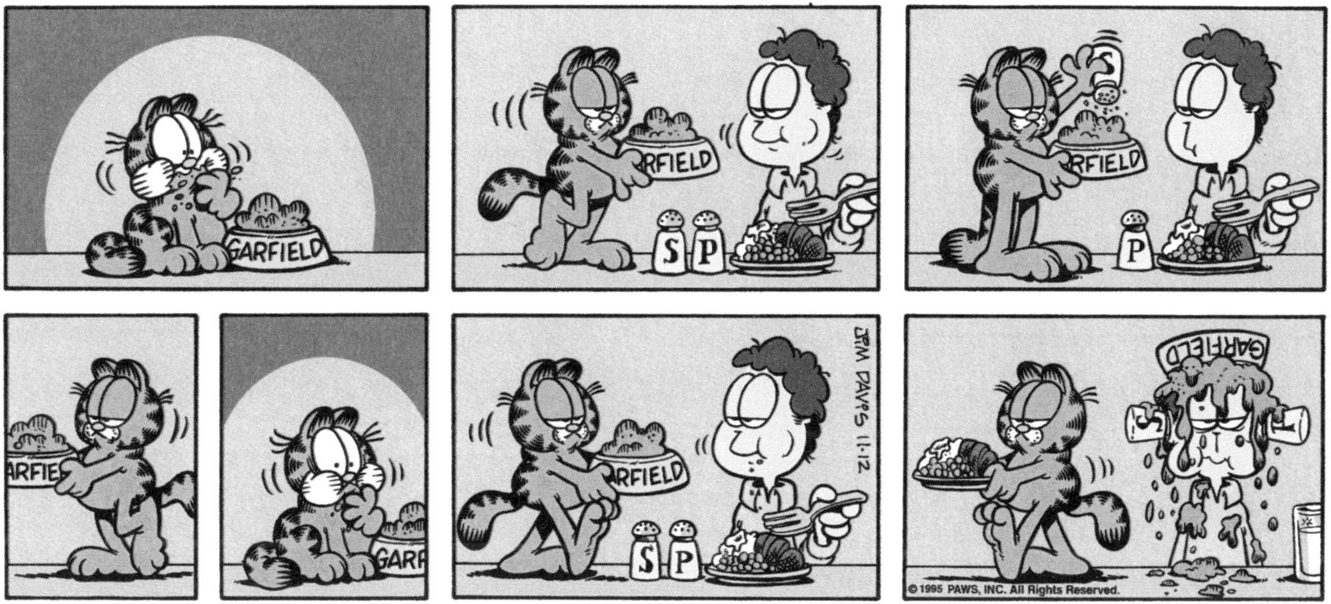
GARFIELD
RFIELD
S
P
RFIELD
S
P
ARFIE
GARF
JIM DAVIS 11-12
RFIELD
S
P
GARFIELD
© 1995 PAWS, INC. All Rights Reserved.

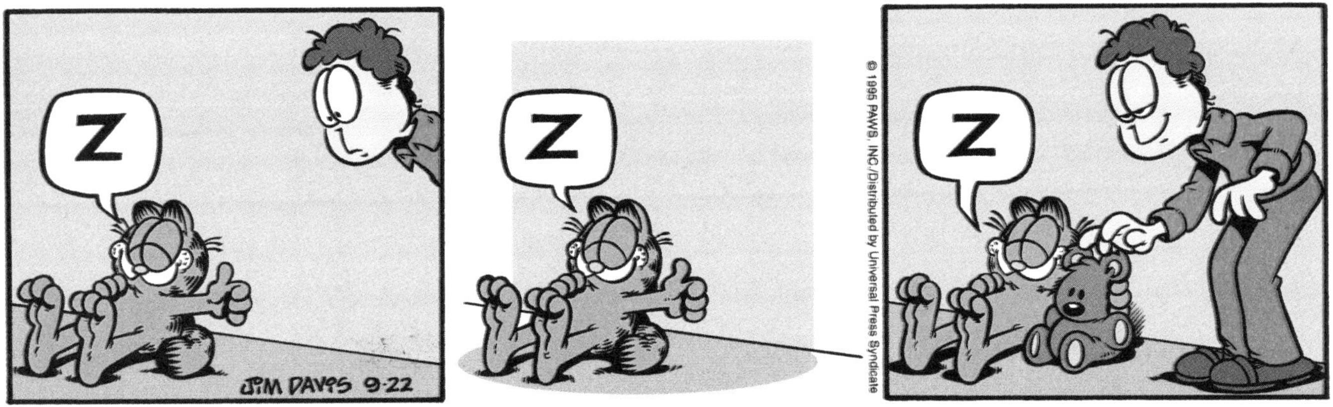
Z
Z
Z
JIM DAVIS 9-22
© 1995 PAWS, INC./Distributed by Universal Press Syndicate

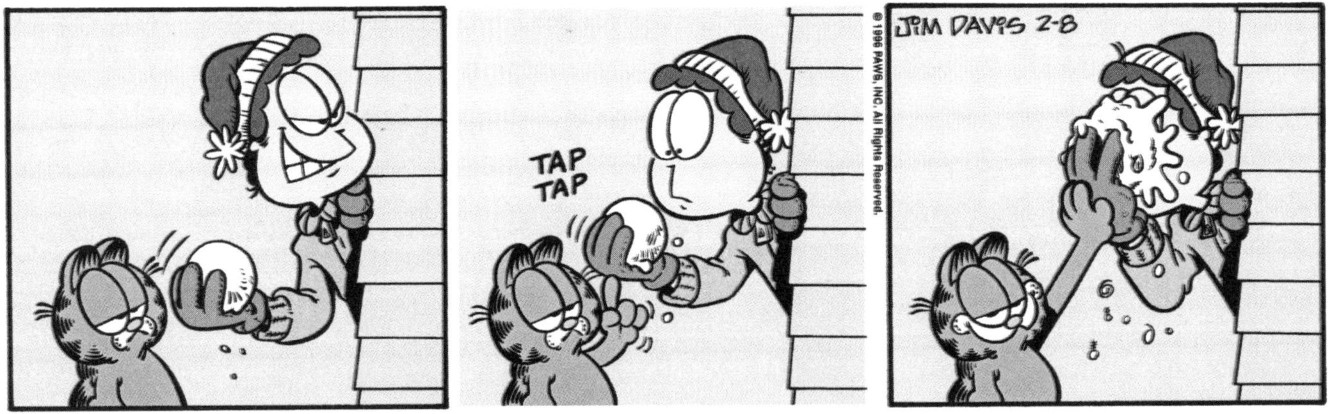
TAP
TAP
JIM DAVIS 2-8
© 1996 PAWS, INC. All Rights Reserved.

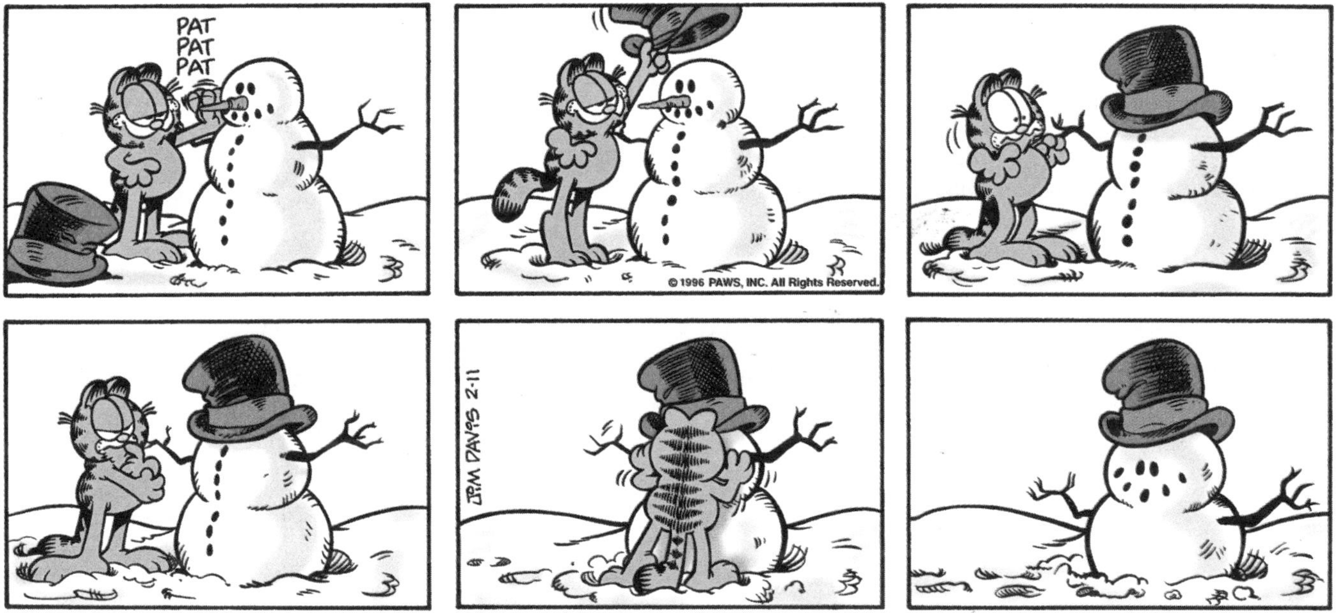
PAT
PAT
PAT
© 1996 PAWS, INC. All Rights Reserved.
JIM DAVIS 2-11

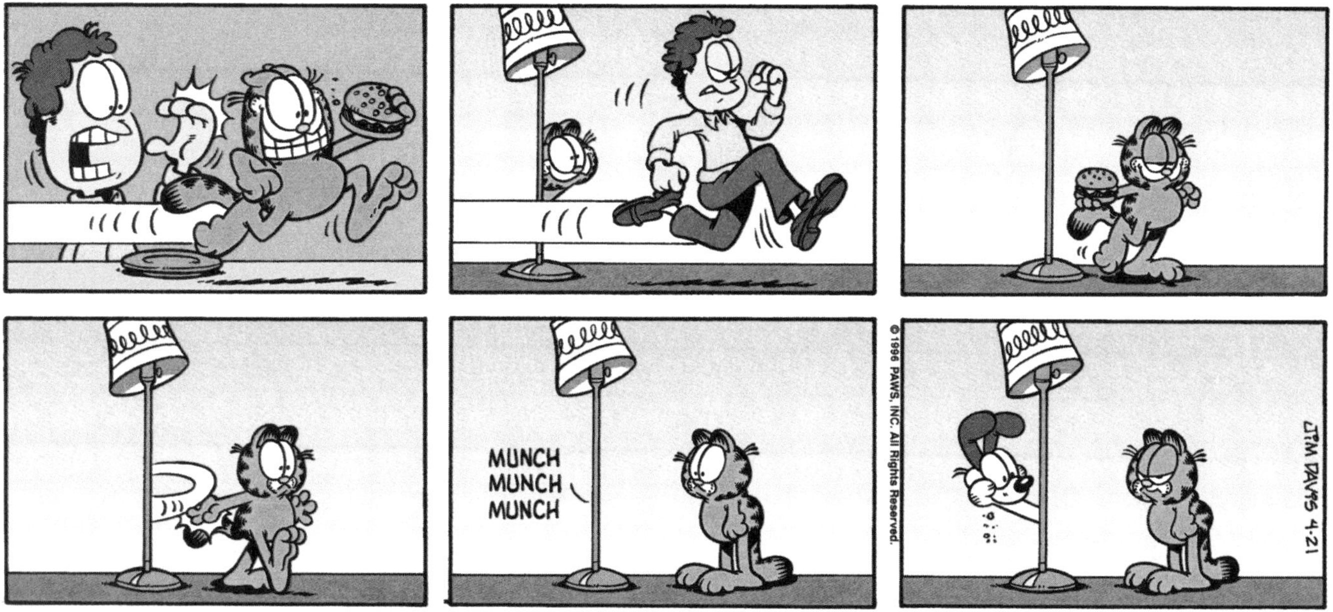
MUNCH
MUNCH
MUNCH
JIM DAVIS 4-21
© 1996 PAWS, INC. All Rights Reserved.

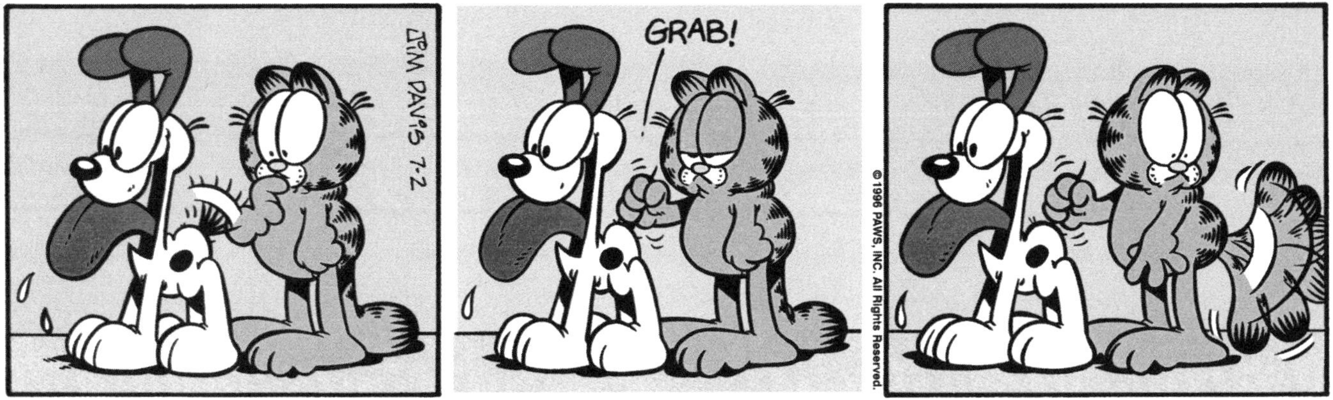
JIM DAVIS 7-2
GRAB!
© 1996 PAWS, INC. All Rights Reserved.

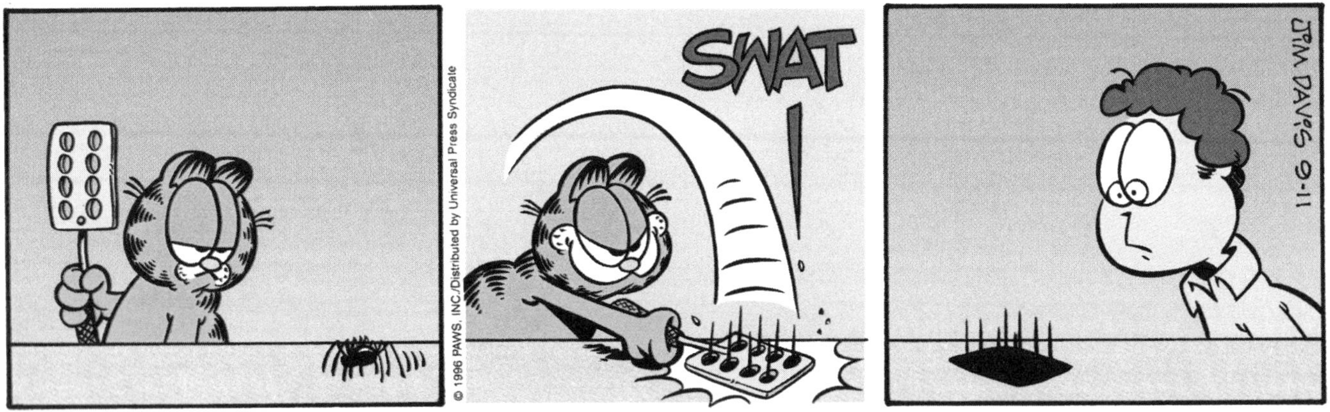
© 1996 PAWS, INC./Distributed by Universal Press Syndicate
SWAT
JIM DAVIS 9-11

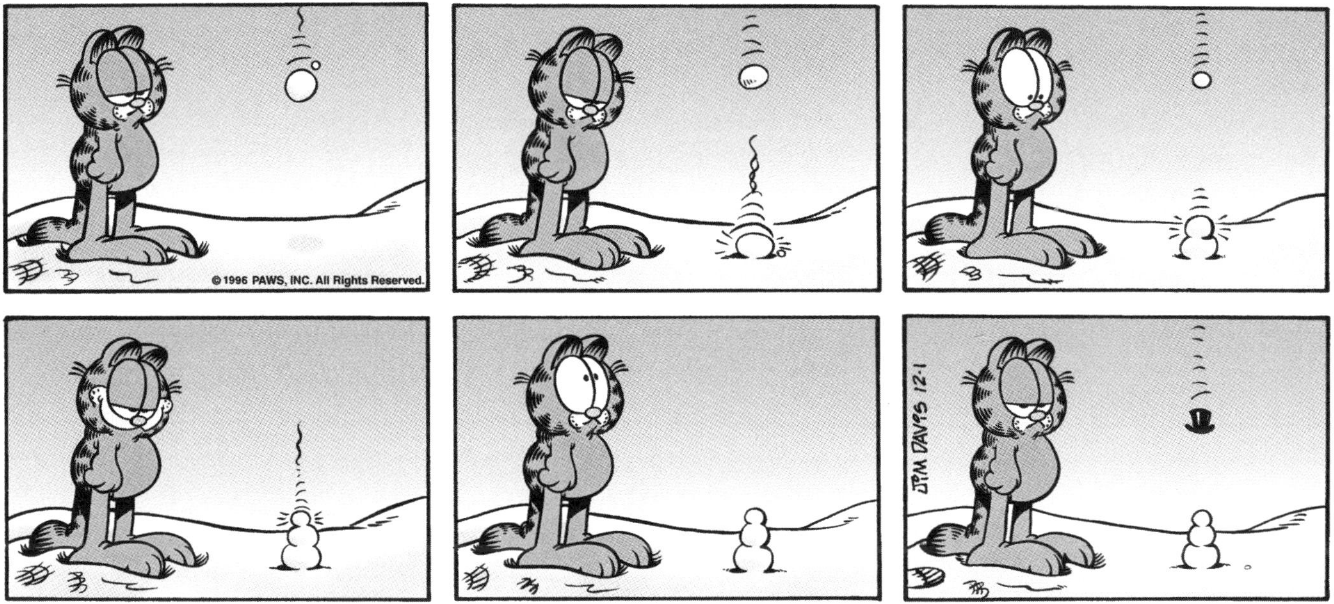
© 1996 PAWS, INC. All Rights Reserved.
JIM DAVIS 12·1

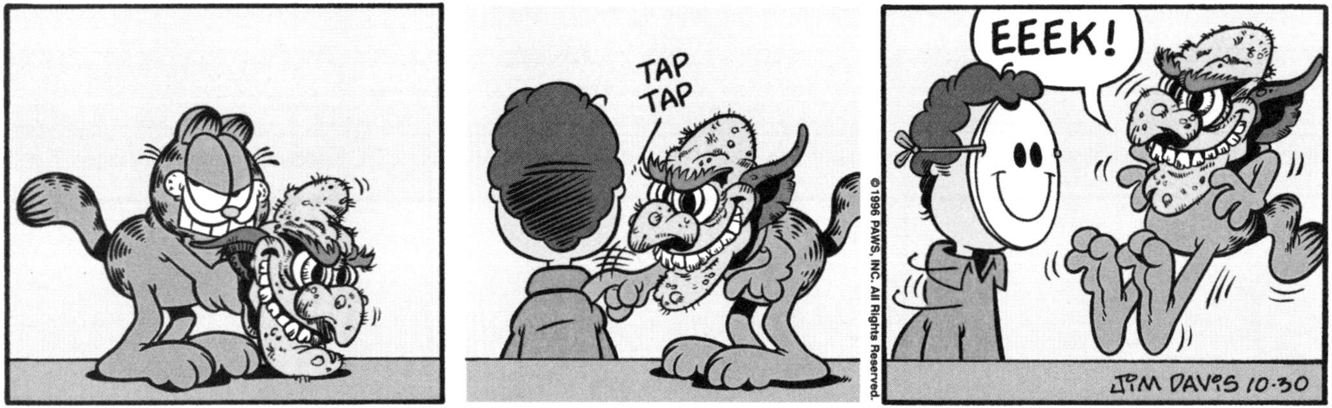
TAP TAP
EEEK!
JIM DAVIS 10-30
© 1996 PAWS, INC. All Rights Reserved.

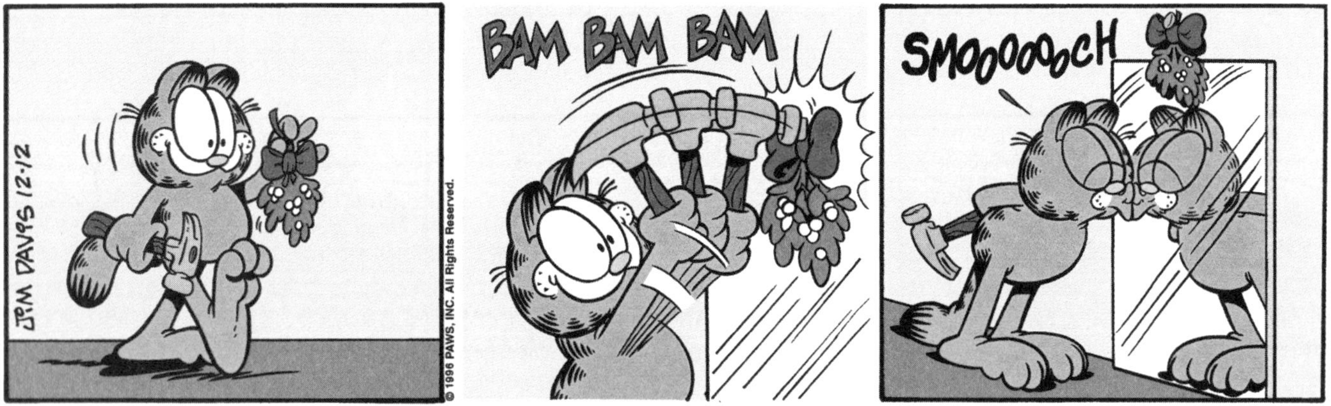
JIM DAVIS 12-12
© 1996 PAWS, INC. All Rights Reserved.
BAM BAM BAM
SMOOOOOOCH

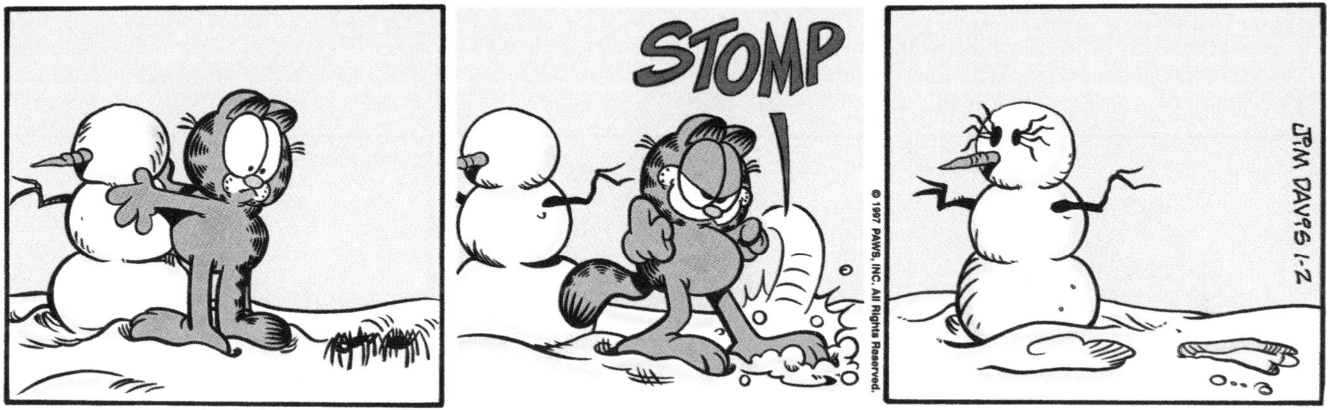
STOMP
© 1997 PAWS, INC. All Rights Reserved.
JIM DAVIS 1-2

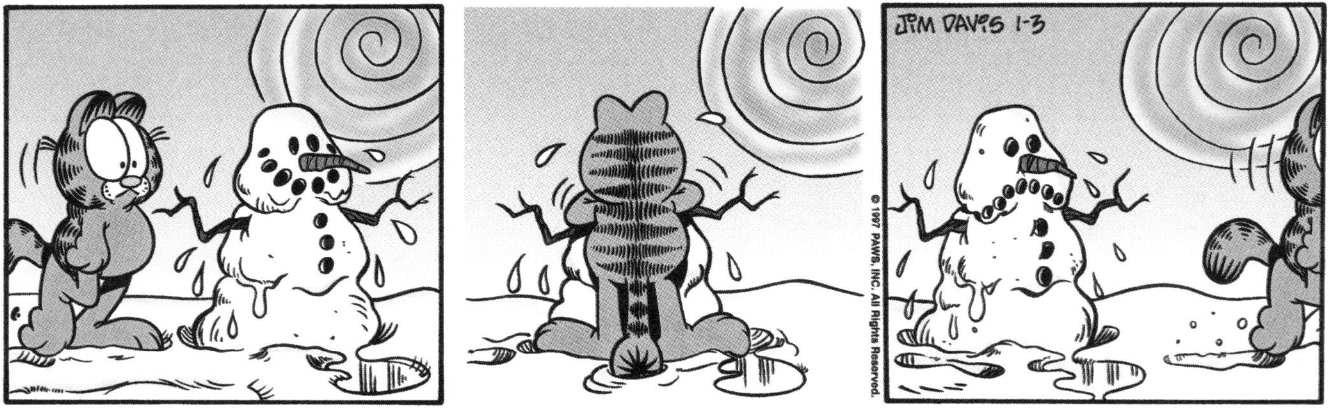
© 1997 PAWS, INC. All Rights Reserved.
JIM DAVIS 1-3

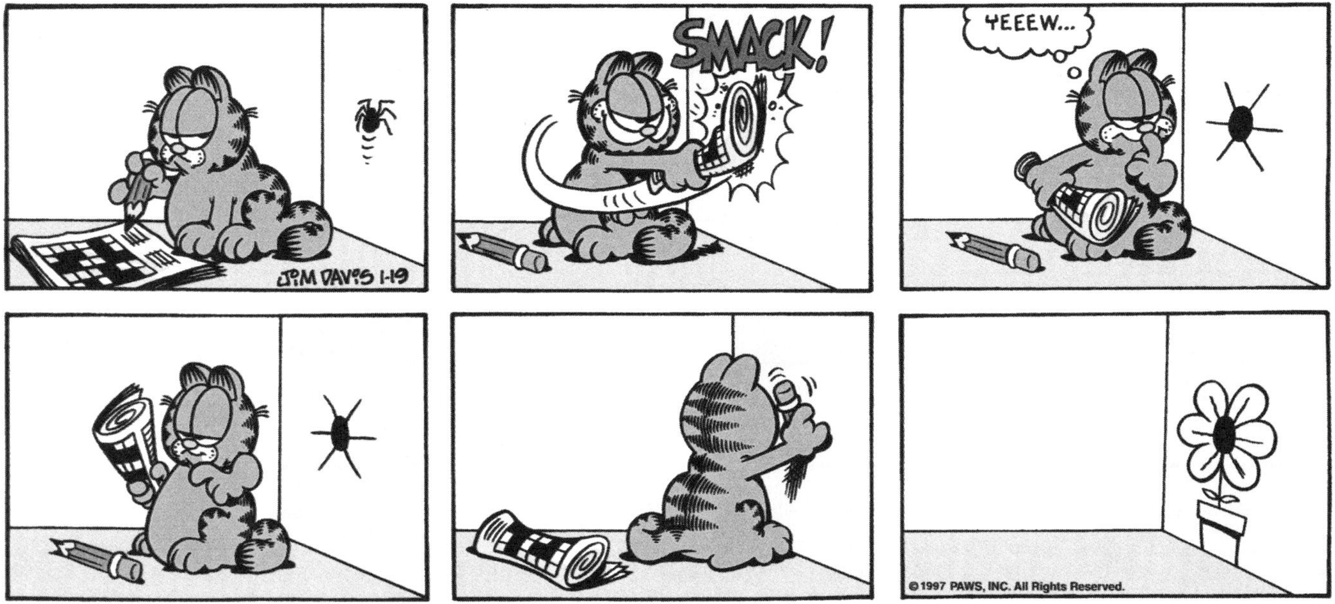
JIM DAVIS 1-19
SMACK!
YEEEW...
© 1997 PAWS, INC. All Rights Reserved.

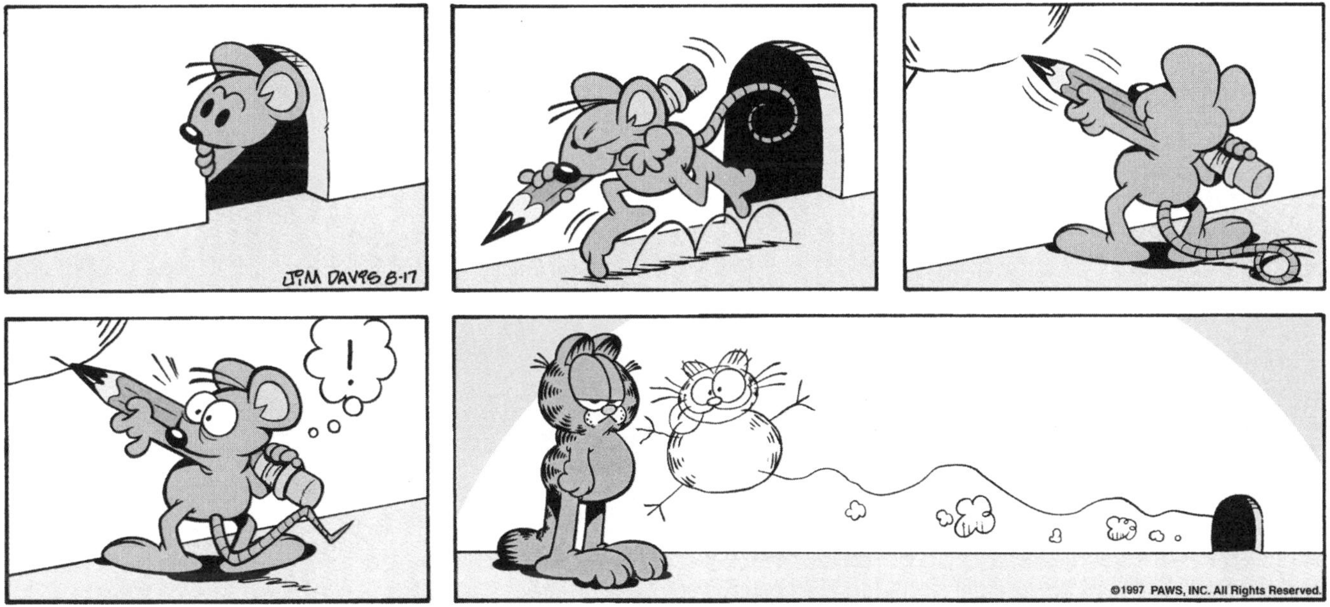
JIM DAVIS 8-17
!

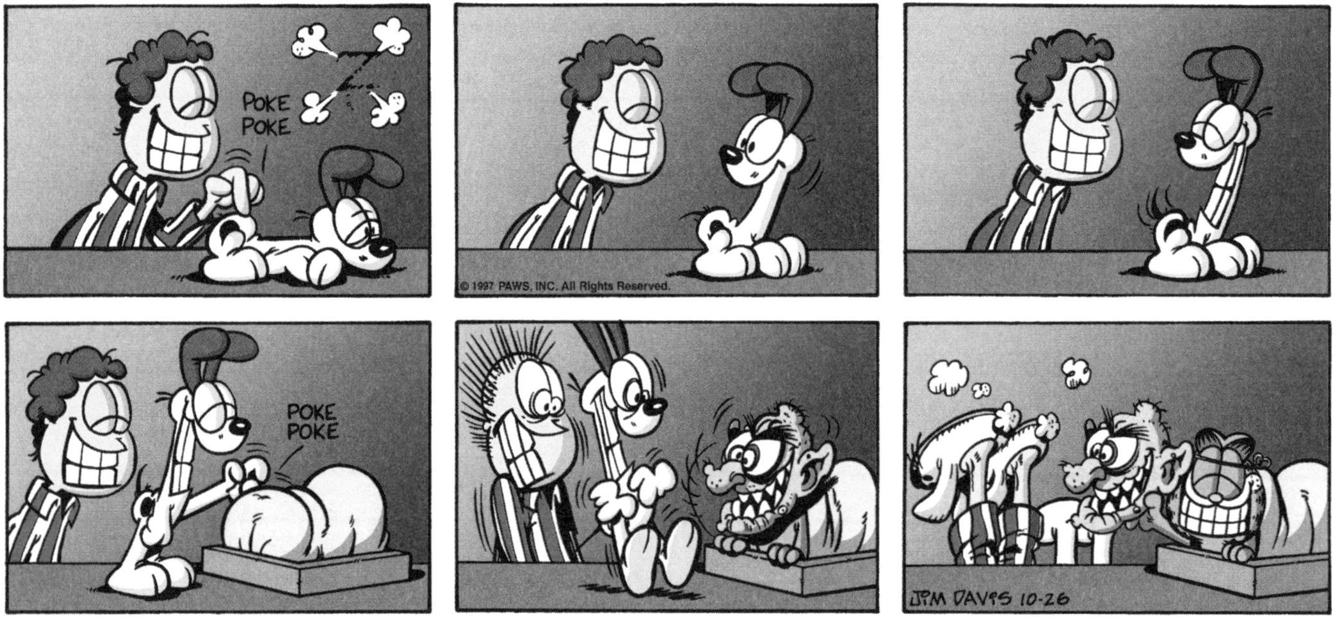
POKE
POKE
© 1997 PAWS, INC. All Rights Reserved.
POKE
POKE
JIM DAVIS 10-26

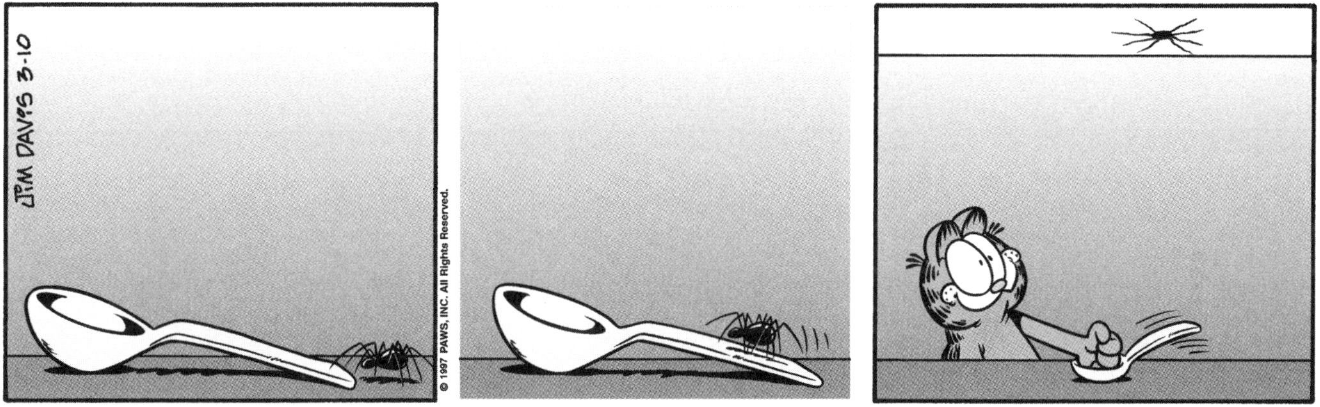
JIM DAVIS 3-10

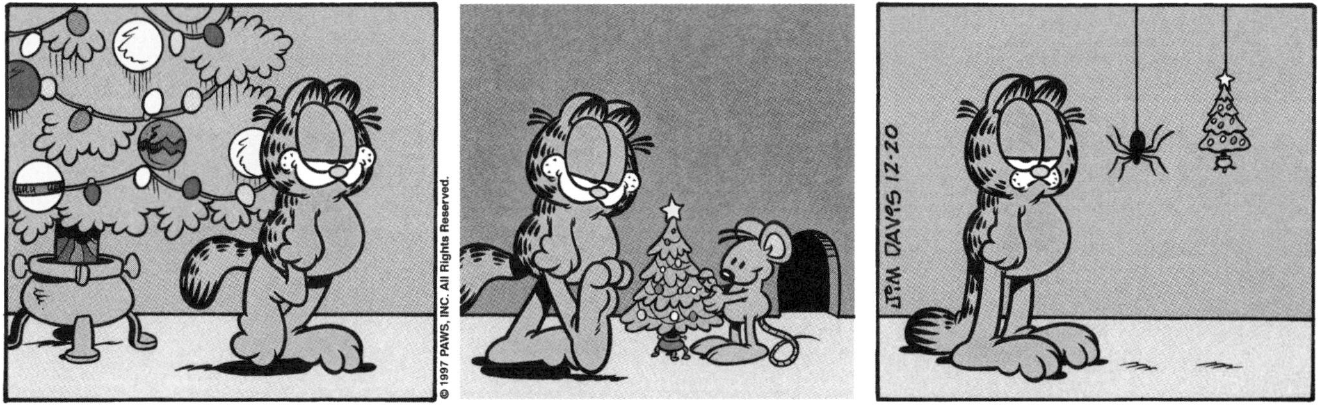
JIM DAVIS 12-20

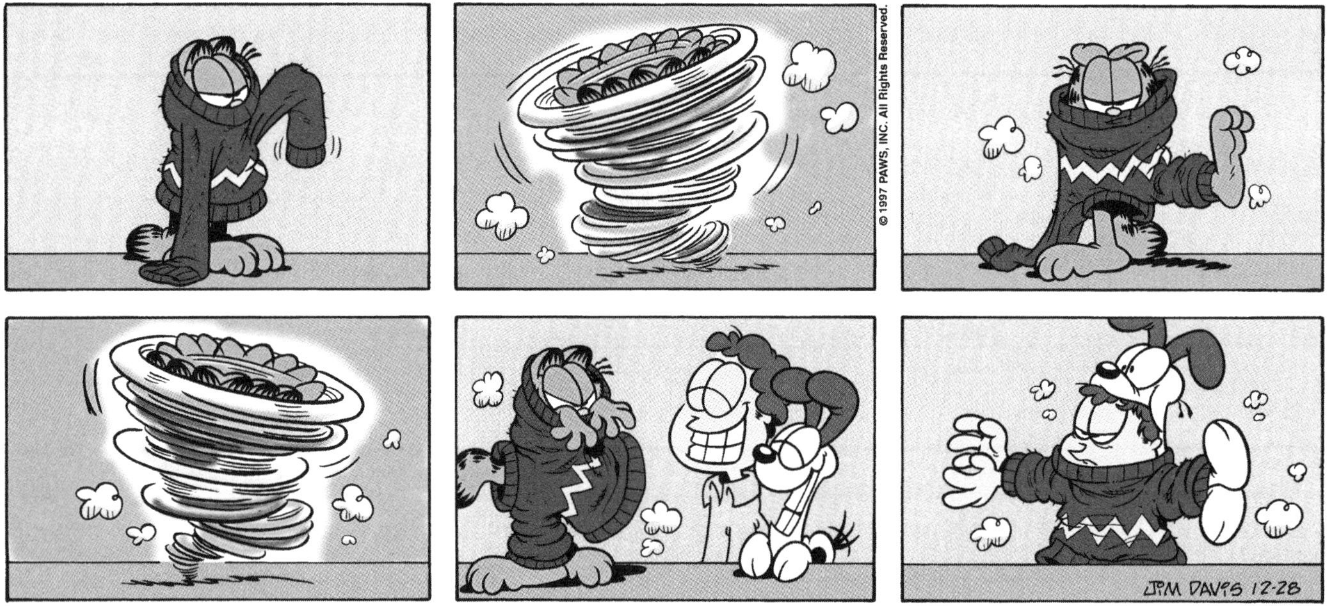
JIM DAVIS 12-28

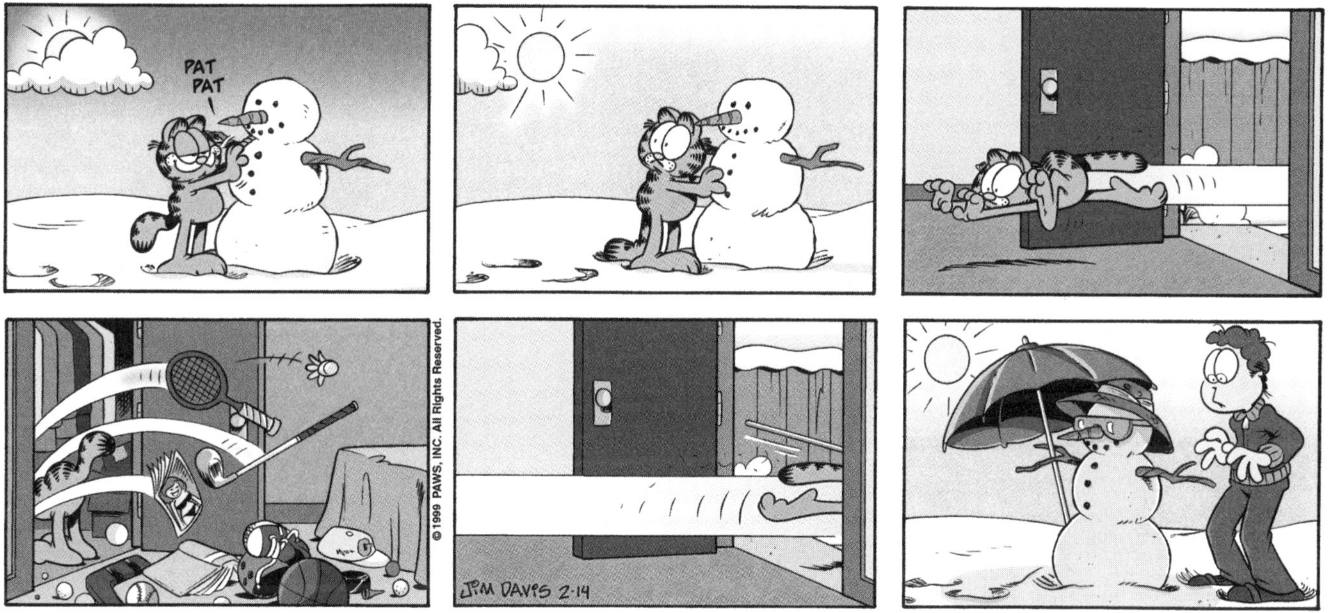
PAT
PAT
© 1999 PAWS, INC. All Rights Reserved.
JIM DAVIS 2-14

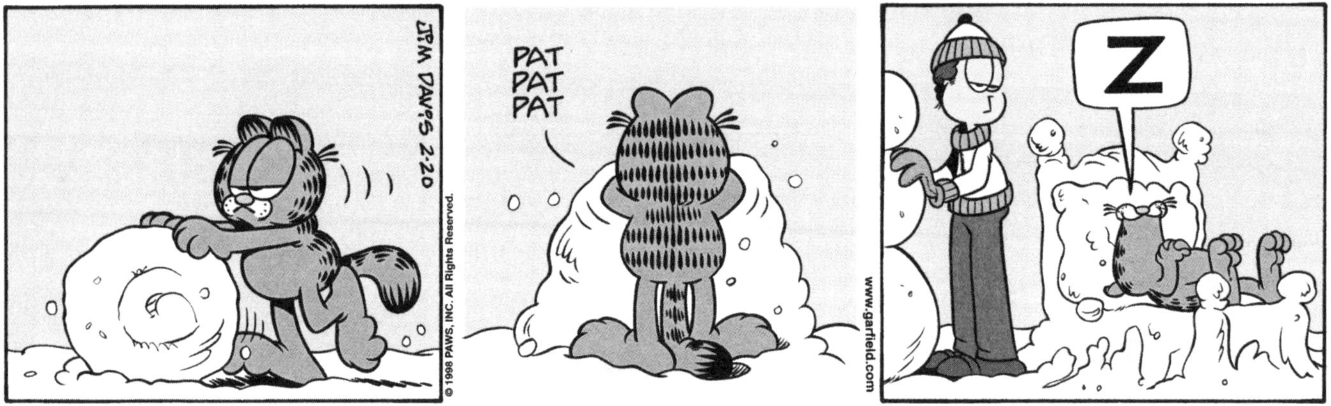
JIM DAVIS 2-20
© 1998 PAWS, INC. All Rights Reserved.
PAT
PAT
PAT
www.garfield.com
Z

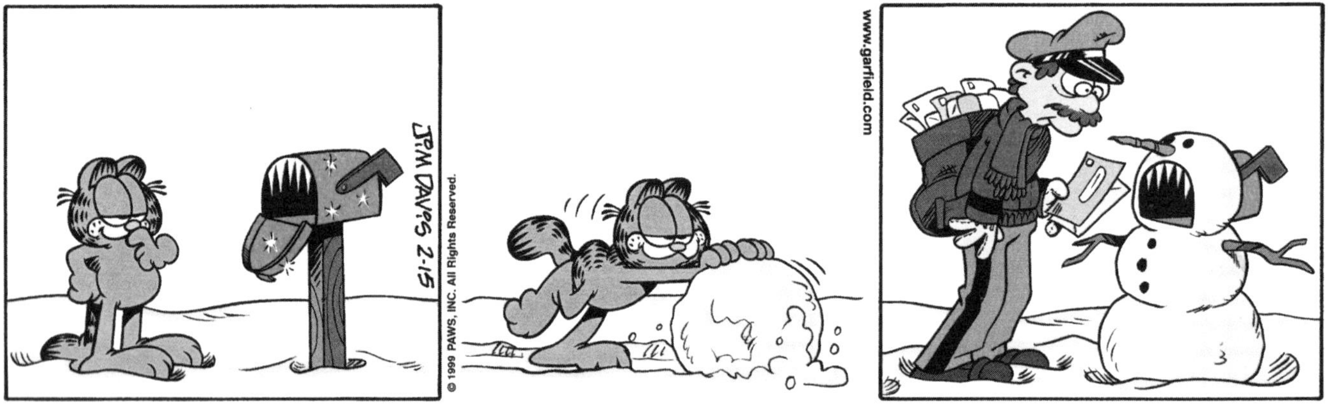
JIM DAVIS 2-15
© 1998 PAWS, INC. All Rights Reserved.
www.garfield.com

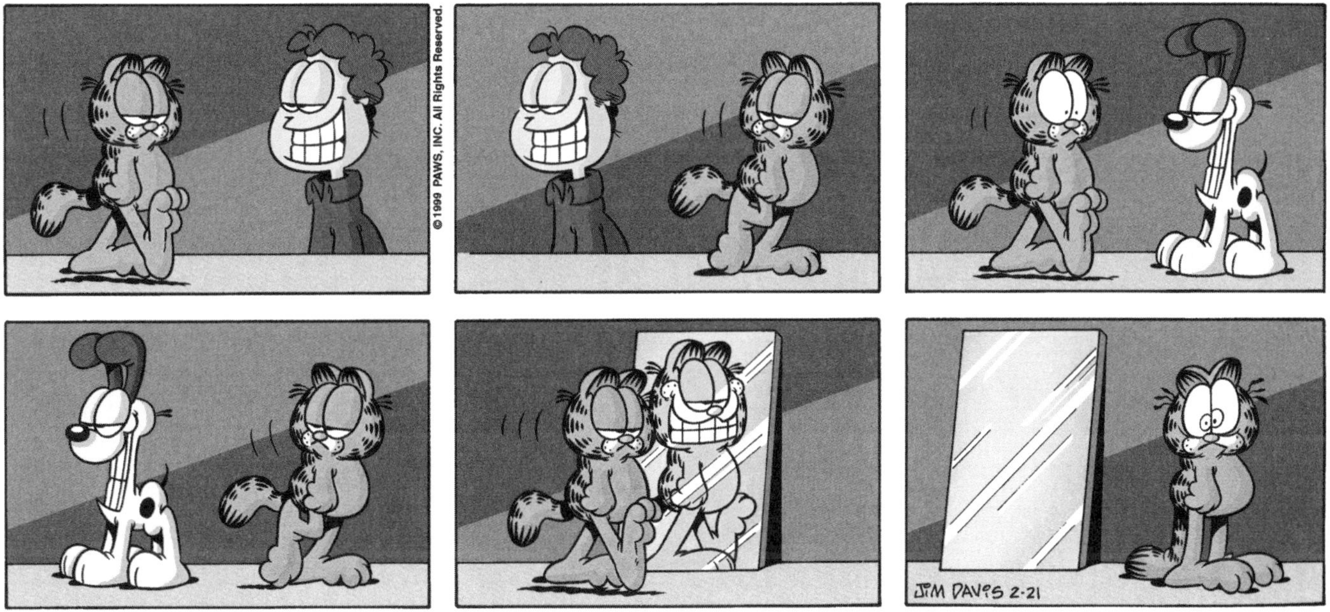
JIM DAVIS 2-21

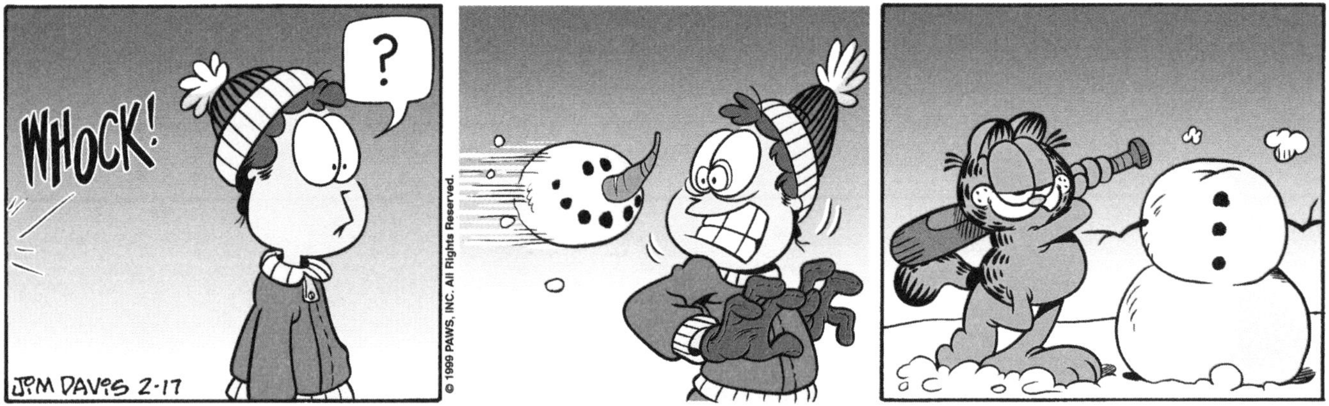
WHOCK!
?
JIM DAVIS 2-17
© 1999 PAWS, INC. All Rights Reserved.

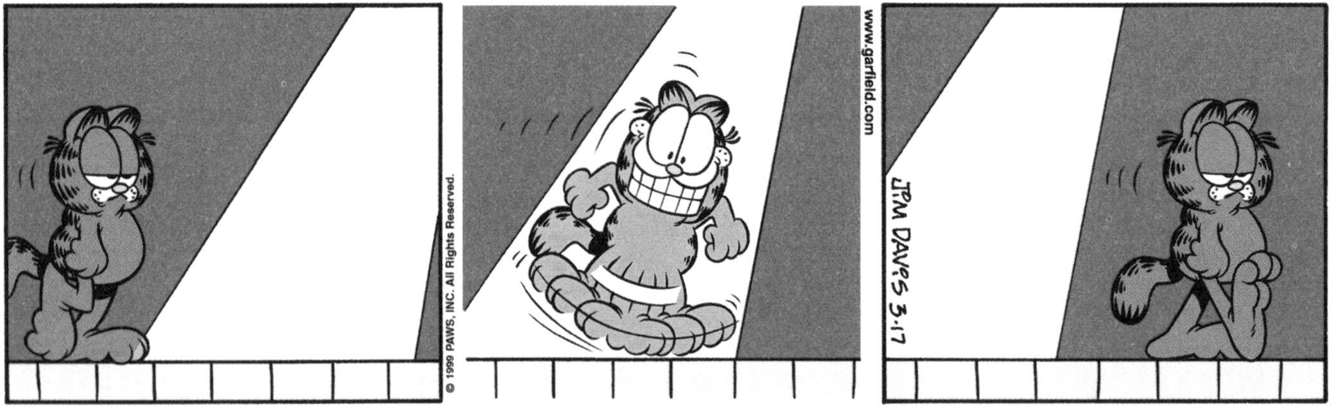
© 1999 PAWS, INC. All Rights Reserved.
www.garfield.com
JIM DAVIS 3-17

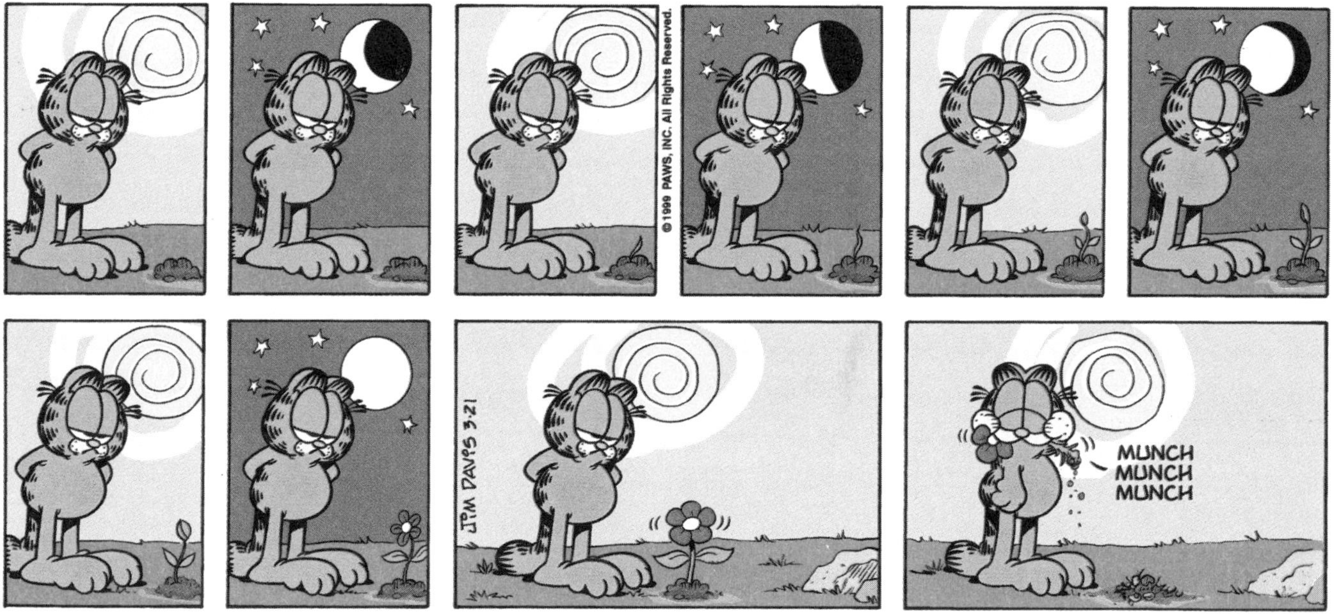
© 1999 PAWS, INC. All Rights Reserved.
JIM DAVIS 3·21
MUNCH
MUNCH
MUNCH

JIM DAVIS 11-9

JIM DAVIS 11-7

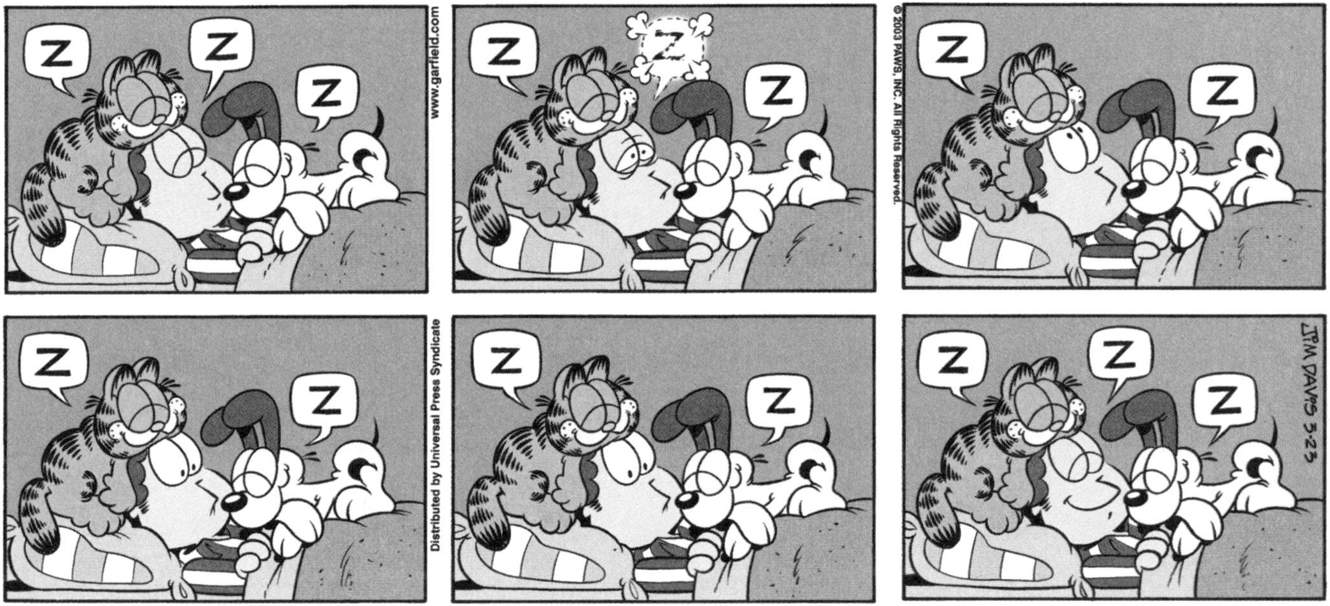
Z
Z
Z
www.garfield.com
Z
Z
Z
© 2003 PAWS, INC. All Rights Reserved.
Z
Z
Z
Z
Distributed by Universal Press Syndicate
Z
Z
JIM DAVIS 3-23
Z
Z
Z

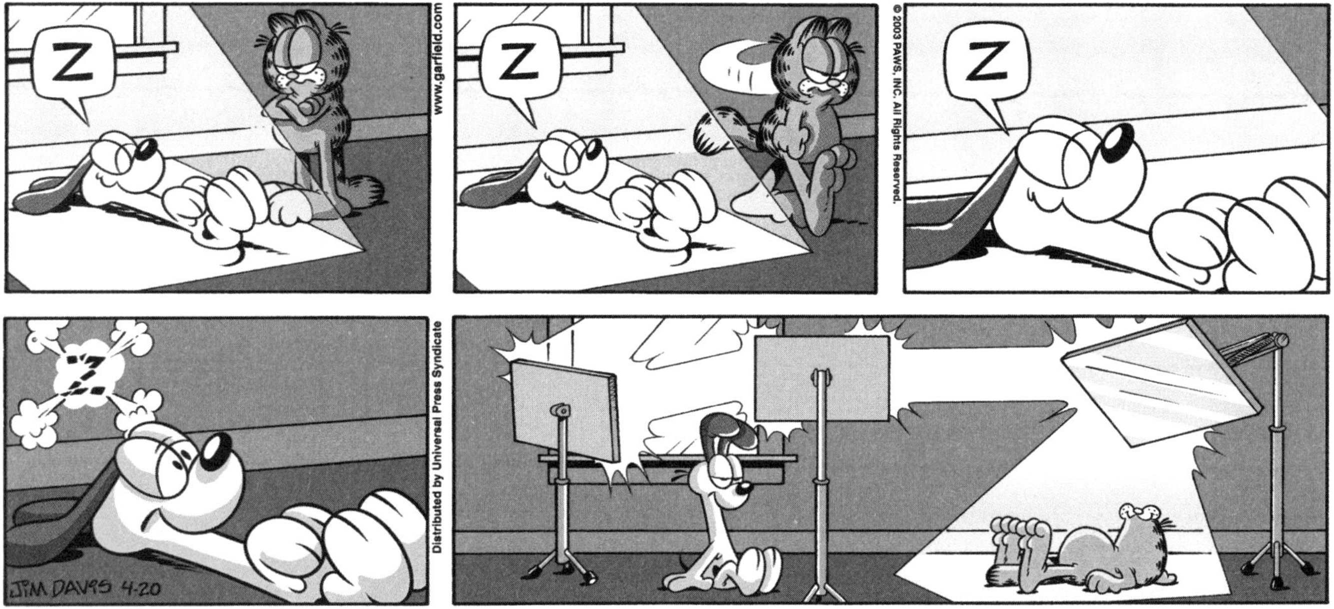
Z
www.garfield.com
Z
© 2003 PAWS, INC. All Rights Reserved.
Z
Distributed by Universal Press Syndicate
JIM DAVIS 4-20

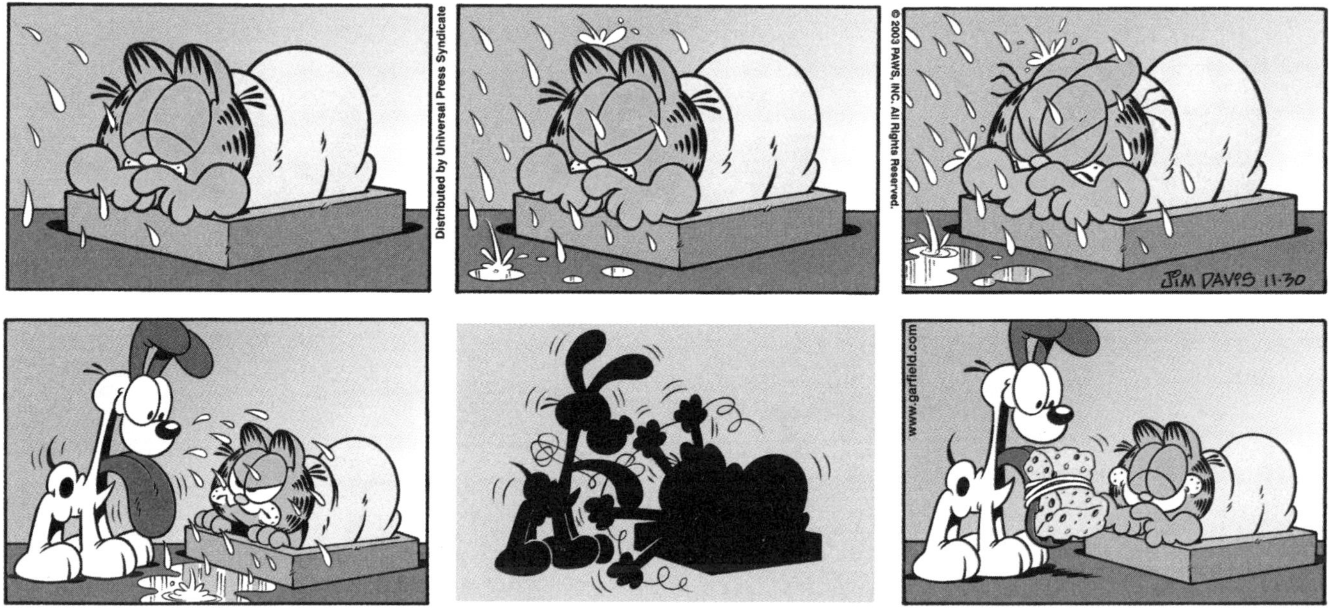
Distributed by Universal Press Syndicate
© 2003 PAWS, INC. All Rights Reserved.
JIM DAVIS 11-30
www.garfield.com

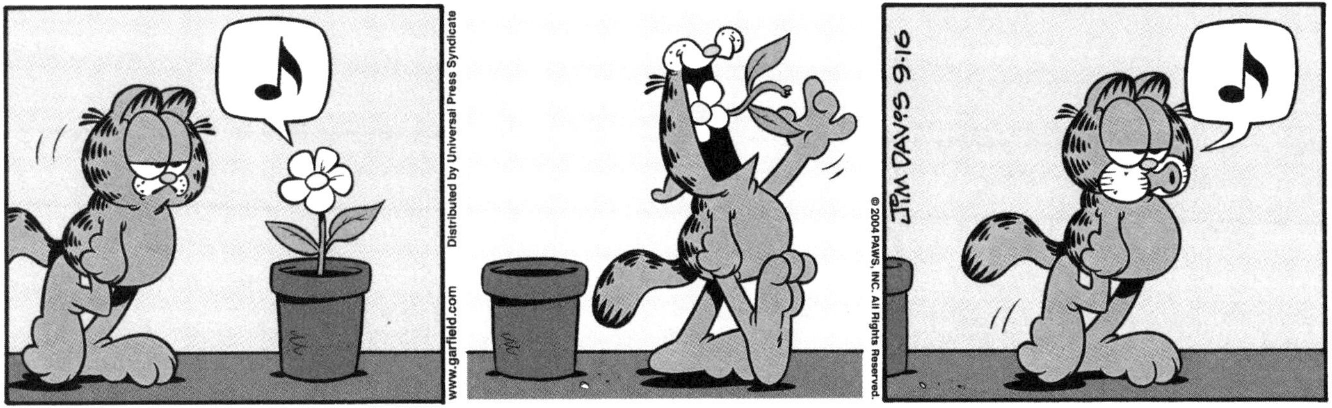
♪
♪
JIM DAVIS 9·16

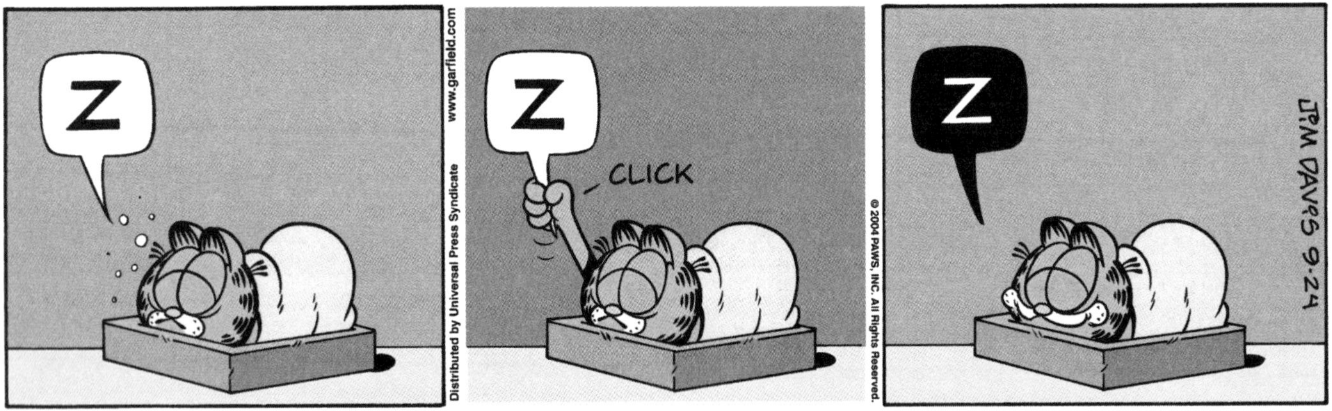
Z
Z
CLICK
Z
JIM DAVIS 9·24

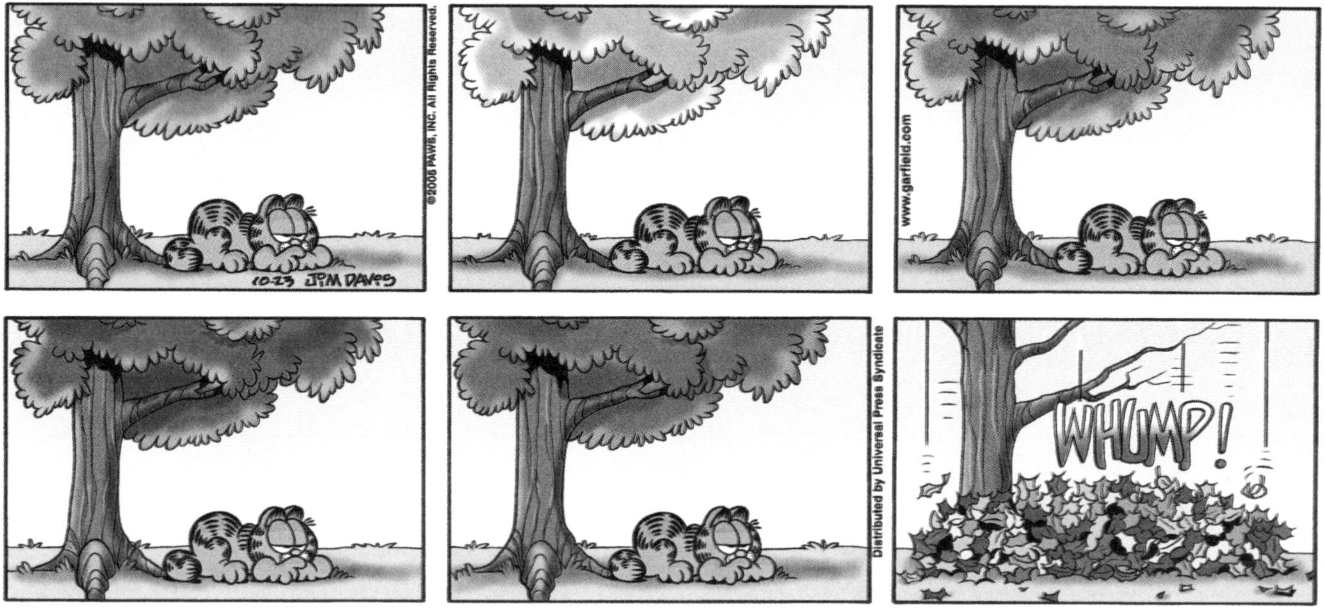
10-23 JIM DAVIS
©2008 PAWS, INC. All Rights Reserved.
www.garfield.com
Distributed by Universal Press Syndicate
WHUMP!

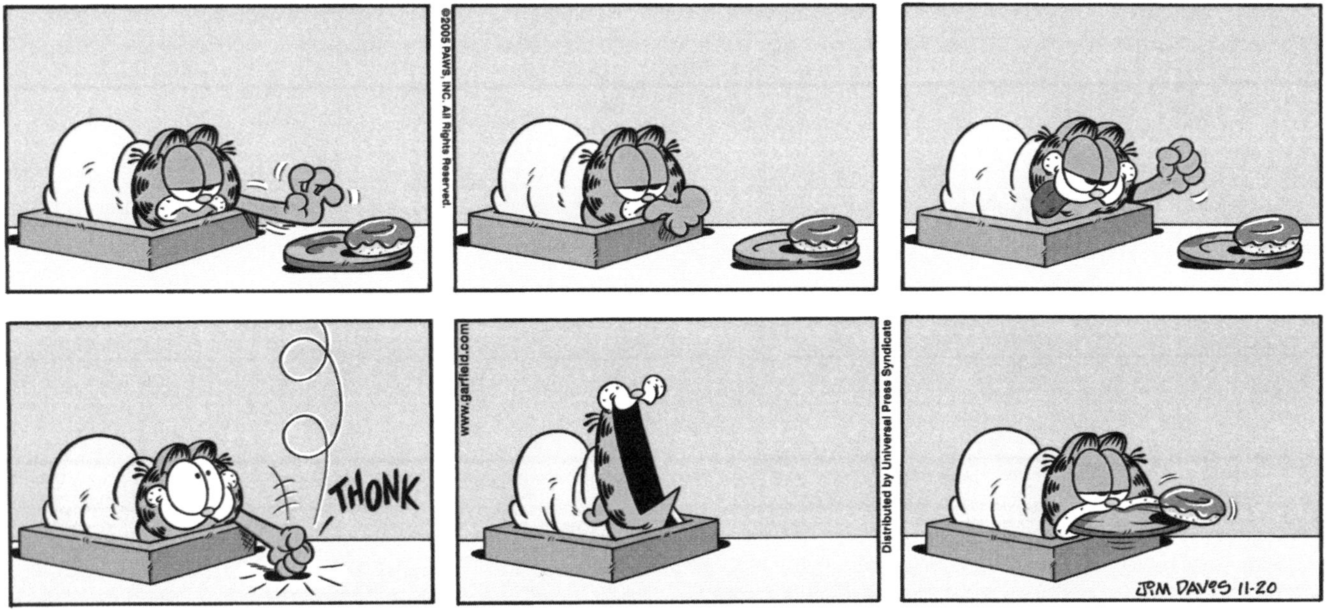
©2005 PAWS, INC. All Rights Reserved.
THONK
www.garfield.com
Distributed by Universal Press Syndicate
JIM DAVIS 11-20

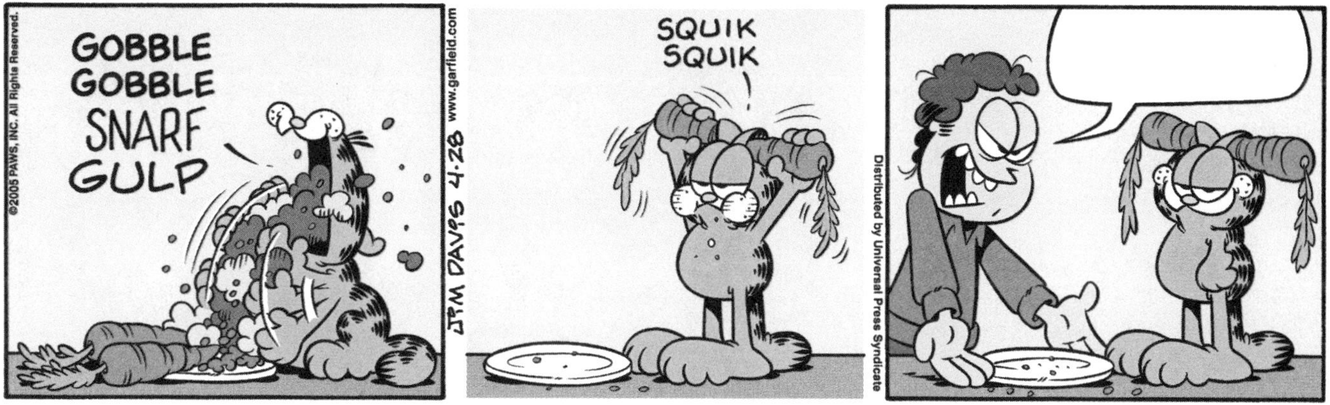
GOBBLE GOBBLE SNARF GULP
SQUIK SQUIK
©2005 PAWS, INC. All Rights Reserved.
JIM DAVIS 4-28
www.garfield.com
Distributed by Universal Press Syndicate

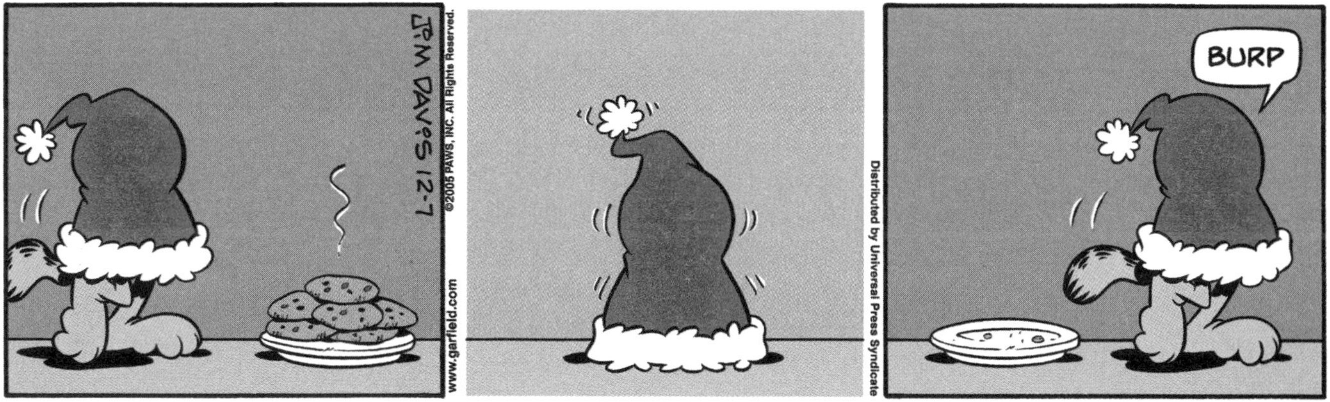
BURP
JIM DAVIS 12-7
©2005 PAWS, INC. All Rights Reserved.
www.garfield.com
Distributed by Universal Press Syndicate

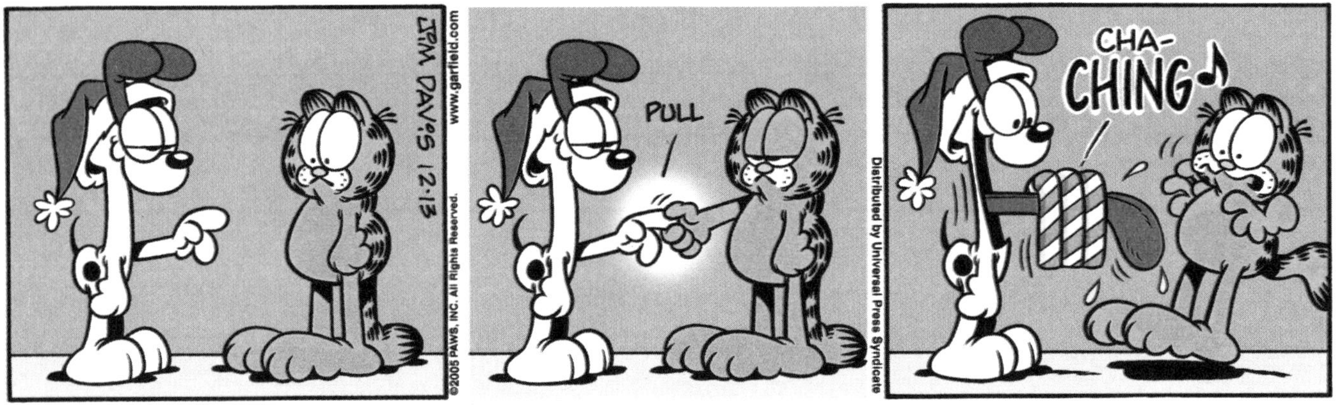
JIM DAVIS 12-13
www.garfield.com
©2005 PAWS, INC. All Rights Reserved.
PULL
Distributed by Universal Press Syndicate
CHA-
CHING♪

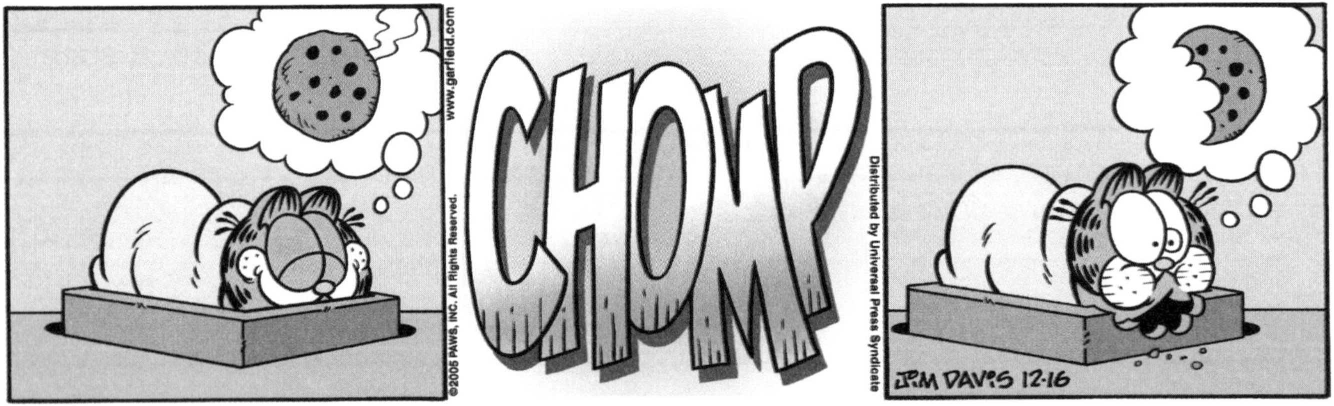
www.garfield.com
©2005 PAWS, INC. All Rights Reserved.
CHOMP
Distributed by Universal Press Syndicate
JIM DAVIS 12-16

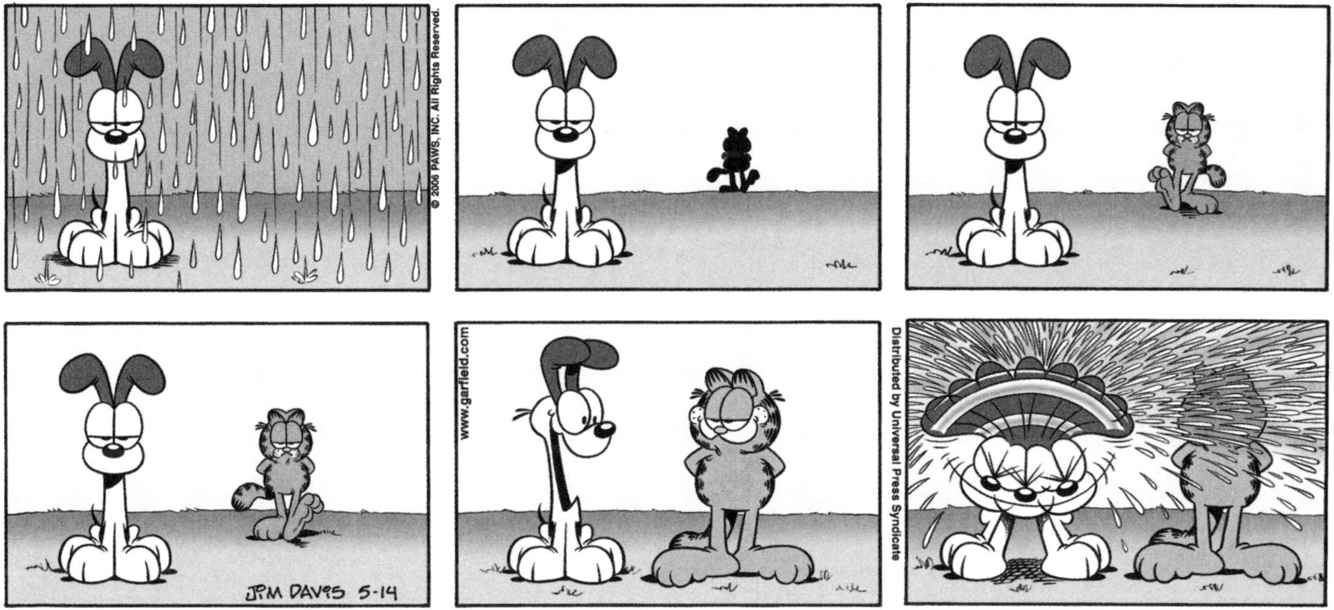
© 2006 PAWS, INC. All Rights Reserved.
JIM DAVIS 5-14
www.garfield.com
Distributed by Universal Press Syndicate

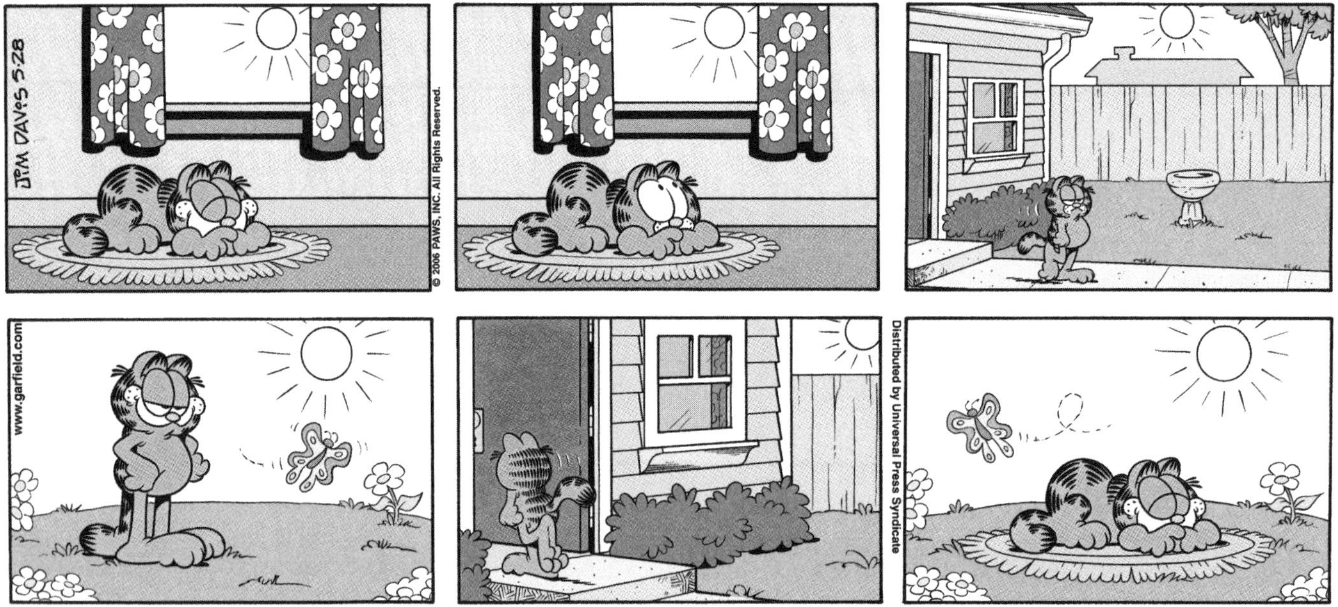
JIM DAVIS 5-28
www.garfield.com

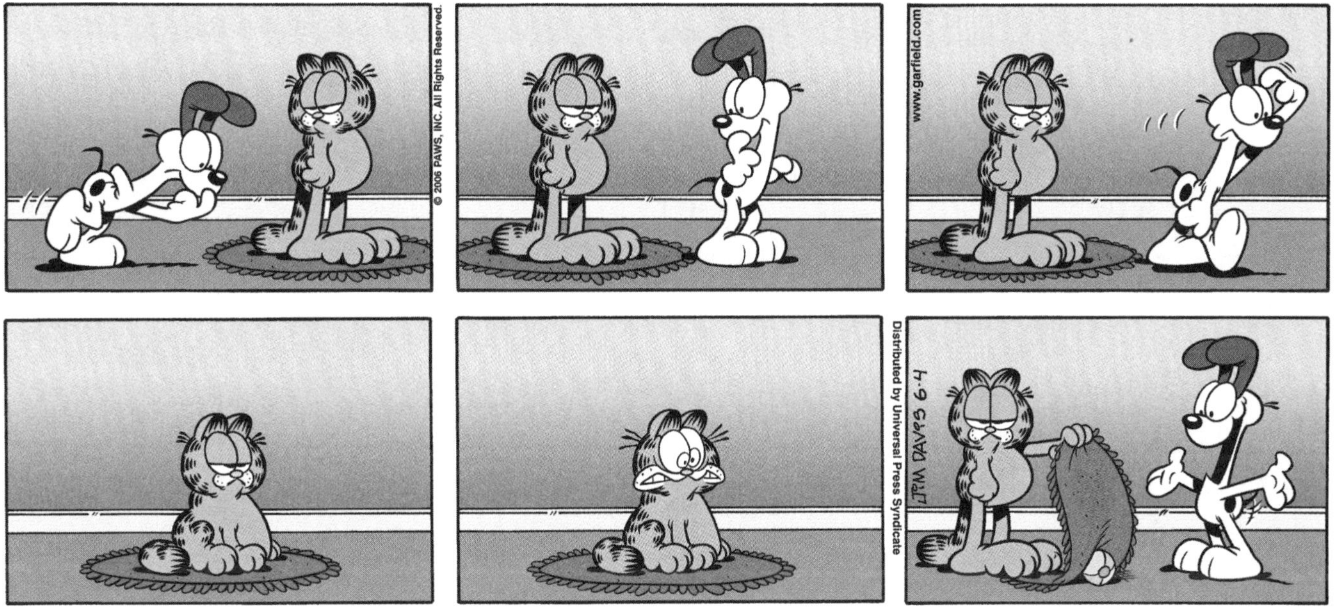
© 2006 PAWS, INC. All Rights Reserved.
www.garfield.com
Distributed by Universal Press Syndicate
JIM DAVIS 6-4

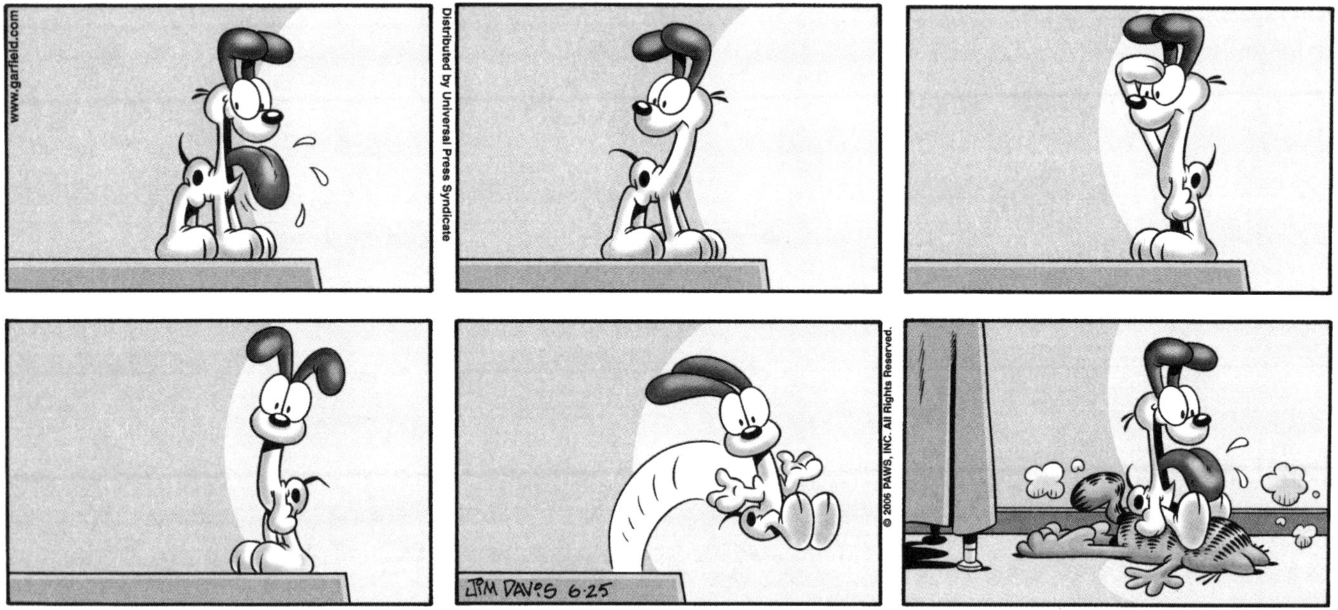
www.garfield.com
Distributed by Universal Press Syndicate
JIM DAVIS 6-25
© 2006 PAWS, INC. All Rights Reserved.

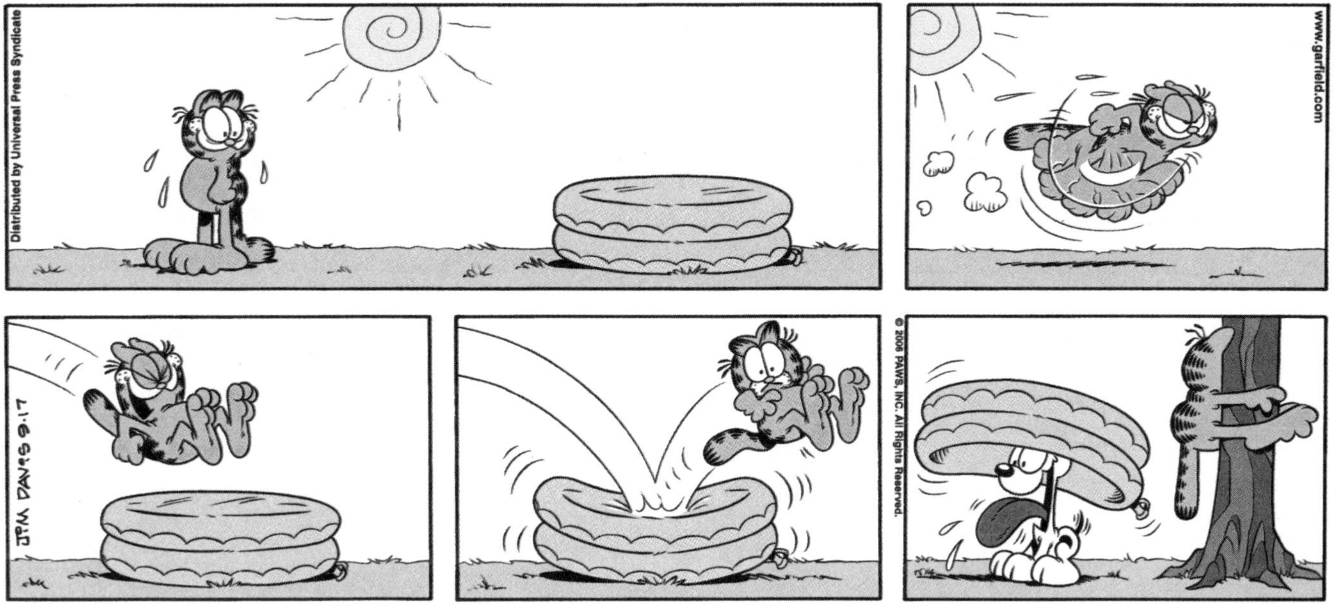

Distributed by Universal Press Syndicate
www.garfield.com
JIM DAVIS 9·17
© 2006 PAWS, INC. All Rights Reserved.

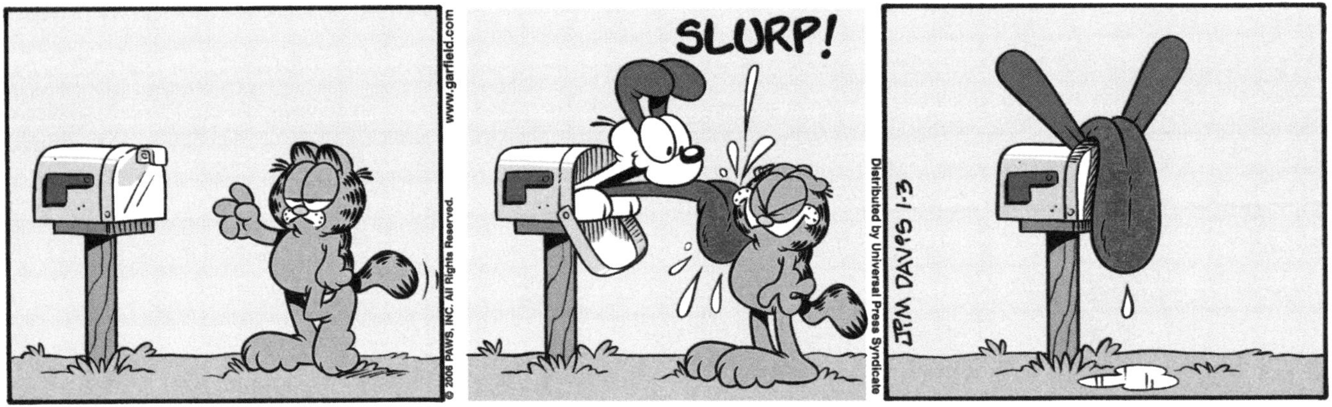
www.garfield.com
© 2006 PAWS, INC. All Rights Reserved.
SLURP!
Distributed by Universal Press Syndicate
JPM DAVIS 1-3

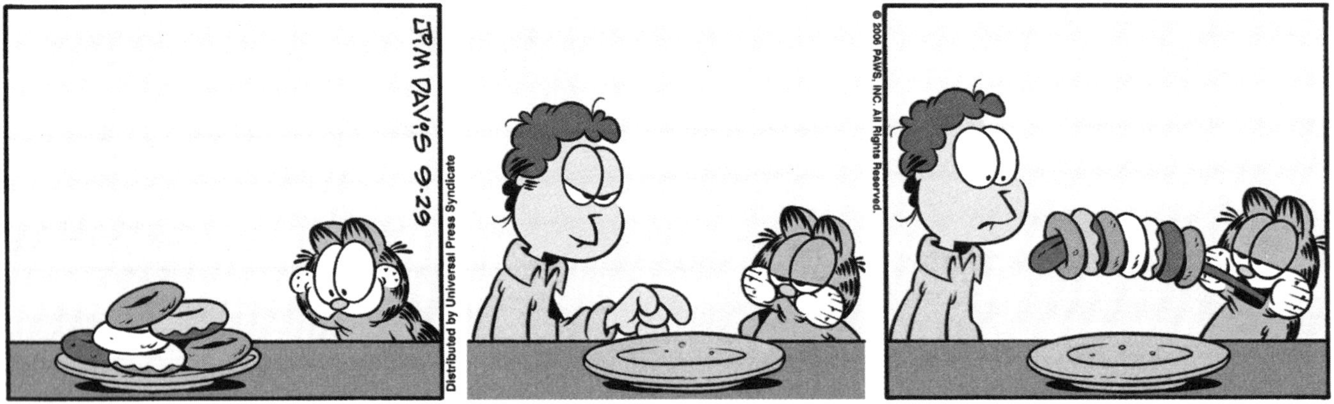
JPM DAVIS 9-29
Distributed by Universal Press Syndicate
© 2006 PAWS, INC. All Rights Reserved.

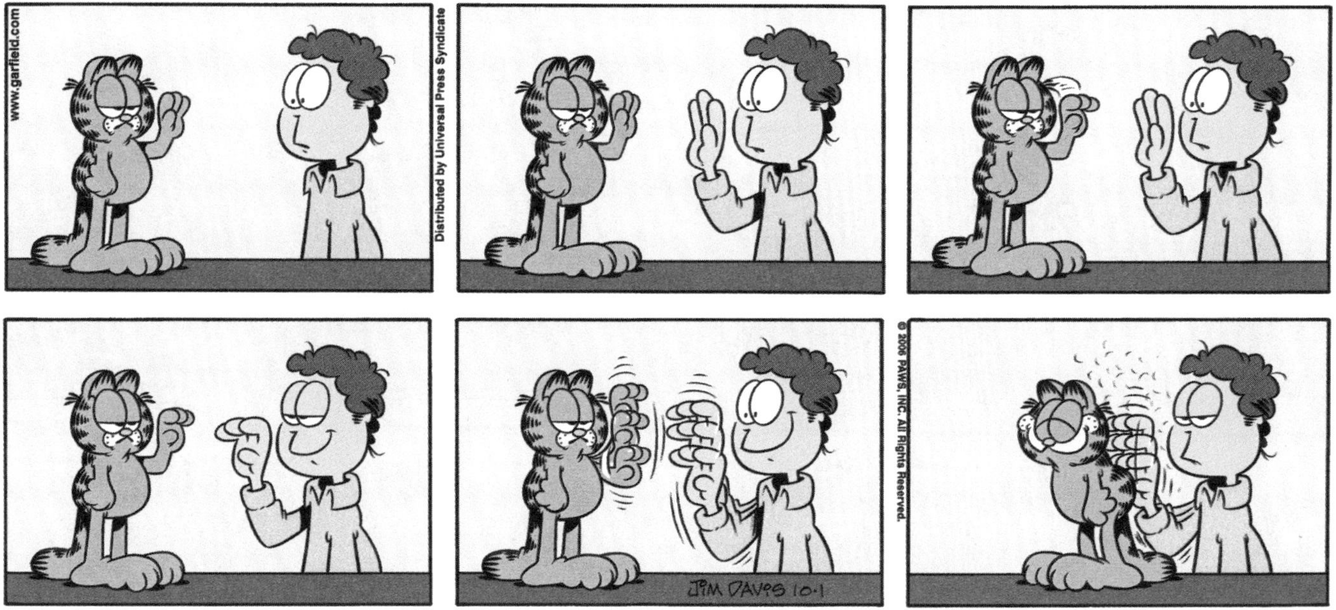
www.garfield.com
Distributed by Universal Press Syndicate
JIM DAVIS 10-1
© 2006 PAWS, INC. All Rights Reserved.

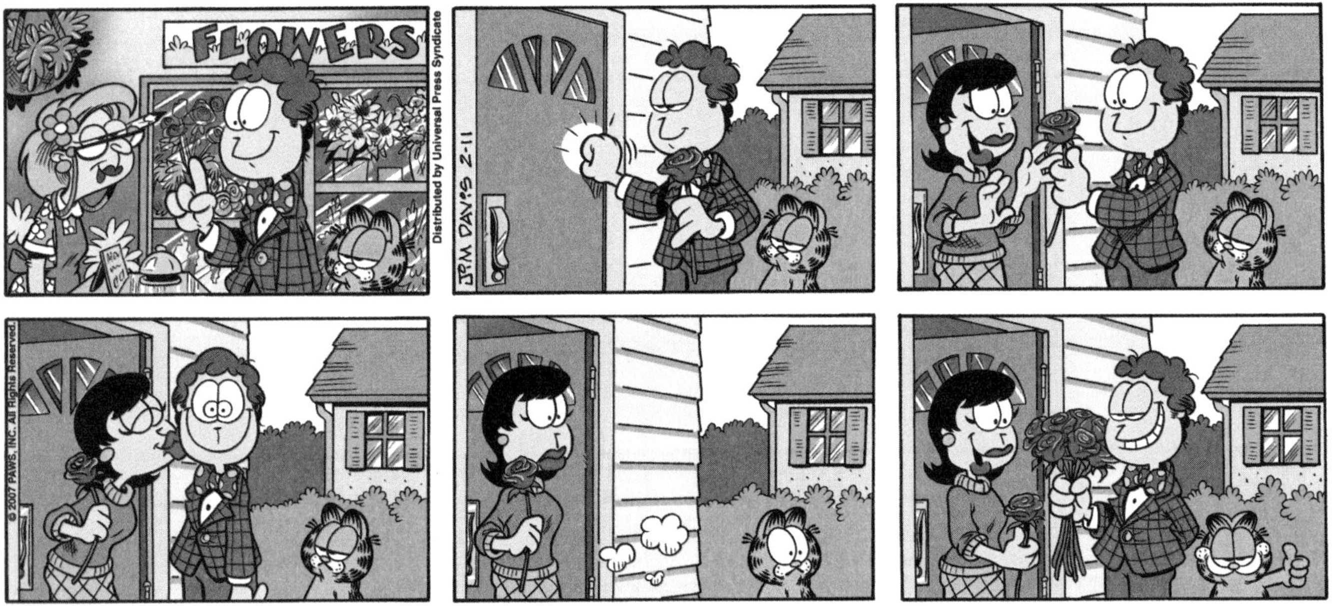
FLOWERS
Distributed by Universal Press Syndicate
JPM DAVIS 2-11
© 2007 PAWS, INC. All Rights Reserved.

© 2007 PAWS, INC. All Rights Reserved.
JIM DAVIS 3-4
www.garfield.com
PLOP
Distributed by Universal Press Syndicate
Kitty Treats

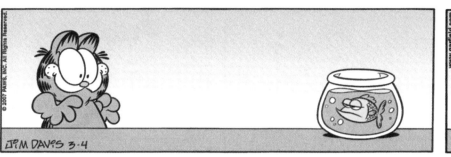

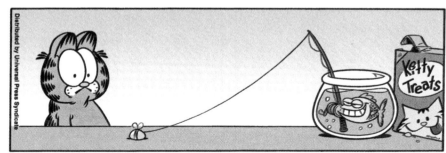

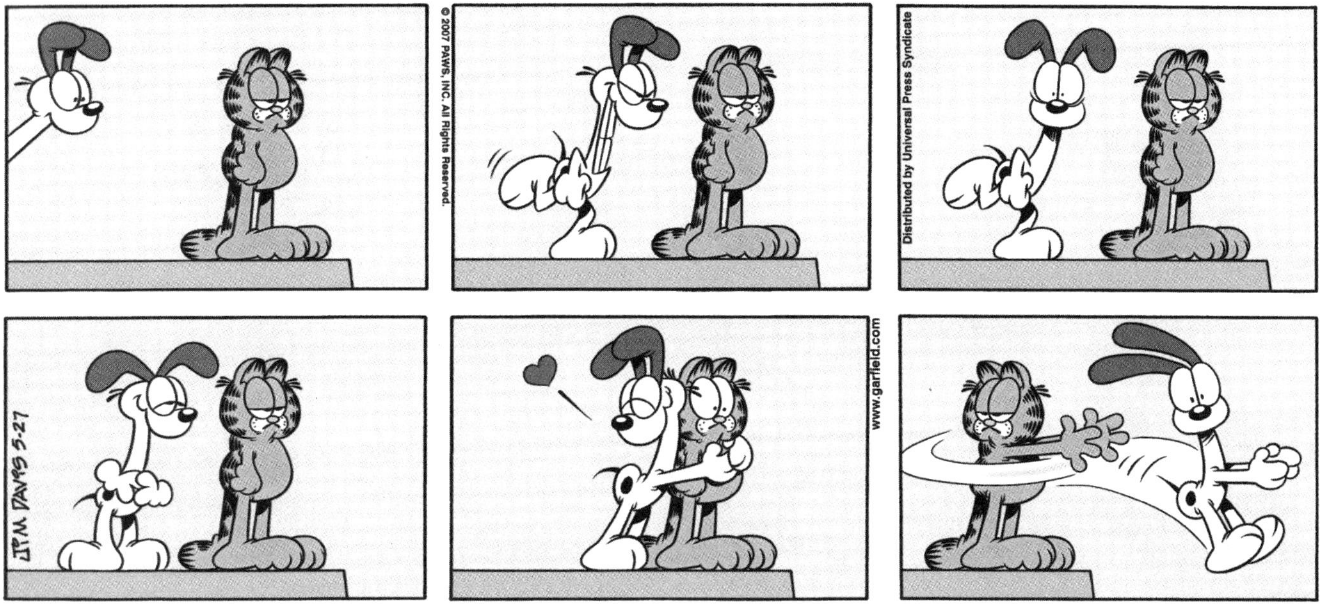
© 2007 PAWS, INC. All Rights Reserved.
Distributed by Universal Press Syndicate
JPM DAVPS 5-27
www.garfield.com

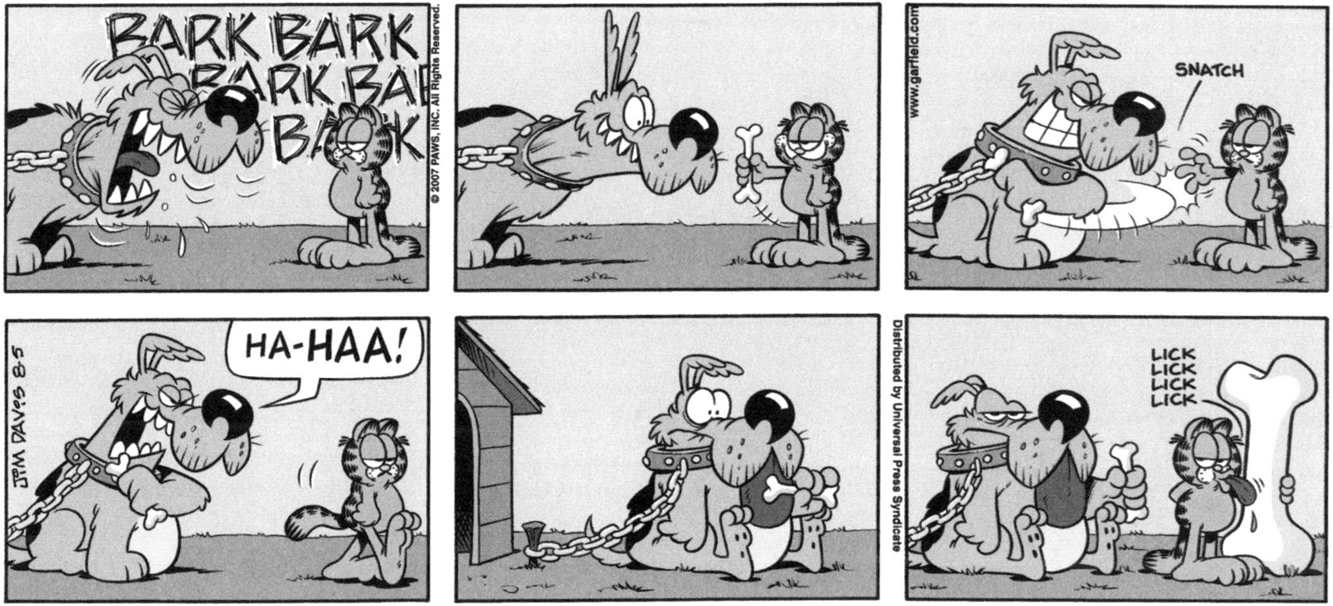
BARK BARK
BARK BARK
© 2007 PAWS, INC. All Rights Reserved.
www.garfield.com
SNATCH
JPM DAVPS 8-5
HA-HAA!
Distributed by Universal Press Syndicate
LICK
LICK
LICK
LICK

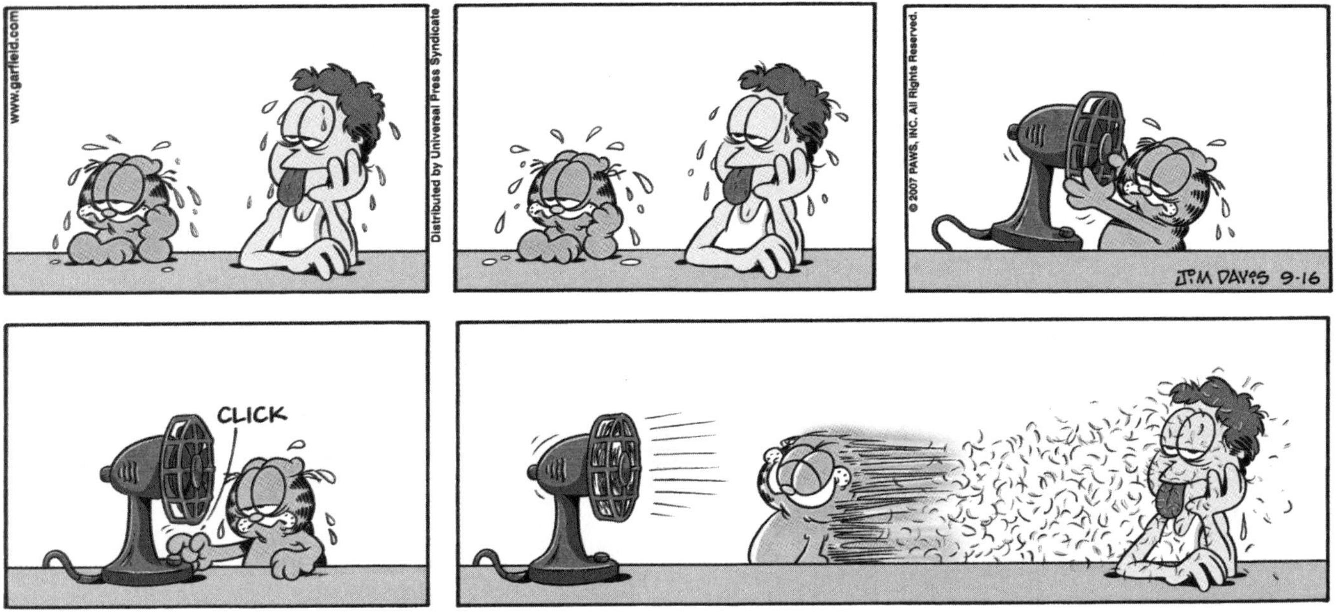

www.garfield.com
Distributed by Universal Press Syndicate
© 2007 PAWS, INC. All Rights Reserved.
JIM DAVIS 9-16
CLICK

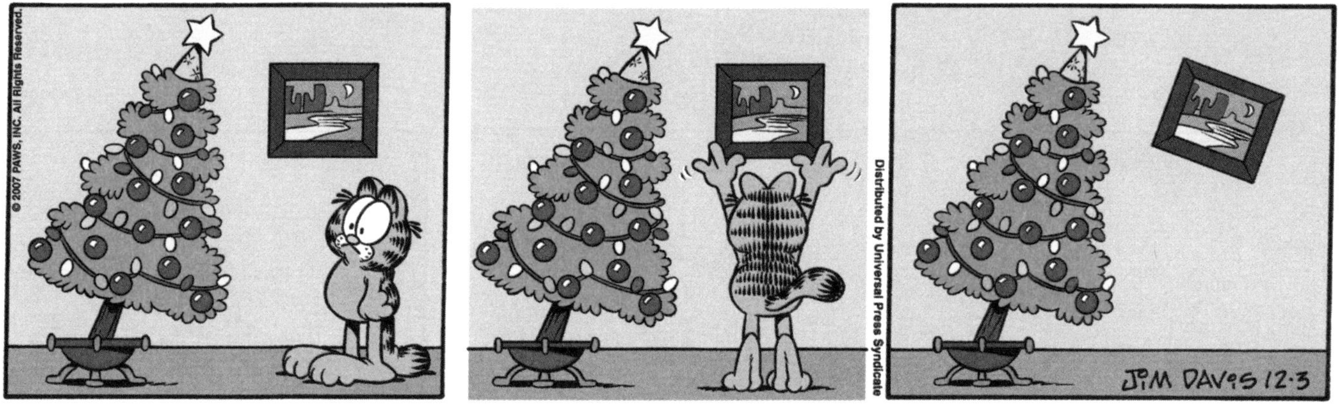
© 2007 PAWS, INC. All Rights Reserved.
Distributed by Universal Press Syndicate
JIM DAVIS 12-3

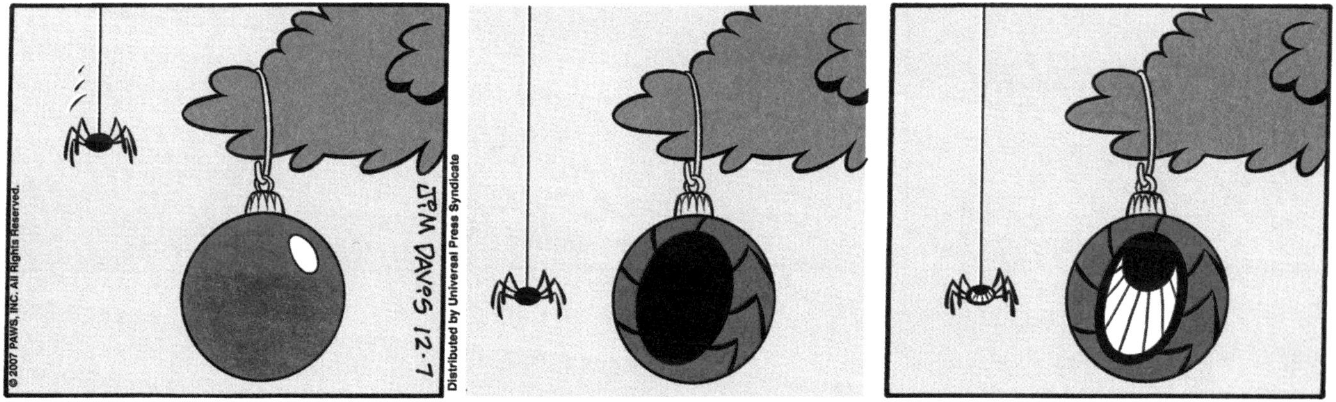
© 2007 PAWS, INC. All Rights Reserved.
JIM DAVIS 12-7
Distributed by Universal Press Syndicate

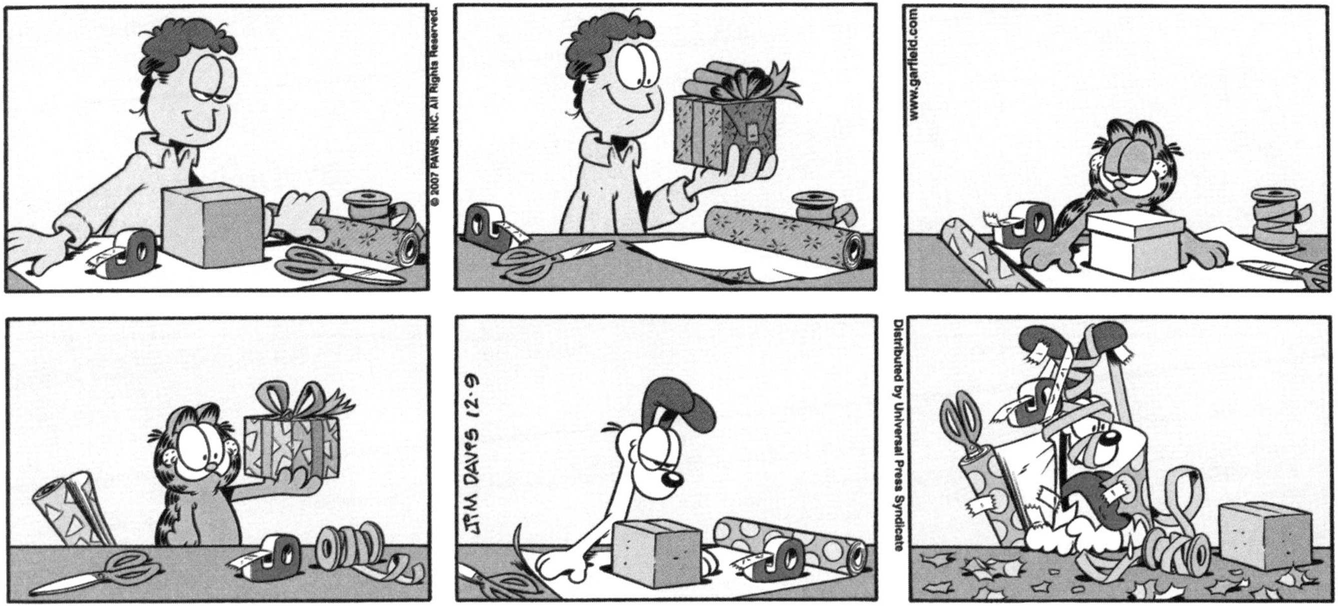
© 2007 PAWS, INC. All Rights Reserved.
www.garfield.com
JIM DAVIS 12-9
Distributed by Universal Press Syndicate

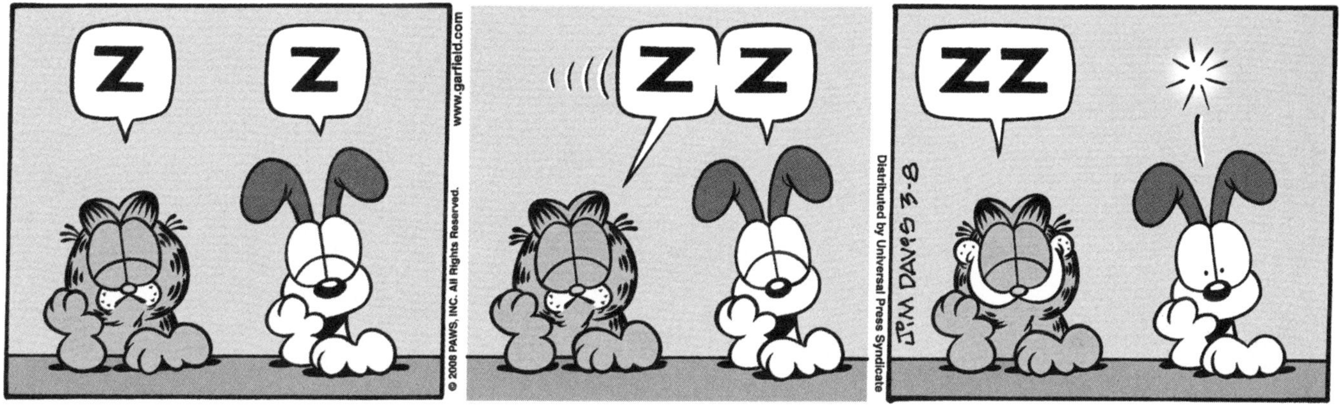
Z
Z
Z
Z
ZZ
© 2008 PAWS, INC. All Rights Reserved.
www.garfield.com
Distributed by Universal Press Syndicate
JIM DAVIS 3-8

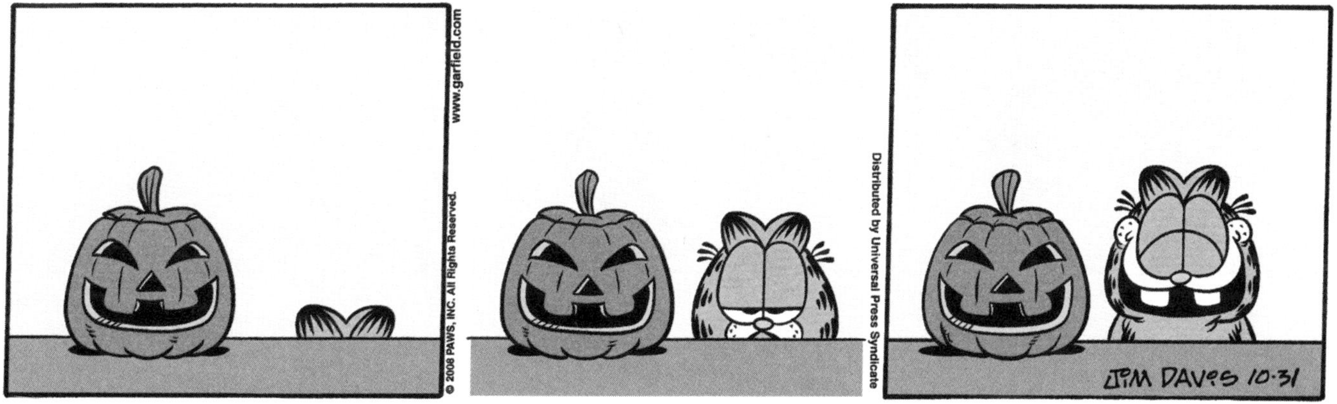
© 2008 PAWS, INC. All Rights Reserved.
www.garfield.com
Distributed by Universal Press Syndicate
JIM DAVIS 10-31

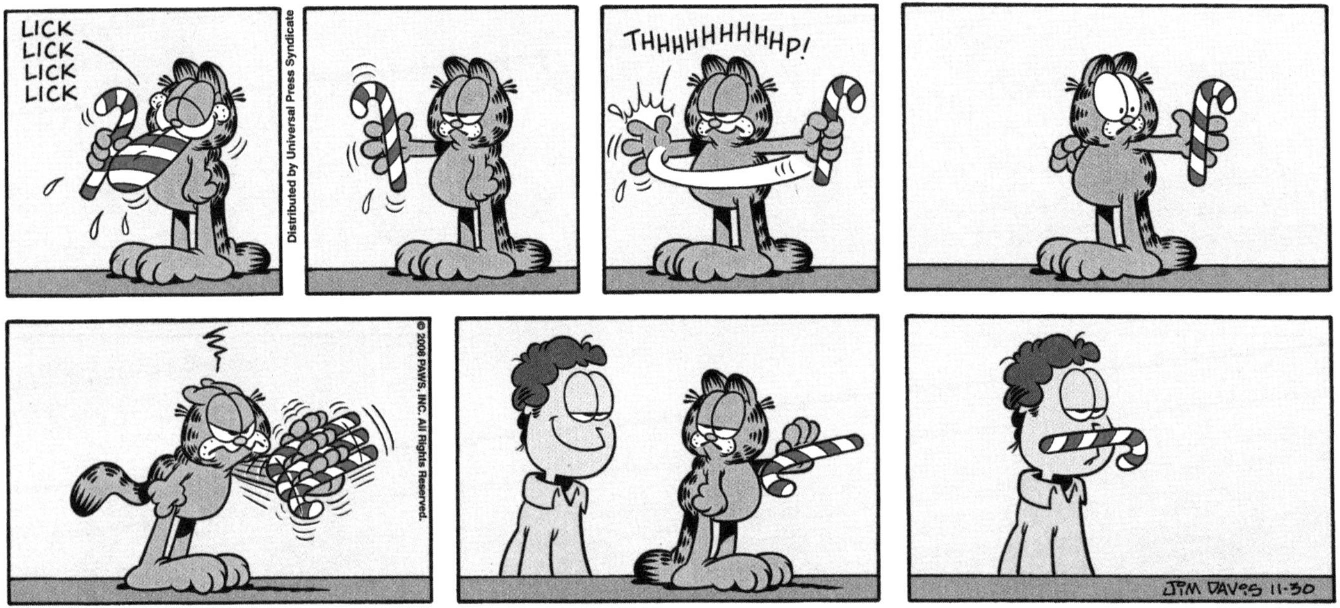
LICK
LICK
LICK
LICK
Distributed by Universal Press Syndicate
THHHHHHHHHP!
© 2008 PAWS, INC. All Rights Reserved.
JIM DAVIS 11-30

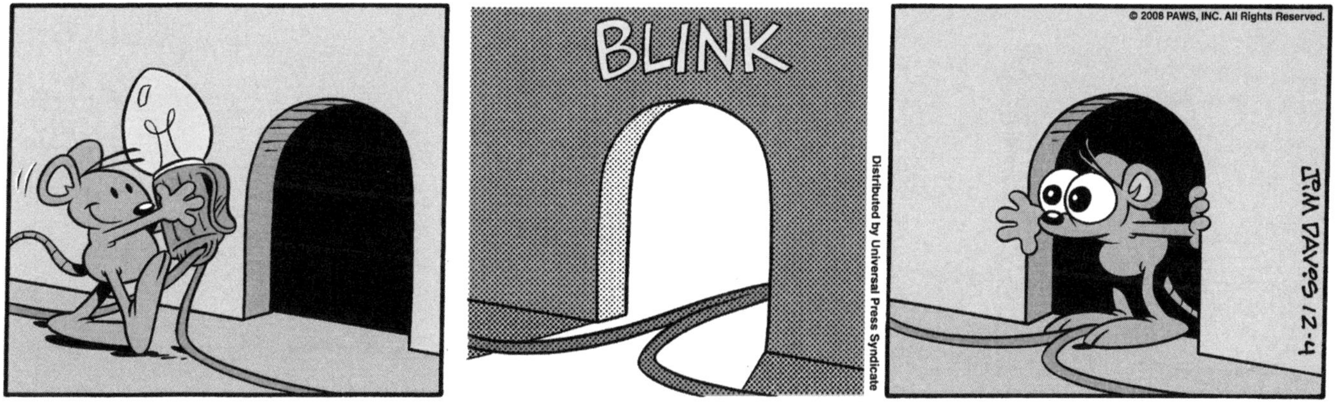
BLINK
Distributed by Universal Press Syndicate
© 2008 PAWS, INC. All Rights Reserved.
JIM DAVIS 12-4

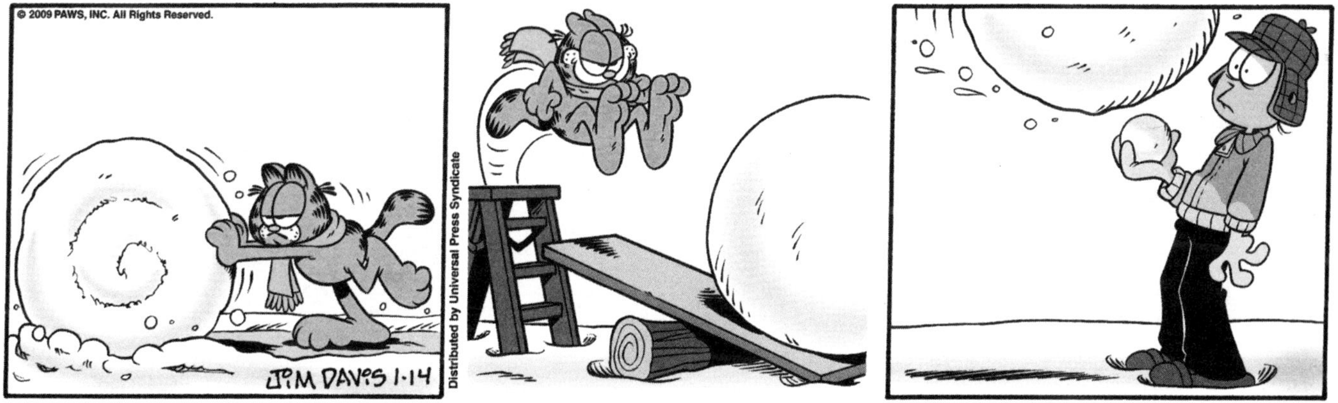
© 2009 PAWS, INC. All Rights Reserved.
JIM DAVIS 1-14
Distributed by Universal Press Syndicate

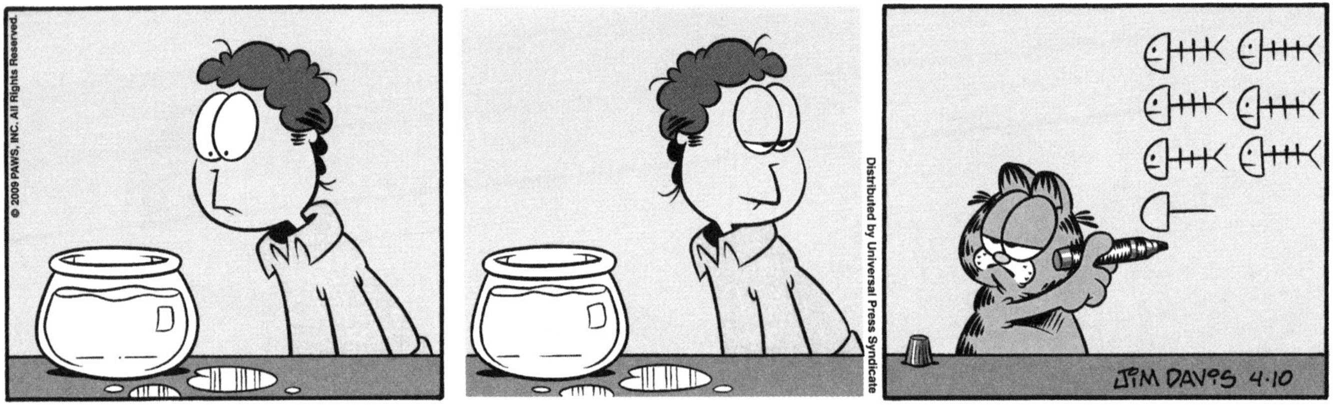
© 2009 PAWS, INC. All Rights Reserved.
Distributed by Universal Press Syndicate
JIM DAVIS 4·10

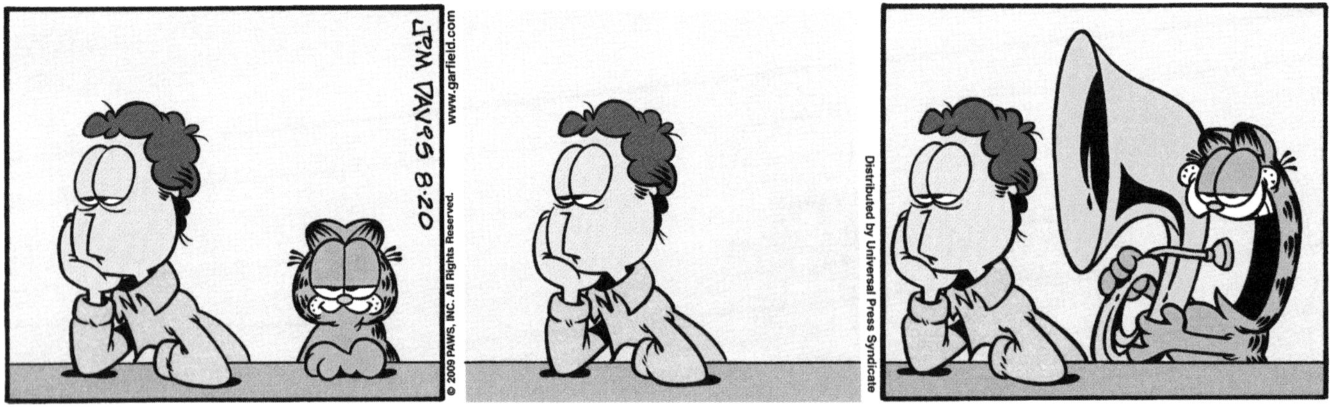
JIM DAVIS 8·20
www.garfield.com
© 2009 PAWS, INC. All Rights Reserved.
Distributed by Universal Press Syndicate

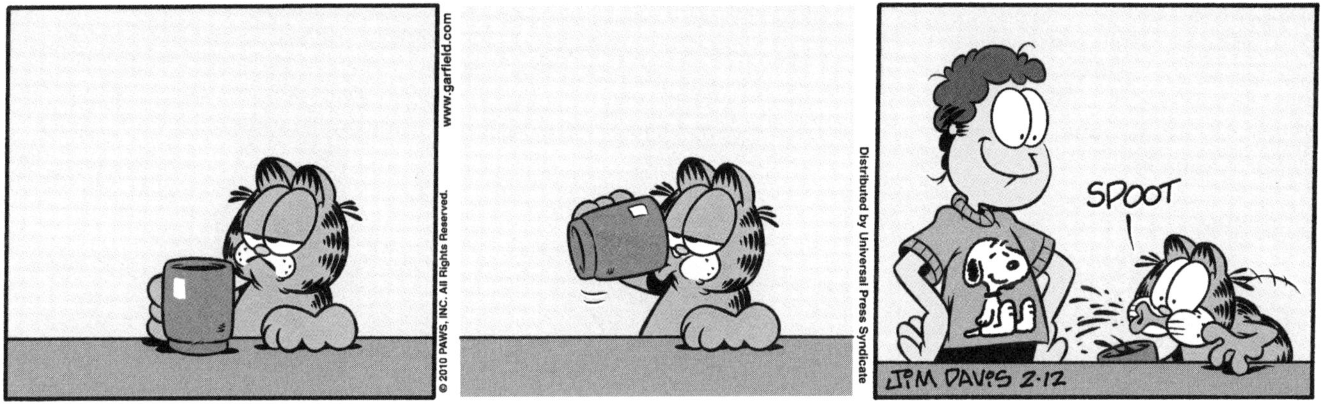
www.garfield.com
© 2010 PAWS, INC. All Rights Reserved.
Distributed by Universal Press Syndicate
SPOOT
JIM DAVIS 2·12

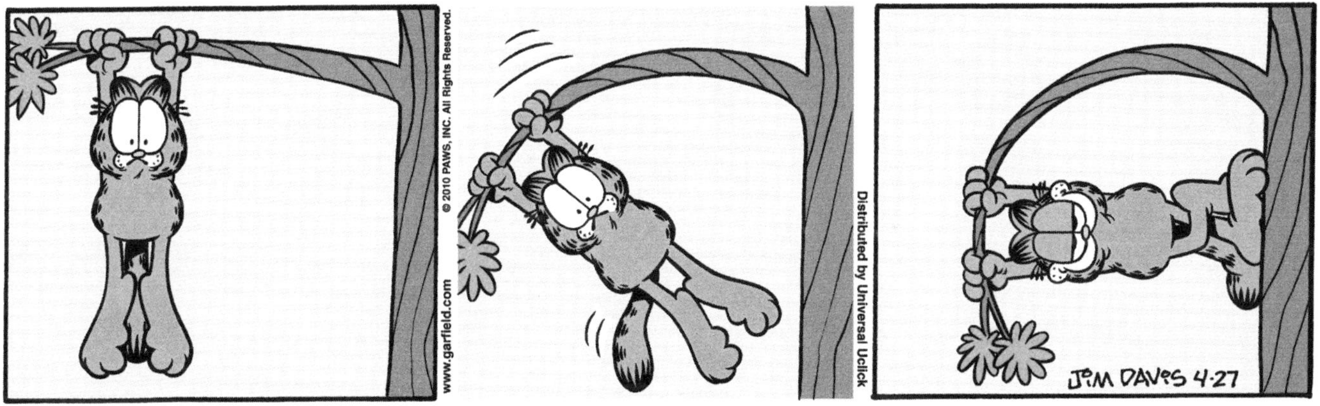
© 2010 PAWS, INC. All Rights Reserved.
www.garfield.com
Distributed by Universal Uclick
JIM DAVIS 4·27

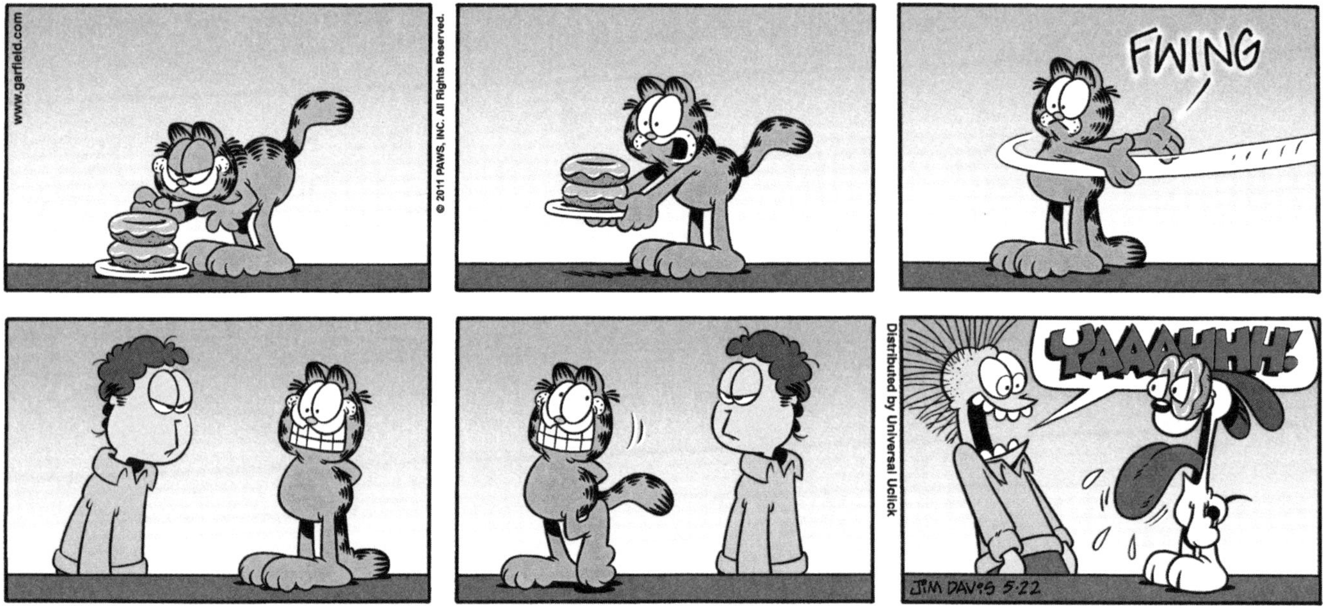
www.garfield.com
© 2011 PAWS, INC. All Rights Reserved.
FWING
Distributed by Universal Uclick
YAAAHHH!
JIM DAVIS 5·22

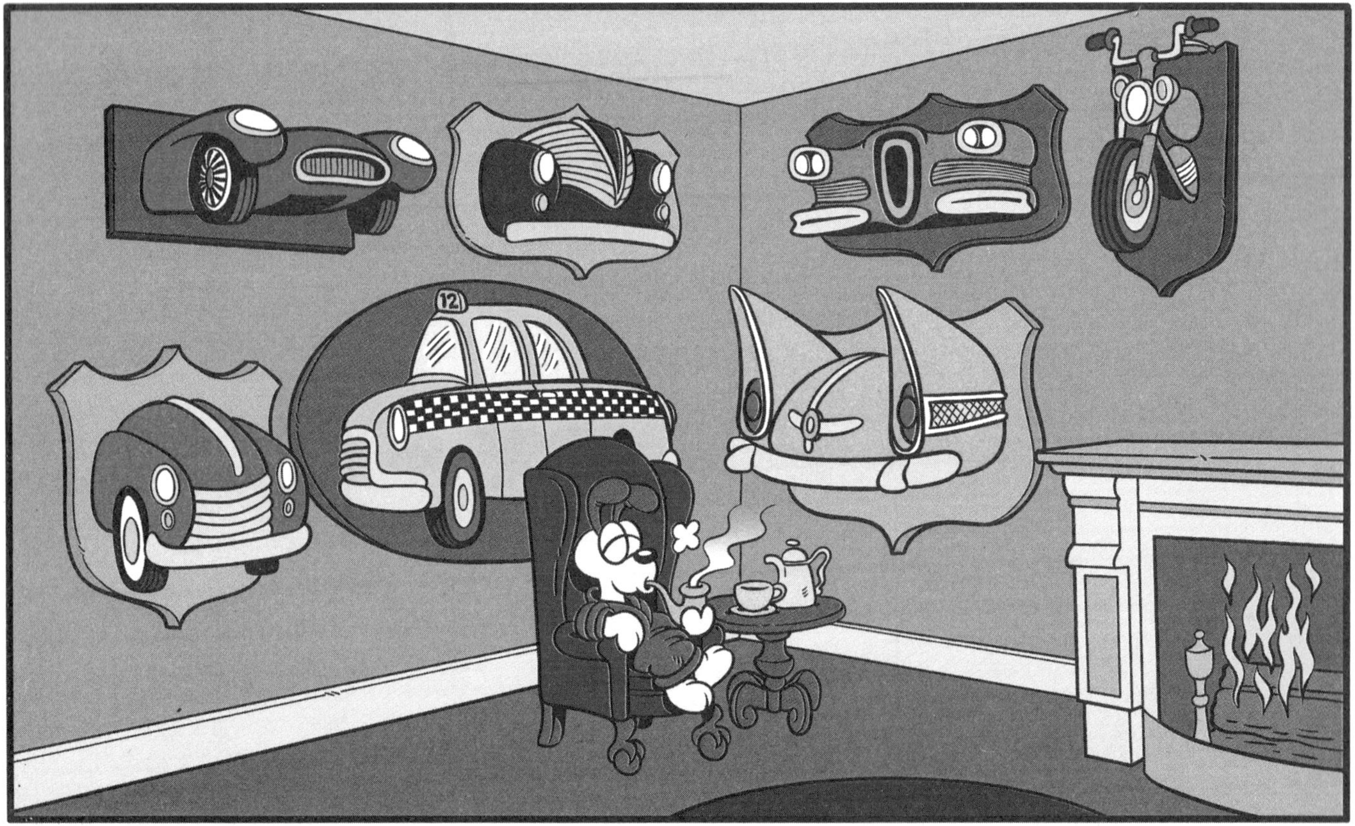
12